Take My Coxcomb

Take My Coxcomb

Shakespeare's Clown-Servants from Late Feudal to
Proto-Capitalist Economies in Early Modern England

Everett G. Neasman

iUniverse, Inc.
New York   Bloomington

*Cover Art Credits: Kevin Coleman as The Fool, King Lear 2003,
Shakespeare and Company. Director Tina Packer. Photo by Kevin
Sprague. Shakespeare & Company 70 Kemble Street Lenox, MA 01240*

iUniverse books may be ordered through booksellers or by contacting:

*iUniverse
1663 Liberty Drive
Bloomington, IN 47403
www.iuniverse.com
1-800-Authors (1-800-288-4677)*

*ISBN: 978-1-4401-5351-8 (sc)
ISBN: 978-1-4401-5352-5 (ebook)*

Printed in the United States of America

iUniverse rev. date: 03/25/2010

Contents

ACKNOWLEDGEMENTS

A book that crosses curricula such as this requires broad visions and deep thoughts; I express sincere gratitude to the scholars who made it possible.

First mention must go to those scholars who have thoughtfully read and commented on the manuscript from its incipience to fruition. Shakespearean Dr. Mary Ellen Lamb was the guiding force whose tireless editing made this endeavor an intellectual project. This book would not have come into being without her. Dr. Mark Amos always challenged my awareness of medieval influences on post feudal social orders. He gave keen insight into the study of societies in transition, viewpoints that helped the study to make a lot more sense with him than without him. I owe a debt of gratitude to Dr. Mary Bogumil for her passion as a dramatist and for her patience with my writing. She truly exemplifies the philosophy of the "little engine that could;" writers must remain tenacious and resilient. Dr. Ryan Netzley showed me some ways to think about critical theory, and they improved my writing. Debating postmodern applications of biblical exegesis in *The Merchant of Venice* provided a bifocal view of Venetian religion and economics. And a word of thanks goes to Dean David L. Wilson and Asst. Dean Pat McNeil who provided a timely and helpful fellowship. I express special thanks to Thespian Dr. Anne Fletcher for teaching dramaturgy to me and for making the stage live in my soul. Thanks Anne for the theatrical journey and for the reality that Shakespeare's plays are more than ink on leaves. For us, Shakespeare's plays live and breathe anew every time people take his written plays onto the stage.

Next, I must thank others who have contributed to this work by suggesting source material, sharing their work with me, discussing possible avenues of research, and nurturing me through the academic process. These include Sidney Harrison, Dr. Pierre-Damien Mvuyekure, Dr. Thomas J. Remington, Dr. Maurice Lee, Dr. Charles L. Means, and Dr. Segun Ojewuyi. In addition, I am grateful for the impeccable professionalism and encouragement by Dr. Houston A Baker; Arthur F. Kinney, Renaissance Society of America; Paul J. Contino, *Christianity & Literature*; and Dr. Pasty Daniels, *The Jackson State University Researcher: An Interdisciplinary Journal.*

And greatest gratitude:

To God;
Farley and Lydia Neasman, my loving parents;
and Dr. Taunjah P. Bell my lover and my friend.

Take My Coxcomb

INTRODUCTION

Enter Dromo, drawing a clowne in with a rope

Clowne.   *What now, thrust a man into the common wealth, whether hee will or noe? What the deuill should I doe here?*

Dromo.   *Why, what an ass art thou? Dost thou not knowe a playe cannot be without a clowne? Clowns have bene thrust into plays by the head euer since Kempe could make a scuruey face, and therefore reason thou shouldst be drawne in with a cart rope.*

Clowne.   *But what must I doe nowe? [. . .] This is fine y faith: nowe, when they haue noe bodie to leaue on stage, the[y] bring mee vp, & which is worse, tell mee not what I should saye.*

The dramatic ideals expressed by Parnassus' Dromo are fairly representative of those of the Elizabethan playgoer's view in general concerning the clown character. The popularity of the clown was one of the most striking features of the English early modern stage. From tolerated intruder to scripted comic, the clown matured into the sphere of plays. There are numerous stage histories of Elizabethan comedies that demonstrate the development of clowns within the plays and from one production to another.[1] Yet, if we the audience grasp Dromo's rope to help tow in the clown, just who and what are we towing onto the stage and into the play?

The early role of clowns as servants makes them an ideal mouthpiece for changes in master-servant bonds so important to this transitional period between late feudalism and proto-capitalism. Clowns establish their dramatic identity through the economics of service roles and master/servant bonds,[2] and these dual roles as clown-servants tie them to the witty complexities of household economics. In this study, economy is the domestic system that pertains not only to the management of a home and its goods and services, but also to the socioeconomic relationships among its members.[3] By clowning on the subject of service, Shakespeare's clown-servants use their stage identity to address through humor the complex, often unpleasant, socioeconomic changes within the Elizabethan servant-class. As clowns' bonds of service change to accommodate economic shifts toward capitalism, master and clown-servant bonds become a source of humor, as do the comical treatments of themes that complicate these bonds. The economic relationships between master and servant reflect the greater economic tensions expressed within the plays and representative of the real world of the time. This book will present Shakespeare's clowns as major characters, whose wit addresses monetary concerns of the period.[4] Just as barometers measure pressures in weather systems, Shakespeare's clowns gauge the tensions within the economies of their plays with regard to Elizabethan economics.

This book analyzes the ways in which clowns of Shakespeare's comedies reflect the rapidly changing conditions not only of their plays, but also of the early modern period in its transition from a late feudal to a proto-capitalist society. The clown-servant characters represent this economic shift: All of Shakespeare's clowns exhibit dutiful service within the late feudal household as well as display characteristics of the proto-capitalist endeavor to prosper. Shakespeare's clown-servants evolve from characters with strong late feudal ties of domestic service to progressive characters of proto-capitalist exchange. This growth of Shakespeare's clown-servant characters occurs against a backdrop of similar clown-development in early modern England. As clown-servant actors adapt the legendary clowning style of William Somer, the fool of Henry VIII, they move progressively away from portrayals of his real life clown service and toward a dramatic characterization of clowning that reflects overall influence of proto-capitalist development of the theater. Rather than cling to portrayals of late feudal order, early modern dramatic clown-servants illustrate proto-capitalist modes of exchange, both as characters in their plays and as actors in the theater. Both pre-Shakespearean drama and Shakespeare's plays illustrate an economic shift. To study this shift from feudalism to proto-capitalism in early modern drama, this study's chronological focus covers roughly from the late 1580s to 1603, a period that witnesses the theatrical waning of the clown's improvised medieval jig and the emergence of the early modern scripted clown. Central to this book is the notion that Shakespeare's clowns refine past trends of dramatic foolery to emerge as comic entities unique to the Elizabethan economic experience. I will refer to clowns listed in *dramatis personas* of Shakespeare's comedies and discuss how they reflect English economic sensibilities for the Elizabethan stage. My historical and literary inquiries into Shakespeare's clown-servants introduce into current Shakespeare studies a fresh perspective on service and comedy in early modern England. A proto-capitalist reading of Shakespeare's clown-servants and the theaters they inhabit uncovers economic elements in the plays often omitted in previous considerations of the clown. Taking as its primary object the economic shifts evident in Shakespeare's clowns and in the plays *The Comedy of Errors, Two Gentlemen of Verona, Merchant of Venice,* and *Twelfth Night,* this book also evaluates these plays against the backdrop of Elizabethan theater. As these plays progress, the change in master/servant bonds reflects the move of entrepreneurial clowns from impromptu solo artists to scripted players.

In this endeavor, I observe clown-servants as progressive characters that employ proto-capitalist modes of exchange, driven by incentives of profit to alter their traditional means of prosperity. I also examine in these clowns the practice of holding fast to feudal domestic order in their efforts to discount new means of doing business. But just as the term " proto-capitalist" looks ahead to widespread commercialism, late feudalism looks back at a reflection of an historical past, a reflection often blurred by historical analysis. Within each of these comedies (*The Comedy of Errors, The Two Gentlemen of Verona, The Merchant of Venice,* and *Twelfth Night*), Shakespeare's clown-servants portray characters with ties both to late feudal domestic economics and proto-capitalist economics. As Shakespeare's comedies develop, so do his clown-servant characters. They evolve from clowns who emphasize traditional domestic order to those who employ proto-capitalist exchange within their traditional households. It is this trend of the development of the clown-servant character that makes him an interstice between feudalism and capitalism. The terms used in this study to describe socioeconomic issues emerge from the great debate on the transition from feudalism to capitalism that began with the publication in 1946 of Maurice Dobb's *Studies in the Development of Capitalism.* According to Dobbs (1946), the term "proto-capitalist" applies to the notion of a transitional phase of commodity production that is post-feudal (Holton

95).[5] As Perry Anderson and later critics of Dobbs's transition theory caution, such an approach tends to exaggerate the extent to which the ending of serfdom from the fourteenth century onwards represents the demise of feudalism itself (95). The term "proto-capitalist" is used here to describe the co-existence of two distinct modes of production– feudal and capitalist, with the latter gradually achieving dominance (95). My argument will focus on the effects of proto-capitalist exchange on socioeconomic relationships. These are shifts in the self-awareness of characters that pertain to the "socioeconomic superstructure" rather than the direct results of changes to the modes of production.[6] Proto-capitalist refers to an economy characterized by some minimum free market conditions such as the increase in private property, i.e. the early modern household and the dissolution of traditional household order, helped along by an adequate monetary system and free wage earners.

This study treats feudalism as a system of "economic self-sufficiency" or "natural economy" (Holton 157).[7] However, unlike early Marxists analysis, this study does not treat feudalism as reflecting evolutionary thought that considers "the past" merely as a "stage" leading up the present (Marx *Pre-capitalist* 356). The notion of feudal order (or *feodalité*) is a product of legal and political discourse from the 16th century onwards (Holton 18). R. J. Holton writes:

> While feudalism continued to be seen primarily as a judicial form, it could scarcely make a prominent appearance in economic theories of social change, that is, as a discrete stage in the evolution of human society. An alternative option was to restructure the notion of feudalism itself by turning it into an economic concept. (23)

This viewpoint is especially evident among Marxists. By

the term late feudalism, this study points to the justification of policies instituted by governing bodies with the specific intent of reinforcing and maintaining the socioeconomic effects of old feudalism from the 16th century onwards. Thus, the term late feudalism applies to Tudor England and to the presence of an entrenched, immensely wealthy elite maintained by low taxes on capital and the absence of taxes on estates. It also applies to a large and growing class of uneducated and to unskilled labor brought in by unchecked immigration (both legal and illegal) controlled by foundational socioeconomic relationships that favored the landed nobility. The use of the terms "late feudalism" also points to debilitating economic factors like enclosure that fragmented large estates and expanded the peasant population.[8] Therefore, as Holton concludes, the judicial and political theory stressing phenomena such as "vassalage" and "political authority" of feudalism within the Marxist perspective became an economic concept—a mode of production—in which serfdom and property forms became paramount and institutions such as vassalage receded in significance (23).[9]

In their research on the transition from feudalism to capitalism, Paul Delany and Linda Woodbridge both examine the great noble household and its number of domestic servants in relation to the socioeconomic responses of service and beggary. Central to foregrounding economic concerns about feudalism in Shakespeare's plays, these works explore in *King Lear* the dissembled household as indicative of changing Tudor economic conditions of household service. Both Woodbridge and Delany draw comparisons between Lear's kingdom and the early modern English home. Delany suggests that *King Lear* represents "the neocapitalist economy of the Renaissance, not directly, but rather through an exploration of philosophical concepts and moral values that are typically associated with that economy" (432). As a philosophical concept of economic order, the home changes to accommodate new economic practices of service, practices that Delany sees in *King Lear* as the change from service for "kind" to service for "cash" (432). Woodbridge points out that

> the play, then, unsettles key Renaissance signifiers of stability: making home dispensable, penetrable, unsafe, it strikes at domestic ideology; allowing England to be dissected, the play unravels the new centralized nationalism the Tudors and King James had so triumphantly constructed. (209)

For both Woodbridge and Delany, an example of a household staff reduced in number is *King Lear* and the disbanding of Lear's one hundred knights, who are, in a feudal sense, also his servants. As domestic fools, Shakespeare's clown-servants inhabit household and stage spaces where servants and employers meet. His plays offer rare early modern depictions of these spaces as upper class characters depend on servants to deliver messages, run errands, and carry out a variety of orders for their masters (81). Wiles notices that few masters were willing to associate their households with emblems of folly (183). The cap-and-bells and bauble represent a traditional ideal of service that has been eclipsed by new bonds of domestic service. For example, Lear's fool continues to offer up his cockscomb, an act that suggests the declining end of his domestic service because Lear is without a house. He depicts the waning of the court fool and the overall dissolution of feudal bonds of service that earlier clown-servants experience in their plays. Shakespeare's clowns combine the court jester's energy to entertain with wit and service ideals. They are wise-fools who challenge domestic economic aspects in the plays. These clown characters abandon the portrayal of the parti-colored fool for the clown-servant and illustrate a dramatic awareness of overall economic changes in Elizabethan England.

The move of the early modern English household away from the rules of late feudal order is evident in the significant shift away from retaining large numbers of household servants. Kate Mertes offers a befitting metaphor for the reduction of the feudal household and its transition into a smaller economy. Mertes notes that the medieval household "did not die out; but rather as it is posited that the brontosauruses and tyrannosauruses dwindled into birds, it became a much smaller, quieter and more domestic beast" (191). In reference to the household of the second Earl of Southampton (1570s), Delany states, ". . . for at this time the great aristocratic households were shrinking, and the status of those who remained in them was declining. Even the richest peers could no longer afford to support hundreds of retainers, as they had done in the Middle Ages" (433-4). Woodbridge notes that in *King Lear*, Goneril questions Lear concerning the service of her domestic staff in place of his one hundred knights (209). Goneril asks: "Why might not you, my lord, receive attendance from those that she calls servants or from mine?" (2.4.45-6). For Woodbridge, the replacement of the feudal knight by a domestic servant as chief household officer illustrates a reconfiguration of household order in early modern England. In the play, Goneril dissolves the one hundred knights in an attempt to establish household order. In early modern England, the dissolution of knights by those in charge reflects the numerous efforts of the Tudors to levy royal sanctions against armed retainers of powerful nobles (210). Thereby, the monarchy changed a decentralized feudal system into centralized government (210). Delany also observes in *King Lear* the Tudor controversy over "maintenance": the noble right to keep an armed and uniformed (liveried) body of retainers for public escort (433). For Delany, by the end of the sixteenth century, the practice of keeping liveried servants was more a show of "conspicuous consumption" than a true gesture of autonomy from the central government (433).

Rather than autonomy, Lear voices royal responsibility for the homeless from the heath (3.1). Woodbridge suggests that

> the poor are poor in *King Lear* because of widespread economic conditions for which the king is not solely responsible, and because the common assumption that the poor are responsible for their poverty impedes action that might change the economic system. Lear is not alone in neglecting the poor; to neglect and despise them is endemic in the play as it was in Renaissance England. (233)

Lear's realm, like the Tudor monarchies, struggles with responsibility for the poor. In Tudor England, royal responsibility ranged from benevolent relief to ill treatment through rigid laws, a notion that, as Woodbridge argues, runs counter to Tudor audiences that equate homelessness and beggary with a "beastly life" (214). Lear reevaluates service and his concepts of unemployed servants as homeless beggars. As not only Lear but also his fool become homeless, they share a social condition with "poor Tom," as acted by the homeless Edgar. Both the homelessness of Tom and Lear's fool results from Lear's mismanaged economy. Just as the image of the home serves as one of Woodbridge's "signifiers of stability" (209), homelessness and beggary illustrate domestic instability in the wake of proto-capitalist change in household order.

By the mid sixteenth century, the Tudor monarchy classified actors as beggars (Woodbridge 262). Woodbridge suggests that "an individual's identity is bound up in where home is. Those who become homeless become strangers to themselves" (227). Bluntly put, identity is a function of place (226). Therefore, just as *King Lear* illustrates, "Lear's fall from the heights of monarchy to the depths of beggary draws on the traditional monarch/beggar antithesis. But, the terms in which the extreme reactions are couched point toward the discourse of vagrancy, which posits 'the common road' as the opposite of 'home'" (218). Along with other company players, Shakespeare's clowns attempted to shed the negative connotation of vagrancy often associated with beggars.[10] In 1572, England's Monarchy passed the "Act for the Punishment of Vagabonds" to address the unprecedented problem of vagrancy by requiring employment within households.[11] Many Elizabethan social reformers used legal means to brand actors as vagrants. Players sought to profit from the theater and united in a system of patronage to deflect the tag of vagrants. The "Act" necessitates a closer look at patronage. For Elizabethan players, the "Act for the Punishment of Vagabonds" was a significant catalyst for patronage. Theatrical players developed at the crossroads of late feudalism and proto-capitalism and used the latter to distinguish themselves from beggars by creating a home in the theater. For players to legitimize their role in dramatic production, they made the theater building home and converted the reputation for panhandling into a reputation for theatrical beggary for applause. In a recent work on beggary and Elizabethan theater, Paola Pugliatti notes that beggary became a social paradox, one in which new proto-capitalist economic developments could not allow the permanence of a social group which not only was unproductive, but also constituted a threat to the private property of productive people (18-19).

Whether changes in social attitudes toward the poor point to monarchical welfare reform of organized alms-giving or the legal intolerance of fraudulent professional begging, the shift is evident in both the enterprises of actors and in the roles of Shakespeare's clown-servants. Beggary responds to proto-capitalist changes to the human condition of service. Woodbridge inquires: "Is it no more than a trope (allied to the humility topos) that speakers of epilogues, who address audiences on behalf of actors and playwrights, often position themselves as *beggars* for applause?" (262). I answer Woodbridge's query with a brief statement by Delany that foregrounds the clown-actor, often misinterpreted as beggar.[12] Delany assesses that Lear's fall occurs because he cannot allow his royal dignity to be measured in monetary terms; "but the Fool well knows the difference between a beggar's life and that of a court dependant, even if his master does not" (435). As Woodbridge suggests, players' conversions into theatrical beggars were more than matters of renaming their practices. The act of begging applause changed the one dimensional act of panhandling into an act of proto-capitalist enterprise and itinerant clowns into players that invested in the business of theater. To view the acts of the clown-servant and the business of theater as proto-capitalist enterprise highlights a difference between the economic concepts of proto-capitalism and mercantilism.

From these perspectives on money, mercantilism and proto-capitalism differ in that this study sees the former as a macroeconomic system that prioritizes the fiscal needs of the government and as a stimulus of commerce.[13] Rather, this study applies proto-capitalism to individual endeavors of characters that possess cash and progress to challenge the traditional economic boundaries of their class and station. For example, in *The Merchant of Venice* Antonio is the non-feudal merchant, a mercantilist with invested argosies in the Mediterranean trade arena based out of Venice. Yet, because his capital is tied up in mercantilist investment, he does not have ready cash in hand to assist Bassanio. Bassanio and Shylock are proto-capitalist. Bassanio desires cash to raise his station, for money to make more money. Shylock operates outside of Antonio's social parameters, yet his usury acts as a proto-capitalist mode within Venetian mercantilism. It produces wealth that in turn inflates his self-worth. In this study, cash is the commodity, both the economic force of trade and the commodity traded.[14] In other words, it is the appeal of money to make money and, in so doing, to create individuals and markets out of traditional business arrangements.

Studies have explored the implications of proto-capitalism for clown figures in an attempt to examine proto-capitalist changes to the service economy in the wake of negative social practices like beggary.[15] Draper evaluates money and its value in relation to social class and human interaction. For Draper, professional fooling suggests that a form of "commercial transaction" occurs in relation to human desire (154-5). Money and morality fuse to determine the value or "profit" of economic decisions. Unlike feudal foolery that tied the clown-servant to the manor in a bond of loyalty for protection and sustenance often with insubstantial cash profits, Shakespeare's clowns progress to market their foolery and earn cash profits used in exchange outside of the household. Nevertheless, Draper discounts the economic behavior of Shakespeare's clowns as beggary rather than business. But, exchange value is not solely based on human desire, and Shakespeare's clowns represent complete monetary systems that emphasize the dynamics of service relationships.

Recent critics analyze Shakespeare's clown-servants to observe their dramatic contributions in relation to Elizabethan servitude. Studies of master-servant bonds by Linda Anderson (9-12), Judith Weil (16), and David Schalkwyk (76) stress characters inter-related within the social economic context of their plays. These relationships suggest intersections of reciprocal behavior that at times appear fixed, yet exemplify the fluidity of an unstable world and conflicting individual interests. But these relationships are insufficient reasons to apply the fluidity present in the theatrical realm to real socioeconomic instability in Elizabethan England. The reflection of the real world of Shakespeare's time must appear in the plays. Although critical emphasis on the dramatic distancing of characters from reality invests Shakespeare's servants with a certain authenticity, that is, Shakespeare's clowns as his own fictional creations, the clown-servants evolve from clowns of the court, wards of feudal service to entrepreneurial proto-capitalists of the stage and in the plays. This shift in service not only parallels significant changes in the Elizabethan economy, but also illustrates Shakespeare's development of the clown-servant. I aim to explore ways in which the role of clown-servants reflects trends away from late feudalism for both the clown and actor within the theatrical worlds of the play. But I also want to show, first, how Shakespeare's clowns, as servants, reflect the social economic growing pains experienced by the servant class of Tudor England.

SOCIAL ECONOMIC CONTEXTS

While my terminology throughout this study, from investment capital to risk management to market economy, is often anachronistic, it accurately describes the economic stresses of early modern England and their presence in the roles of Shakespeare's clowns. Estimates show that one quarter to one half of the population of England in pre-modern times were household servants (Laslett 13). The dynamics of servitude dictate the importance of completing domestic tasks like food preparation, house maintenance, and valet duties, and the servants and their labors ascribe class status to both themselves and householders. The new economy of early modern England creates a shift away from a servant class securely affixed to lifetime household service.

Economic reality in late sixteenth-century England is that many servants count as the unemployed. William Harrison's descriptions from the late sixteenth century describe "superfluous heaps of them . . . great swarmes of idle seruing men" that he hopes "would be brought to labour . . ." (134-5). An example of a late feudal lifetime clown-servant is Will Somer, servant to Henry VIII. The stage clowns that follow Somer, like Tarlton, Kemp, and Armin, have one foot in the feudal tradition and another in the proto-capitalist one.

This book examines the acting of Dick Tarlton, Will Kemp, and Robert Armin and Shakespeare's clowns the Dromios, Launcelot Gobbo, and Feste to establish a trend of clowning-servant both on the Elizabethan stage and in English society. I posit that Shakespeare's clowns are microcosmic representations of an overall capitalist shift in early modern England economics. While sixteenth- and seventeenth-century England did not experience an abrupt triumph of capitalism on a grandiose scale, the gradual transition from feudalism to capitalism was already evident in its social institutions. It is the variable interaction of late feudalism and capitalism, two ultimately irreconcilable modes of production, that shapes the heterogeneous social formations of the age (Wiles 82-83). The late sixteenth century saw the rise of urban capitalism that led to Elizabethan economic instability. Proto-capitalism became evident throughout society and continued to develop within the residual late feudal order.

Proto-capitalist economics prospered with the growth of cities: "London swelled from a town of fifty thousand in 1520 to a bustling metropolis of over two hundred thousand in 1600" (Yancey 19). The powers of an aristocratic hierarchy were challenged by the growth, in numbers and in power, of an urban middle class of merchants and craftspeople. Elizabethan playwright Thomas Dekker depicts a capitalist London:

In every street, carts and coaches make such a thundering as if the world ran upon wheels. At every corner men, women and children meet in such shoals, that posts are set up on purpose to strengthen the houses, lest with jostling one another they should shoulder them down. Besides hammers are beating in one place, tubs hooping in another, pots clinking in a third, water tankards running at tilt in a fourth. Here are porters sweating under burdens, there merchants' men bearing bags of money. Chapmen (as if they were at leap frog) skip out of one shop into another. Tradesmen (as if they were dancing galliards) are lusty at legs and never stand still. (qtd. in Brown *How Shakespeare* 154)

However, economic growth did not mean prosperity for all. Noise, traffic, and trash, the by-products of Dekker's capitalist metropolitan, had negative implications for London society. Historian Marjorie K. McIntosh's most recent work, "Poverty, Charity, and Coercion in Elizabethan England" suggests that although the Elizabethan economy grew and became diversified, with signs of early capitalism in agriculture and industry and increased overseas trade, this expansion was insufficient to provide employment for all male household heads by the late sixteenth century; moreover, inflation outstripped rising cash profits (460). Yet, as Theodore Leinwand argues, "Then as now people responded to and acted upon their economic encumbrances and opportunities in various and often unpredictable ways" (1). Noise and traffic represented work and production, both positive aspects of budding capitalism that accompanied the proto-capitalist fervor to survive. Transience, often an adverse effect of such rapid population growth, plagued the whole of Elizabeth's reign. From 1550-1600, England struggled vigorously with the question of what behaviors reinforced positive work ethics and what constituted vagrancy. For the Elizabethan government, the problem rested not so much with recently established guildsman or the dedicated apprentice, and not even with recently arrived skilled day laborers, but with the free movement of its citizens through an ambiguous public sphere.

Rather than merely reinvigorate social control of theatrical performance, the "Act for the Punishment of Vagabonds" set in motion proto-capitalist interactions driven by both prestige and revenue. As a system of gift-giving, patronage brought to bear two distinct economic effects of capitalist growth on Elizabethan Theater: exclusive royal patronage and heightened economic emphasis on the audience as patron.[16]

As discussed above, patronage became the legal mark that separated the lawful player from the illegitimate vagrant. Itinerate playacting resembled the movement of transient vagabonds, and actors were often deemed vagrants and were subject to legal penalties for unlicensed travel. In 1598, an amendment to the "Act for the Punishment of Vagabonds" abolished the power of magistrates to license players, leaving only the nobles with the authority to lend their names to playing companies (Gurr *Stage* 19). As "middleman" between crown and stage, the magistrate was not completely removed from the business of playacting, but was absorbed into its monarchical control. Exclusive royal and noble patronage empowered law-abiding acting companies in the midst of a shifting economy to earn profits in exchange for playacting. Although money from patrons points to a traditional relationship between noble and performer, money from box office sales added a proto-capitalist aspect of share-earning to the business of theater. Royal patronage and "box office" profits were not mutually exclusive. As Suzanne R. Westfall describes, "the theater was rapidly becoming commodified and patronage shifted from the upper strata of society to include the general public" so that "by the end of the sixteenth century . . . companies like Shakespeare's clearly had two patrons--both the monarch and the paying public" (White and Westfall 41). Playing companies depended on both forms of revenue and the social economic bonds that accompanied them. Often in the course of a playing-year, a company vacillated between royal and aristocratic, seasonal employment during holiday festivals and frequent stops at "public" playhouses during the course of the year. Shakespeare did not benefit solely from either elite or public support but managed both simultaneously. Even though royal and aristocratic patronage gave the monarchy some degree of control of the theater, this patronage was the immediate catalyst for commercial theater.

Royal and noble patronage of the plays created a system of exchange mutually beneficial to the Court and the players rather than existing merely as a self-aggrandizing appendage of government propaganda. Intricate were the economic influences of theatrical production on late Tudor England, and "patronage" helped to sustain aspects of service in the rapidly growing commercial theater. But patronage was not a unidirectional exchange of royal favor or mere compensation for dramatic services rendered. It was a complex system of exchange, gift-giving with benefits for both giver and receiver. Even though proto-capitalist values were emptying out an ideology of service so crucial to a feudal system and ushering in principles of entrepreneurship and profit, patronage held in place the time-honored bonds between wealthy nobles and working artisans. Royal courts provided the most illustrious venues conducive to playacting not only to maximize dramatic appeal, but also to illustrate the pageantry of palace life (Astington *Court* 96). M. D. Jardine notes that "monarchs did use theatrical display to perpetuate the service ideal, and it was certainly a vital, calculated element of their strategy for maintaining power" (302). Ostentatious productions separated royal from public venues and bonded players to the aristocracy through the reciprocity of service. As Stephen Greenblatt notes from Bishop Goodman's account of Elizabeth's "staged" exits from Council, play going was as much about theatrical ostentation as it was about admiring Queen and court (*Renaissance* 167). Visual splendor in the forms of spacious torch-lit theaters, elaborate props, and decorative costumes ensured the most artistic productions for the wealthiest playgoers.[17] Yet, to assume complete ideological control of the theater by the monarchy and its aristocracy is to overlook the complex nature of the service ideal and the patronage system in a fluctuating economy.[18] Jardine notes that patronage "typically operates in a covert way, unlike coercive power-wielding; its power and influence are based on an ideology of service and interdependency designed to maintain the status quo by arrangement rather than force" (287).

It is within the system of patronage that playing companies began economic associations. Jardine states that "Patronage study leads to a focus on circular relations of mutuality rather than conflict of interest between groups bidding for power" (287). For the Elizabethan court, playacting was more than just a social appendage or a symbolic show of state power. Rather, an exchange of power endowed playing companies with royal approval, artistic prestige, and public celebrity important to financial success in the public theaters. Greenblatt reasons that "royal power is manifested to its subjects as in the theater, and the subjects are at once absorbed by the instructive, delightful, or terrible spectacles and forbidden intervention or deep intimacy" (237). Greenblatt's idea of "deep intimacy" plays out more so in court halls among royal audiences and to a lesser degree between court and artists. It was the establishment of playhouses that deepened the intimacy among playwrights, actors, and their "public audiences" since playhouses were financial investments in audience support. With the play as a commodity, its audience "demands" the "supply" of new plays.[19] Gurr contends that while the influence of a royal patron on his company may be hard to demonstrate, the influence of the audience is direct (*Playgoing* 32-35). Like the market, the theater is a place of exchange, where entertainment is offered in return for a fee. Therefore, the play is a commodity.[20]

For the "public" theater of the late sixteenth century, patronage was a reality of lawful dramatic production.[21] In the physical absence of the royal or noble patron, his livery became for players a label of royal or noble favor as well as a badge of legitimacy against harassment and arrest. The badge or name of playing companies legitimized the players as lawful laborers and the plays as the products of exchange in a "no money, no show" economic climate (Leggatt 296). However, play production takes capital. Roslyn Lander Knutson's work, *Playing Companies and Commerce in Shakespeare's Time*, turns away from the theory of theater wars as the economic force behind playing companies and turns to one of financial gain. Similar to the hierarchical structure of royal patronage, actors formed fraternal relationships through companies and sought mutually beneficial associations within the theater (Knutson 22-3). Knutson notes the Elizabethan presence of "both the variety of guilds represented by players and the ubiquity of freemen in the men's companies from the 1570s to the 1590s when commercial relationships among the London-based companies were being developed" (22). Prosperity for freemen-actors came in the form of profits and was sustained through economic bonds like membership within a greater player-community.[22] This is to suggest that players, like many of their characters, worked for cash profits within a traditional grouping system like a company. Like other institutions, the acting companies sought to maintain a balance of noble patronage and lower class labor in the midst of commercial venture for profit.

In this way, theatrical profits became the driving force of company relations. Joint investments among players refer to strategic alliances between two or more actors to undertake economic activity together in the business of theater. The players agree to create a new entity together by contributing equity, and they then share in the revenues, expenses, and control of the enterprise. Economic bonds among actors tied players to companies and provided capital for joint investments.[23] As a commercial model, the joint investments of players do not antiquate royal patronage or monarchal hierarchy since, in fact, company membership is in itself a hierarchical structure. Rather, joint investments complement royal patronage and endow players with a proto-capitalist means of financial security in times of economic misfortune, changes in membership, changes in patrons, playhouse closures, plague, and personal feuds. Another form of player insurance against economic duress was the instance of companies playing together.[24]

Evidence of acting companies playing together in the 1590s suggests that the need to do business was greater than the desire to perpetuate wars among the playing companies.[25] Playing together reflected the economic understandings of business amid constantly changing rules of operation.[26] In the provinces, records of the Admiral's Men show extensive cooperation with other companies. Playing itinerate shows away from London required coordination to produce shows when audiences were in season.[27] As Knutson illustrates, it was not uncommon for playing companies to combine with other companies and also to take on acrobats and jugglers to suit festive audiences and raise profits. To track theatrical relationships in this period of economic change is to view the players as both servants to their patrons and to their audiences. This dual form of service allows play actors to profit from the conflict between two models of service, one emergent, playacting for a paying audience, and one residual, traditional patronage. In the character of domestic worker, the clown-servant gives a humorous voice to tensions between servants and masters in early modern households.

This book posits that Shakespeare's clown-servants address both the masses of laborers and the noble playgoers through a balance of downstairs humor and upstairs wit that permeates all class levels. The cross class appeal of the clown-servant allows him to bridge social gaps through servant-class humor and makes comedy of household service. Clearly, the waning of late feudalism is evident in the portrayals of household economics and the shift away from traditional service. In this period of transition, the late feudal, courtly fool changes to household servant/clown. Thus, his witty comments take on more of a humor that puns and jests about familiar household economies rather than buffoonery of kings and courts. Puns are the stuff of the household because they endow the clown-servant play with meaning. The meaning and understanding of words is central to the master and clown-servant relationship. By manipulating words through puns, the clown-servant is able to influence household order. Household business becomes the center of humor. Examples are the clown humor that surrounds dinner preparations and etiquette among E. Dromio of *The Comedy of Errors* (1.2), Launce and Crab in *The Two Gentleman of Verona* (4.4), Launcelot Gobbo of *The Merchant of Venice* (3.5), and Feste of Twelfth Night (2.3). Emphasis on household business causes many of Shakespeare's clowns to resemble country simpletons of the servant class.

The country simpleton model for Shakespeare's clown would be very flattering to a city audience because much of London Elizabethan population migrated from less urban dwelling places. The country simpleton, with his common sense approach to life, struggles to succeed in the city like many of the unemployed servants who left the country-side and ties of domestic service to seek prosperity in the city. Dromios, Launce and Speed, and Launcelot either serve private masters or are household servants loosely connected to housewifery. Although Touchstone is a court jester, he speaks from a greenworld seat of displacement, reasoning through wit the advantages and disadvantages of courtly and pastoral life. Because Shakespeare's plays reflect aspects of London life regardless of their setting, it is crucial to view servants as individuals hailing from within London, from the vast English countryside and numerous townships, and from a world spurred by varying social-economic forces to the capital city with its burgeoning economy. London's burgeoning economy did not do away with feudal order, and domestic service continued to adhere to many of its codes of decorum. By noting the movement of servant class laborers from settings with more traditional employer-worker relationships to London, it becomes clear that the clown-servants in Shakespeare's comedies must manage the new economic relationships within old forms of order.

HISTORICAL CONTEXTS

Understanding the economic significance of Shakespeare's clowns requires grasping not only their roles in plays, but also the history and relevance of clown-servants to changes in England's economy. Like the guildsmen in society, the clown-servant on-stage reflected the concerns of English citizens struggling to prosper in an economy with competing traditional and proto-capitalist forces. Once inside the theater, fellow citizens, servants and employers embraced and accepted the clown-servant for creating comedy out of real social economic change. Central to this book are Shakespeare's clown-servants of the 1590s, with a rich ancestry in feudal service and a late Elizabethan stage presence motivated by proto-capitalist free enterprise. As early Tudor audiences changed in class and tastes, playwrights drew from many dramatic cousins akin to the English servant clown. Playwrights knew of the real feudal bonds between kings and their fools. England's courts and great medieval households had their fools. Thus, the fool of the court directly influenced the fool of the playhouse. In one instance, Sidney Anglo, the editor of Henry VII's court Account books, points out that "the most mentioned entertainers . . . are the fools" (Angelo 15). In another, Henry VIII's fool, Will Somers, often brightened the king's mood with a bawdy rhyme (33). Even the humane thinker Sir Thomas More maintained a master/servant relationship for wit's sake with his fool, Patterson (Goldsmith 6).

The witty truthfulness of Shakespeare's clowns may be applied to the economic topic of service. His comic clowns depict service relations that are familiar to Elizabethans, a familiarity stemming from their own lives and other dramatic traditions. Influenced by many forms of pre-modern clowning, the popularity of the early modern staged foolery also stems from the parallel development of European and English theatrical devices. Shakespeare's clowns depict rustic reflections of the English countryside, servant–class characters who appeal directly to the economic sensibilities of Elizabethan audiences, yet Shakespeare's clowns evolve within a dramatic tradition of clowning that lies outside the court or household as well. Thelma Niklaus notes the clown's ancient Greek origins and suggests that "It seems probable that all mimes, clowns, drolls, and mummers known to Europe were engendered by the Satyr of Greek Old Comedy, a form of entertainment known to derive from the phallic ritual and ceremony of Dionysos" (18). William Willeford views the dialogue between Greek stage clowns as the impetus for the later Italian zanni (11). He distinguishes the clown through verbal and physical theatrics: scatology, fertility, propagation, and phallephoric humor. Greek, Italian, and English clowns with respect to their cultural origins employ these verbal and physical theatrics even though their outward appearances change.

David Wiles and others view the ancestry of the early modern clown as firmly planted in the Tudor Vice of medieval morality plays, an accepted fact of theater stage history (1). Just as Shakespeare's clowns speak in prose rather than in verse, so does the vernacular of the morality Vice set him apart from other characters. Their speech complements the servant qualities of both Vice and clown and permits them to comment on monetary conditions. In dialogue with other characters and well as with the audience, the Vice and the clown broach the topic of money. The ancestor of Shakespeare's clowns, the Vice's language of money predates the proto-capitalist shift of Elizabethan economic trends. Mischief, the Vice of *Mankind* (c. 1470), offers an early example of a clown-servant character who markets his talents within a traditional setting. Mischief stops the play to market his services to the audience in return for fees to be collected before the play may resume.[28] For both Vice and clown, the marketing of their acting was made possible by their connections to economic actions in the play. Mischief not only solicits money directly from the audience, but he does it in the guise of Devil. Wiles notes that Mischief physically implicates audience members as spectators of Mankind's downfall by charging them to see the Devil; and also, Mischief is the character on stage that orchestrates the demise of Mankind. By linking Mankind to horse stealing, Mischief and his accomplices get both Mankind and the audiences to trust the Devil and question economic morality. Thus, Vice and clown share a profound closeness with the audience that allows them to break the financial relationship between the actors' box-office and the paying audience and freelance for additional monies. In the same way that Mischief is able to solicit money from an audience already engaged in the play, later clowns like Tarlton and Kemp are permitted to gig for tips.

Influential in the development of Shakespeare's clown-servant, the often Vice-like Italian Zanni also shares service status with Shakespeare's clowns.[29] Roma Gill sees traits of two traditional zanni, in Shakespeare's rustic clown, the awkward booby who indulges in perjury and word play, and the witty servant who parodies the actions of his master. In *Commedia del Arte*, a Zanni often uses the language of money to influence service relationships within the play. The servant clown, Ambidexter of *Cambyses* speaks in broken four beat meters, a pace lending itself to improvisation, to upset the balance of class among his fellow servants. In her seminal work on Shakespeare's fools, Olive Mary Busby notes that in the early days of regular drama, improvised dialogue of *Commedia del Arte* and the appearance of the masked clown on the English stage helped to make him a jesting servant (22). Busby posits that by late Elizabethan drama, the foolish qualities of clowns give way to more witty and intriguing characters, clowns that Robert Hillis Goldsmith later refers to as Shakespeare's "wise fools."[30] The early modern stage fool reflects a blend of these classic clowning traditions as well as the move toward the wise fool. As the wise fool develops, his costume changes from motley dress to the coat of the rustic simpleton. Gelasimus, in Grimald's *Archipropheta* (1547) was probably the first clown in cap-and-bells on the English stage (Goldsmith 32). Yet, somewhere between the stage fool and Shakespeare's servant clown, cap-and-bells are shed for a hood and a cockscomb and bauble for an old rugged stick and bladder.

This book suggests that Shakespeare's clown-servants wore the conventional tawny livery of domestic servants, rather than the pied, cap-and-bells and bauble of the court fools. This change in dress points to changes to service in the noble households. By the 1590s, clown-servants appeared less in the extravagant dress of noble trains and more in the modest array of domestic households.[31] Regardless of Shakespeare's play-settings, the clown-servants vividly reflect aspects of Elizabethan service-economy. In relation to domestic service, the terms "noble" and "household" must be explained. Economics points to household while domestic labor within the home points to relationships between family and non-blood relations. This book considers the recent works of Kari Boyd McBride (2002), Wendy Wall (2002), Judith Weil (2005), and others within the scope of Kate Mertes work on the early modern noble household of England. According to Kate Mertes ". . . noble and aristocratic are used as general terms to cover the rich landholding classes, those whose wealth came from the land but who did not need to till it themselves" (4). This study observes the grouping of peoples by nobles into families to form domestic socioeconomic hierarchies. Wall suggests that the early modern "family" was a "primary unit of production" headed by both men and women, with children, servants, apprentices, infants to be wet nursed, and live-in guests (7-8). I stratify Wall's family unit into upper and lower classes with regard to those who serve and to those who receive service. My view of the family units as representative of proto-capitalist development amid residual feudal order incorporates McBride's assessment of early modern domestic arrangements:

> Early modern England inherited from a mythologized vision of an ideal past, an ideal that had currency as a traditional touchstone even in the country becoming decreasingly rural and

agrarian and increasingly urban and mercantile. Perhaps because of the rapid changes in social, economic, and political life (the pace of which contemporaries noted with some alarm), the late medieval country estate remained the symbol of good housekeeping: a moral economy wherein all classes and all peoples lived in right relationship with each other and with the rest of creation. (5)

From the time of Shakespeare, McBride's study focuses the historical look back, a view that allows this study to ground notions of domestic economics in the plays to overall notions of household order in early modern England.

In this book, the term "household" stems from but is not restricted to the noble family unit. Household refers not only to a domestic unit of blood and non blood relatives, "all of whom live together under the same roof(s) as a single community, for the purpose of creating the mode of life desired by the noble master [or noble mistress] and providing suitably for needs (Mertes 5), but household also refers to the splintered representations of family units outside of the nobility. For example, my analysis of *The Two Gentlemen of Verona* views the removal of the household from the court and its gentle subjects to the forest with outlaw kinsmen. The forest home combines traditional expectation of order with entrepreneurial economic practices. I observe in *The Merchant of Venice* changes to the family unit within merchant class households in the absence of true nobility. In this play, there is no landed or blood-aristocracy, only mercantile wealth and the family units that assemble around it. Weil's research takes into account strict household regulations that govern relationships in the traditional homes between masters and servants (26). Weil notes that servants may constitute "incipient monsters" who behave disorderly (20), desire to be treated as equal family members

(20), and attempt to undermine household decorum (59). Importantly, from the perspective of the "all licenc'd fool," Shakespeare's clown-servants exhibit all of these behaviors. It is the relationships between clown-servant and master/ mistress within household settings that concern this study. I move from the most traditional of household relationships between noble courtly master and, ideally, esteemed clown-servant to attenuated ties between nobles holding onto old forms of domestic order and clown-servants who seek alternative socioeconomics.

A look at Shakespeare's immediate predecessors suggests that only a handful of early modern English plays employ some aspect of a servant class clown. Shakespeare's comedies portray developed clowns who are integrated into the main action of their plays usually as servants to primary characters. Nowhere other than in Shakespeare do clowns distinguish themselves as trustworthy commentators of their play's economic tensions. Yet early modern England does show a shift towards clowns who jest on the topic of service. Such are the servant clowns Trotter in *Fair Em* (1591) and Miles in Robert Greene's *Friar Bacon and Friar Bungay* (1598).[32] Once the humorous appeal of early modern English clowns-servants moves further away from time-honored traditions of clowning like scatology and buffoonery, Shakespeare's funny clowns instigate dialogue charged with witty exchanges on service that move the clown-servant toward proto-capitalism. A significant leap in clown development, yet akin nonetheless, joins *Friar Bacon's* Miles and *Merchant's* Launcelot. Humorous situations occur when the master/servant bonds of these clowns dissolve. Although Miles does not achieve the psychological introspection of Launcelot, he too converses humorously with a counseling entity believed to be the devil on the subject of service.[33] Similarly, both Miles and later Launcelot converse with fiends and heed their counsel to flee from angry masters for seemingly more prosperous employment. Miles conveys the comic appeal of a lazy servant beguiled by the devil that is later seen in Shakespeare's Launcelot. However, unlike Shakespeare's clowns, Miles and other pre-Shakespeare clowns are not woven into the social economic fabric of their plays. Unlike Launcelot's service to Jessica, Trotter's job as a "tapster" in hell affects only Trotter. Shakespeare brings to the Elizabethan stage a new breed of clown whose parodies mirror social economic conditions in early modern England. The advantage of the master/servant bond is obvious; the clown follows his master. But, since servants were less feudalist than capitalist in their service, Elizabethans looked to the clown-servant and their dramatic portrayals of master/servant bonds to address skepticism concerning changes to the domestic service industry. All in all, as economic barometers, Shakespeare's clowns provide commentary regarding the nature of financial relations within plays. Shakespeare employs clowns to voice seemingly personal opinions of monetary concerns that supersede their limited wordplay. Their perspectives encompass the acts and motives of other characters, often those characters that experience economic ambiguities.

BOOK CHAPTERS

Just as the clown-servants develop in the early modern theater and move progressively away from their feudal roots, so Shakespeare's clown-servants develop proto-capitalist insight and move away from their traditional domestic economics. In chapter two, I examine early modern English clowning to trace the theatrical development of the simpleton clown servant as found in Shakespeare's comedies. Although influenced by classical dramatic forms like *Commedia del Arte* and the archetypal Vice, Shakespeare's clowns reflect late Tudor and early Stuart senses of humor. My study begins with Henry VIII's clown servant William Somer to examine the waning appeal of classical clowning. From Somer, I trace the progressive development of early modern clown-servant to Shakespeare's day. Direct influence of early modern English clowns on Shakespeare's characters begins with foolery of Richard Tarlton. I look to historical records of Tarlton and his clowning devices to bridge the gap between classic European clowning and the clowns exclusive to early modern England. His renowned clowning influences Shakespeare's clown actors William Kemp and Robert Armin. I investigate changing patterns in their approaches to comedy that move from traditional comic devices to Shakespeare's full integration of the clown-servant into the plot. Although William Willeford in *The Fool and His Scepter* cites early modern English jest books to suggest no significant difference in the "gags and jokes in a clown's routine" (xxi), this book shows how the humor created by Shakespeare's clowns influences the economic perceptions of other characters.

In my third chapter, I argue that the Dromios of *The Comedy of Errors*, Shakespeare's first clowns of comedy, present Shakespeare's humorous commentary on bond relationships. Shakespeare's comedies reflect an awareness of changes in service class economics and the humorous intersection of progressive ideas and waning feudal orders. I observe household economics in conflict with the commercial exchange of the Mart and the problematic that money adds to bond relationships. When applied to verbal exchanges between master and servant in *The Comedy of Errors*, money magnifies the dialogue between Dromio and Antipholus of Syracuse to illustrate that the master/servant bonds are the glue of the play's economics. Plot complications test these bonds, producing humor. I then turn to Launce and Speed in *Two Gentlemen of Verona* and argue that their master/servant relationships illustrate the progressive development of Shakespeare's clown humor along capitalist lines. Additionally, Launce and Speed represent Shakespeare's early servant humor that extends to animal comedy. I see Launce's dog, Crab, as an extended member of the servant class. I use Launce's view of Crab as his servant to observe exchanges of behavior between masters and servants, exchanges that point to the differing approaches to service and profit between the two.

Chapter four evaluates Launcelot Gobbo in *The Merchant of Venice* as a traditional clown-servant who moves laterally between masters. This chapter considers exchange particularly relevant to the market strategies of speculation, mercantilism, and risks representative of visible early modern capitalist discourse. I suggest that Launcelot's service choice to leave Shylock's employment for Bassanio's characterizes a deliberate move from late feudal to proto-capitalist business. The economic aspects of Launcelot's dichotomous masters may be more thoroughly understood through his answer to *Merchant's* implied financial query: What is good business? Primarily, I posit that as the entrepreneurial "middle man" between these dichotomies, Gobbo proves advantageous to the play's merchants, Christians, and mercy-seekers. As the play's broker, I see a witty Launcelot who disrupts Shylock's household orders and physically repositions people, money, and services based on profitable exchanges both for those characters and for himself.

In my fifth chapter, I observe in *Twelfth Night* how Shakespeare positions Feste to reflect changes in domestic service. As both an entrepreneur entertaining for coins and also a member of a traditional domestic staff, Feste illustrates a laborer within the economic transition between feudal and capitalist worlds. Feste's position reflects early modern England's move away from large numbers of household servants toward the smaller households. Within the festivity of *Twelfth Night*, Feste brings awareness to the waning holiday fun in the feudal twilight of two noble homes. He uses for his medium the oscillations between flexible and inflexible social economic class climbing. These tensions result from challenges to social expectations of a dying feudal order. What proper behavior governs the relations between masters and servants in the midst of social economic change? I submit Feste's witty commentary on service, entrepreneurship, and the classes as a new brand of humor representative of the proto-capitalist growing pains of early modern England. In this chapter, I address Feste's songs as comic devices relevant to the overall economics of the play.

In sum, this book seeks to join scholarly debate concerning the economic relevance of Shakespeare clowns. By emphasizing aspects of service, the comedy of the clowns is tied to economic tension in the plays. Although moments of economic tension directly concern masters and major characters, the clowns as servants provide sound economic counsel. By understanding clowns as servants in relation to the economic themes within the plot, audiences of Shakespeare may better discern the inclusion of economic uneasiness in the plays as well as the solutions sought by other characters. The economic paradigm of the late feudal/proto-capitalist shift in early modern England provides the chronological plane upon which to measure changes to the service ideal and its influence on characters and actors as servants of the stage. As a paradigm of history, the late feudal/proto-capitalist shift allows the development of Shakespeare's clown-servants to be traced between plays and along social economic influences.

CHAPTER I

THE DEVELOPMENT OF THE ENGLISH CLOWN-SERVANT IN EARLY MODERN ENGLISH DRAMA

> *Will Somer.*   *This bit Harry I giue to thee, & this next bit must serue for me, both which Ile eate apace: This bit Madame vnto you, and this bit I my selfe eat now, and all the rest vpon thy face. (Armin 46)*

As Elizabethan stage clowning moves forward into Shakespeare's time, the dramatic portrayal of service relationships between clown-servants and masters progresses from late feudal to proto-capitalist displays of exchange. An initial characteristic of this economic trend is the commodification of the domestic clown-servant himself. I foreground an economic view of Shakespeare's clown-servants by way of their development from the court fool, William Somer. The spelling "Will Somer" refers to the real clown-servant to the court of Henry VIII, and "Will Summer" refers to the dramatic character and stage persona representative of Somer. Charting the dramatic development of clown-service from Somer, the court clown-servant to Will Summer, his theatrical persona, illustrates theatrical and literary historiography in the lineage of Shakespeare's domestic clown-servant. This lineage opens a window into the merging worlds of early modern English theatre, London economy, and the actors who reveal this picture in their portrayals of clown-servants. By centering on the clown-servant rather than usual protagonists (like Lear, Orsino, and Portia) as an agent of economic action central to plot structure, I am able to observe, as commodified personae, clown-servants.[1] Rather than relying on a Marxist view of commodities,[2] I am using the term "commodity" in its most general sense to mean on object marketed for sale.[3] This sense underlies Falstaff's exclamation, "I would to God thou and I knew where a commodity of good names were to be bought" (2.4.448). Similarly, when the Bastard in *King John* reasons, "And why rail I on this Commodity?" he relates the term commodity directly to the market: he has not yet received the "fair angels" that would salute [his] palm (2.1.587-8). The anonymous writer of the 1609 letter to the reader prefacing the quarto *Troilus and Cressida* uses the term "commodity" specifically to refer to the marketability of comedies, if only "the vain names of comedies" were "chang'd for the titles of commodities." It is in this sense that clown-servants develop into what Phillip Vannini would call a "commodified personae," or a star or celebrity of popular culture. These characters perform within the growing theatrical market of early modern England, an economic environment of monetary exchange for dramatic entertainment. Ultimately, this lineage reveals that Shakespeare's proto-capitalist clown-servants like *The Merchant of Venice's* Launcelot Gobbo and *Twelfth Night's* Feste, whose loose bonds of service give them entrepreneurial leverage within their plays, evolve in part from an English tradition of court service.[4] Likewise, Elizabethan clowns Richard Tarlton, William Kemp, and Robert Armin evolve from the clowning of William Somer, fool to Henry VIII, to achieve entrepreneurial leverage in theatrical production. David Wiles applies Grock's views of clown lineage to his study of Shakespeare's clowns, a view that this book shares (11-12). According to the great modern clown Grock, the clown is, as much as any artist, a product of tradition. Just as a painter uses the experiences of his forerunners, and as an author owes his experience to literary predecessors, so is every eminent clown but a torch-bearer of the clowns who preceded him or who still work with him (226-7).

As proto-capitalists, clown-servants of early modern English theatre emerge from a history of court fools. It was the charitable custom of royalty to keep an innocent fool, imbecilic or mentally retarded by birth, as an expression of alms (Southworth 61-69). The keeping of court jesters was based on pity, a sense of feudal alms together with the belief that the simple state of clowns, by birth, was divinely inspired. Since the clown was believed to be a simpleton incapable of comprehending late feudal law, he was immune to its corruptive forces. Thus, the court jester had a familial association with the court and was valued as a speaker of unblemished truths with impunity.[5] As the court jester becomes the play actor, the gifts attributed to real court service find their way into dramatic plots. The clown's talents of profound situational insight, and language manipulation, and the ability to out think and out wit his adversaries allowed him to act deliberately simplistic, odd, or eccentric, in an attempt to entertain as well as advise.

WILLIAM SOMER, COURT FOOL TO HENRY VIII

By the 1590s, the name Will Summer has achieved theatrical notoriety, and his characterization meets audience expectations concerning the appearance of the clown-servant. The movement of a real clown-servant William Somer onto the stage and the altered spelling of his character's name (from Somer to Summer) move a tradition of late feudal court fooling into the proto-capitalist theater of early modern England. But why begin with Somer, and what makes his brand of clown-service relevant to the development of Shakespeare's clown-servants? Somer's chronological proximity to the advent of early modern theatre in England and the subsequent appearance of his name in plays as a "brand name" or watchword for clown-servant antics make him the pivotal force of the transition from court jester to commodified public servant of the theatre. Like brand names that distinguish one commodity from another, the name "Will Somer" came to signify a kind of clowning. As a brand name for clowning, the title Will Summer names clown characters in plays as well as characterizes the real clown actors who play under that title and grow in popularity. As the pivotal force of clown-service, Somer's fame moves from the feudal court of Henry VIII to the proto-capitalist theatre of Shakespeare.

Next, this chapter examines the first documented dramatic treatment of Somer as Cacurgus, the fool of *Misogonus* who illustrates that servant status is foundational to his clownish humor. It is servant status that commodifies the stage clown who, as a servant, exists as a product that reflects significant changes in England's service economics. Cacurgus's domestic service in the play illustrates a significant shift from traditional domestic service to joblessness and subsequent homelessness. His plight mirrors many unemployed working class servants of early modern England. *Misogonus* displays Cacurgus as both a domestic clown-servant and a dejected and lord-less vagrant. The chapter also looks to the charismatic foolery of Richard Tarlton in *The Famous Victories of Henry V*, which illustrates a commodified clown-servant, a "theatrical commodity," with a recognizable brand name that has evolved within shifting early modern theatre economics to exist as a product that reinforces its productive origin.[6] When viewed from the perspective of the clown-servant, these plays illustrate the progression of household service economics to theatrical profitability.

Misogonus' morio

In *Misogonus*, Somer's persona goes beyond the obvious concern with master-servant loyalty and the inheritance of land and goods, to make visible the complexities of familiar economics that lead to the breakdown of clown-service and dismissal of the clown-servant from the early modern English noble family.[7] The relation of his name to his station first commodifies Somer's domestic service to the king and later to characters on the stage. Although the dramatis persona lists Cacurgus as *morio* or fool, he is summoned by the recognizable pseudonym of Will Somer.[8] Later in Shakespeare's time, in Thomas Nash's *Summer's Last Will and Testament*, Will Summer wittily narrates the seasonal debates concerning the service of the other seasons and cosmic forces to Summer (the season, a character separate from Will Summer).[9] Somer's legacy of foolery helps to develop the popularity of the stage clown. It may be strongly contended that the clown-actor was the first English stage performer to achieve star quality. Star quality or celebrity is evident later in the clowning of Dick Tarlton. Early reflections of Somer's clowning style appear in the clown-servant Cacurgus in *Misogonus* and in Tarlton's portrayal of Dericke in *The Famous Victories of Henry V* (Shaughnessy 7).

William Somer's domestic service in the court of Henry VIII firmly grounds this study in late feudal domestic order. While scholars have traced dramatic plots of clowns and their service to their masters, a clear look into the commodification of "Will Somer" and his particular brand of clowning sheds new light on both literary and theatrical development of clown-service in early modern England. When Cacurgus morio, the fool in *Misogonus*, declares to the audience, "Ha ha! Now will I goe playe Will Sommer agayne" (2.3.79), he assumes the persona of "Will Somer," a commodifed brand of sixteenth-century foolery with a semiotic "gold standard" or brand name for jesters (Barber 61). Barber's notion that Somer's real legendary court fooling becomes a measurement of quality for clown characters in plays complements economist Grant McCracken's idea that "brands are complicated bundles of meaning partly because they have been picking up meaning through the efforts of several generation of managers" (179). When applied to the development of the English stage clown from Somer's real court origins to Shakespeare's fictitious clown characters, McCracken's view of brands shows how the "managers" of clowning shift from generations of monarchs of the court to actors of the stage. The legend of Will Somer, the court fool of Henry VIII, became Will Summer, a fictitious character in plays that reflects generations of feudal development prior to appearing on stage. As a brand name for fooling known for his impromptu wit, Summer's proverbial shrewdness accents verbal forthrightness allowed to the fool.

In England's early modern period, noblemen still practiced selecting simpletons from the countryside to reside in their households as clown-servants (Billington 32). A practice that sheds light on the economics of domestic service, the hiring of clown-servants into homes represented an attempt to surround the simpleton with the type of security extended from nobles to vassals. Sandra Billington suggests that as noblemen traveled the countryside, it was their duty to discover and refer simpletons for court service (32-3). These dullards were mostly of rural origin, and were inclined to prove their "natural" clownishness before induction into noble service as a clown-servant. As a feudal example, Billington consults Thomas of Chobham's *Summa Confessorum* (1215) for economic rule that governed the noble annex of country simpleton as domestic naturals:

A man proven *purus idiota* (a simple idiot) by a jury became the property of the Crown, and his personal property could be bestowed on someone else. Applications were known as 'begging for a fool' and with the inducement of property, it seems that the law, *de idiota inquirendo* (examining into the witlessness of a man) was open to abuse. (33)

Worth mention is the actual wording in which "a man" is synonymous with "property," and yet property may be separated from a man, its owner. The practice of noble annexing of country simpletons continues into the late feudal period in England. A point that applied to Will Somer suggests he became royal property at the advent of his hire to Henry VIII's court. In the context of the *Summa Confessorum*, Somer's only property corresponds to the list of his allowances.[10]

As property, Somer lived in domestic servitude to the King, and received neither wages nor payment for his entertainment. "Domestic life," writes Linda Anderson, "consisted of a master who was owed various kinds of service by his wife, children, and servants. All these kinds of service are regarded as in some degree analogous, so that the master of a household might be regarded as a kind of king in his own household" (19). As the property of a domestic king, Somer, the servant, retains certain worth not based on the value of his household labors in exchange for wage earnings but on the subjective assessment of his verbal wit in exchange for sustenance. The realm provided for Somer's necessities, whether he was at court or traveling with Henry VIII through the provinces. Financial statements dated January 1538 show the purchase of "velvet purse for W. Somer," as well as allowances for "2 pair of black hoes," "2 pair of summer buskin" (Southworth 71). The hierarchal conditions of Somer's domestic service determined that he was available to jest the king out of sadness, the very purpose for which he was supplied the buskin and hose.

Somer's actual acts of service to the king required his ability to jest Henry out of moods of depression, an act that employed verbal wit rather than clownish skills like acrobatics and juggling. "When he was sad, the King and he would rime, thus Will exiled sadnesse many a time," says Armin in a poem that characterizes Somer's service to Henry VIII as the employment of words to vanquish emotional sadness (Armin 40). "The object of jest," Freud wrote, "is to bring about the resultant pleasure of playing and at the same time appease the protesting reason which strives to suppress the pleasant feeling. To achieve this, the senseless combination of words or absurd linking or thoughts must make sense" (720). According to Freud, "jest makes use of almost all the technical means of wit" (720). The tedium of Henry's reign correlates to Freud's "protesting reason," royal tension that Somer appeases by translation of words into wit. Somer's ability to alleviate the tensions of court for Henry points to two noteworthy conditions of their service bond: The first is, for the King, Somer's jests are therapeutic acts of stress-relief that move Henry to accept Somer as a familial companion. This friendship is depicted in *Henry VIII's Psalter* (Plate 11b) and in the large portrait, *The Family of Henry VIII* (Plate 12) that is reported to have hung in the Presence Chamber at Whitehall (Southworth 73-5). The second is that this familial closeness cultivated a relationship in which humor became the bridge between noble and peasant. This humor was made possible by their mutual enjoyment of bawdy comedy; yet at the same time, the responsibility of servant to king was kept intact by their awareness of customary service decorum.

As court jester, Somer's service entails the responsibility of understanding the King's disposition, a responsibility that requires Somer to know the limits of Henry's sense of humor. Seminal to their bond of service is a friendship based on their shared sense of scatological humor, a humor that in itself gives insight into the nature of clown-servant/king relationship. Armin's *Nest of Ninnies* gives clues to the nature of Somer's service of words and his relationship with the king. Taking into account the license of the clown-servant to speak with impunity, bawdy humor may be used in conjunction with word play and witticisms to entertain Henry. Armin reports that "The King vpon a time being extreame melancholy and full of passion, all that *Will* could doe will not make him merry" (44). After secluding himself behind the "arras" to think of a jest to brighten Henry's mood, Somer emerges with three questions of jest, the third jest (or "show-stopper") revealing the king's approval and enjoyment of bawdy humor. Armin writes that in other words, it is the bawdy humor that allows two individuals from extreme economic disparity to laugh together, an act that reinforces the familial acceptance by the king of his jester, who remains, however, his lowly servant who sleeps with the spaniels.

> Now tell me sayes *Will* if you can, what it is that being borne without life, head, lippe or eye, yet doth runne roaring through the World till it dye?this is a wonder qd the King, & no question, I know it not. Why qd *Will* it is a fart. At this the King laught hartely, & was excéeding merry. (44-5)

From these perspectives, it may be reasoned that the bond of service between Henry and Somer (master and clown-servant) was a relationship of words within the parameters of comical etiquette set by the king. The clown, although aware of the parameters, uses his wit to push the parameters as far as the master's humor will allow. If for whatever reason Somer may have felt that his jests displeased the king, he may have opted out of the jesting game. The refusal to play displays a degree of independence that later helps the court jester to evolve into the stage clown. Like later stage clowns, court fools worked with the possibility of comic failure. Thus, to play the "Will Summer" signals the clown-servant's use of words to provoke thought as well as outwit his verbal opponent. As a mannerism of verbal foolery, Somer's bawdy talk evolves in later clown-servants whose jests reflect their household allegiance within the traditional ideal of social hierarchy. As with Henry VIII, the masters in Shakespeare's plays set the parameters of humor for their clown servants. Like Somer, Shakespeare's clown servants push the limits of allowed humor.

As clown-servant, Somer's domestic allegiance to Henry rests on the contemporary authority invested in the Great Chain of Being, an ideal of order in early modern England that everything except God has a superior.[11] As an essentially feudal concept, this great chain was under increasing stress in this period. Aspects like the social mobility of entrepreneurship and cash rather than vassalage as payment for labor threatened this hierarchical order. This notion of divine hierarchy at play in the earthly realm underpins social class order in its relation to service. The clown-servant appeals naturally to key pillars of the pre-established domestic organization, of one's cosmic position as universal servant. In particular, Linda Anderson helps to illuminate the interplay between God and service, for she describes how the lords of great households might interpret the service obligation of their domestics in relation to human service obligations to God. Anderson asserts that "Although relationships between master and servant were acknowledged as a human creation, it was nevertheless often described as being as natural and basic as that between husband and wife or parent and child" (22). Adherence to the Great Chain of Being within domestic order elevates the relationship between master and servant above human conception, and likens it to natural or divine conceptions of order. Thus, noble household order that attempts to correspond to divine order includes the clown-servant as a valued worker within the domestic structure of royal home. When this domestic structure, with Somer at its base, appears on the stage, it emphasizes changing socioeconomic relationships in the play and in early modern England.

The first documented dramatic treatment of Somer, *Misogonus*, begins the dramatic history of the proto-capitalist shift from the clown-servant innocent in service to the court to the entrepreneurial clown-servant of the theatrical market. As the clown-servant of *Misogonus*, Cacurgus is the first known dramatic portrayal of Somer. Cacurgus's importance is that his character marks the first step of the dramatic clown-servant away from the traditional economics of noble household employment and into the open job market of a shifting economy. His representation of the clown-servant's move from legendary court fame to a commodity of theatrical production is made evident in his portrayals of clown service. In hindsight, the play's dating (ca. uncertain, perf. 1564-1577) suggests that it may be seen as a contemporary treatment of the issues current to mid-sixteenth century England. By the end of the play, it is easy to view Cacurgus as one of England's seemingly nameless faceless unemployed masses. An England in the midst of social reform appears to await the jobless clown-servant.

In *Misogonus*, Cacurgus is forced out of Philogonus's household to enter an economy of commercial risks, a shift that exemplifies a branching off of a proto-capitalist domestic servant. The service bond between Cacurgus and his noble patriarch and master Philogonus and Misogonus, Philogonus's prodigal son, not only reflects the plight of the domestic clown-servant who attempts to maintain his sustenance by clinging to late feudal bonds of service, but also reflects the plight of the clown-servant who faces proto-capitalist challenges to relationships of service. The focus of this two-part section is Cacurgus's feigned allegiance to late feudal domestic duty and his proto-capitalist modes of exchange. He assumes both personas in an attempt to gain economic leverage. In Cacurgus, we see the evolutionary beginning of the theatrical term "Will Summer," first as a direct reference to the traditional acceptance of the domestic clown-servant, then later as the brand name for the theatrical clown-servant.

When Cacurgus announces to the audience, "now will I go play Will Summer again" what follows is his rendition of Will Somer's fooling. The significance of the rendition and his mention of Somer is that, on one level, it introduces Cacurgus as a character clinging to bonds of service of earlier times. His service bond to Philogonus suggests nostalgia for pre-modern domestic arrangements. On a deeper level, it begins the development of Will Somer's commodified personae as a brand name for clown-servant foolery. Just as brand names are used to distinguish one commodity from another, so Will Somer's name functioned as a brand name distinguishing his particular form of clowning. The importance of viewing Somer as a theatrical commodity lies in the relation of his service as a domestic clown-servant to his displays of wit. This relation is significant to the development of the dramatic clown-servant from the conventional noble household to proto-capitalist stage. It is service that commodifies the stage clown who, as a servant, exists as a product that reflects significant changes to England's service economics. In *Misogonus*, Cacurgus embodies three distinct aspects of Somer's fooling as clown-servant: first, in the expectations of servant and master; second, in the use of word play and wit when conversing with the master; and third, in a domestic position of service within a domain of hierarchical order.

As clown-servant, Cacurgus enjoys elevated servant status that keeps him in the company of nobles while at the same time he is a domestic servant and must interact as a servant with other servants. A duality that continues in Shakespeare's clown-servants, the clown-servant's humor illustrates his access to upper and lower classes. Cacurgus illustrates that servant status is foundational to his clownish humor and alters this humor to fit the expectations of his masters. He accomplished a great feat for a servant by convincing the master of his regard for late feudal domestic authority and that he expects to be cared for in the tradition of the court jester. As the character "Will Summer," Cacurgus brags to the audience about his benefits from his master's belief in a fixed station:

> If [I] [cannot help lau][ghi]ng as oft as I think
> How like a f[ool p]ut out my head
> With bacon in my hand and my bowl full of
> drink . . . Ha! Ha! Ha! (1.2.225)[12]

Like Somer, Cacurgus offers a lifetime of service to subsist as Philogonus's clown-servant, a position of domestic service that will take care of his worldly needs. Lifetime service points to customary domestic arrangements, wageless relationships that give way to money earning servants. Armin notes that once, when Somer had pleased Henry with clever jests, the King encouraged: "*Will* aske any reasonable thing, and he would graunt it" (45). Notably, Somer's answers reemphasized the bond to Henry and its requisition of a lifetime of service. Armin continues, "Thanks *Harry* saies he, now against I want I know where to find, for yet I néede nothing, but one day I shall, for euery man sées his latter end, but knowes not his beginning" (45). As a court clown, Somer's response suggests that he is aware that he resides in the care of the monarchy for life, and he is also aware of death as the great leveler of kings and peasants regardless of their birth. In other words, Somer knows and accepts his position as court clown-servant in the social hierarchy of his time. The expectations of the court jester to be cared for in return for wise conversation affixes the clown-servant to economic advantages of service and charity. One particular advantage of the clown-servant was that unlike other household servants, the clown-servant enjoyed the companionship of his noble lord and was allowed to accompany other nobles. Robert Hillis Goldsmith argues: "The natural fool or idiot was tolerated and was allowed a measure of freedom not permitted the other lower servants" (6). Like Somer, Cacurgus expects to be at the constant behest of his master, a station that elevates him above other servants that he refers to as "knaves." In an aside, he exclaims:

> What, ho! with his man's voice he calls for Will Summer!
> "[Wh]ere have you put him? Bring him hither, you knave.
> [And] when I am come, my properties he tells:
> [How sim]ple, how honest, how faithful, and true;
> [And gi][veth] my points and many things else.
> (1.1.248-52)

These characteristics of a court fool suggest similarities between the character Cacurgus and Somer that illustrate their loyalties to the nobility. Yet with the advantages of allegiance to the nobility come the realities of servant status. When Somer's jests were done, reports Armin that "*Will* laid him downe amongst the Spaniels to sléepe" (45). Likewise, Cacurgus returns to the world of the servants when done conversing with Philogonus. In these respects, Cacurgus, the dutiful servant, not only has a unique social position between two distinguished aristocrats and the servant-class, but also provides verbal clown-service that must be tempered with truth.

As a clown-servant, Cacurgus enters into a traditional bond with Philogonus his master and caregiver in return for faithful (truth-telling) service as his domestic fool.[13] The benevolence of a powerful man (the good shepherd) toward his lessers points to the clown as the worthy poor. Philogonus bases the choice of Cacurgus as his clown on the notion that in addition to Cacurgus's poverty, he speaks wise words. Philogonus equates this wise element in Cacurgus with the inability to lie. Cacurgus tells the audience in an aside that

> [A fool], he think[s], can neither lie nor flatter.
> [I tel]l him that I hear a very good rumour:
> He is wild, but what though? he is not yet come to age.
> I know that this tale will de[light his] humour.
> Hereafter, they say, he'll be sober and sage.
> (1.1.257-261)

While this report suggests the lechery of youth, Cacurgus frames its words to play to the late feudal expectations of Philogonus for his son. By pleasing Philogonus, Cacurgus maintains the benefits of his traditional domestic service. In fact, it echoes the primary advice of trustworthy friends. Later, the supportive neighbor Liturgus applies the same logic to the problem of Philogonus's immoral son: "Why, Sir! he hath not yet sown all his wild oats; He is but young, truly; he must needs run his race" (2.1.220-21). While he plays the customary dutiful servant, Cacurgus voices the sentiments of Philogonus's trustworthy friends and echoes the hierarchical order that governs domestic service.

Cacurgus also adopts key aspects of Somer's jests with Henry as he uses word play and creates wit when conversing with the master. The service of Somer's verbal wit continues into early modern drama as seen when Philogonus greets

Cacurgus with inquiry: "What, Will Summer! from whence com'st thou" (2.1.266). By addressing Cacurgus as "Will Summer," Philogonus sets in motion their service bond and the expectations of the verbal word games like those shared between Somer and Henry. Rather than answer in direct discourse, Cacurgus invites his master to humor through the instance of jest, and says: "And you'll give me some dingdongs to hang at my sleeve, I'll tell you, by my troth! Both whither and when" (2.1.283). Hanging dingdongs, the dress of earlier court fools, suggests that if Philogonus will figuratively accept Cacurgus as the dutiful servant, he will engage Philogonus in verbal sport. Philogonus enjoys his bawdy humor. In the same manner that Henry VIII's scatological sense of humor established the parameters of decorum for Somer's jest, so does Philogonus's bawdy reference to his genitals for the "dingdongs" set the tone for Cacurgus's verbal wit. With Somer-like style, Cacurgus answers his master's inquiry of Misogonus, his son, by launching into a jest that puns on Philogonus's hunting reference as whoremongering. Again, it is the master that begins the pattern of jest to be followed by the clown-servant:

Philogonus.	Hold thee, and tell me true too, and thoust be my lurding.
Cacurgus.	Aha! this a trim one, indeed-has a golden nose; I'll tell ye vort, a went in right now a-birding.
Philogonus.	A-birding! like enough, I think, to catch a bunting! Had he any dogs with him or no, knowst thou well?

Cacurgus.	I am sure, I, he is gone a very
	whore-hunting; Had a brace
	of hounds with him that were
	good o' th' smell. (1.1.286-92)

Philogonus's allusion to Cacurgus as his "lurding," or hunting hawk allows Cacurgus to relay that Misogonus is "a birding" for seedy female companionship. The above dialogue contains *homographs* ("same writing") the type of pun that employs a word or words with two or more meanings, e.g. "a-birding" and "bunting," as terms for both cardinals/sparrows and girls, and the term "dog" for both hunting breeds and Misogonus's band of unsavory familiars.[14] Walter D. Redfern asserts that these types of punning "illuminate the nature of language" and that the punsters "practice linguistic serendipity" (9). Cacurgus's definitive service as a clown is the illumination of language and thereby the illumination of his master's thoughts and emotions. Playing the dutiful servant, Cacurgus plays his master's agent and reports in a Somer-like style of relaying news within puns and wordplay. For Philogonus, Cacurgus measures to the gold standard of Somer since he tells what his master perceives to be truth.

The domestic clown-servant who subsists as the property of a noble lord reinforces practices of noble household economics that help to maintain economic hierarchy. Cacurgus exists within *Misogonus's* domestic hierarchy. He adheres to a domestic hierarchy that reflects Somer's position within the court of Henry VIII. *Misogonus* addresses the relationship of the clown-servant in its adaptation of early modern social class order and its relation to service. The traditional fool of the court appeals to key pillars of this construct, of one's cosmic position as a universal servant. Anderson's work on God and service applies directly to *Misogonus* and its emphasis on the cosmic hierarchy in relation to domestic service, with God at the top, then King Henry (through allusions to Somer), Philogonus (noble master), and Cacurgus (clown-servant). Anderson reasons that

> theoretically, since God had established the hierarchies of earthly life and determined who would command and who obey, there should be no conflicts among service . . . Nevertheless, there were conflicts of various kinds: between God and monarch, God and employer, king and employer, king and one's kindred, . . . between employer and another social superior, etc. (177)

Anderson also accounts for the basic conflict between master and servant, a condition of service that changes once Cacurgus is no longer accepted as a domestic clown-servant (22).

Conflict for Cacurgus occurs when he fails as Philogonus's dutiful domestic servant and is found to be a masquerading proto-capitalist. For Cacurgus, verbal wit marks an important shift toward capitalism and a step toward the use of words to earn a profit. Cacurgus's hire by Philogonus simply astonishes Misogonus because as Cacurgus's master, he knows that the true nature of Cacurgus's service is opportunistic rather than dutiful. As the *Summa Confessorum* illustrates, the abuse of this kind of traditional domestic placement was not beyond the practice of a clown-servant.. Allardyce Nicoll's early work on the origins of fools directly applies to Cacurgus's masquerade as a dutiful servant and his later wordplay with Philogonus: "The freedom to indulge in wanton talk, truth-telling, and parody proved an incentive strong enough to enlist many perfectly sane men in the ranks of counterfeit fool" (54). William Willeford defines the stage clown as a professional counterfeiter of folly (10), a deliberate joker, and as aforementioned Lippincott sees clown-servants as

> wise enough to play the role of fool without themselves being actual idiots. The audience's knowledge of their playing a role is a large part of the joke, and much of the comedy in the plays comes from the fool's ability to exist simultaneously in two worlds, that of the wise and that of the foolish. (246)

CLOWN-SERVANT AS MORAL VICE

The quality to deceive, to masquerade, likens the proto-capitalist clown-servant to the deceptive nature of the Moral Vice. The Vice acts as a theatrical middle man between the court fool of late feudalism and the proto-capitalist stage clown (the Vice-like clown-servant is further discussed in the section on Tarlton). In the development of the early modern clown-servant, it is the Vice that moves the clown-servant away from portrayals of conventional domestic ties to create a clown-servant who reflects domestic changes in England's service economy. Like his feudal predecessors, the proto-capitalist clown of the early modern English stage shows signs of the Morality Vice. The clown-servant's shift toward proto-capitalist endeavor evolves from the self-serving nature of the Moral Vice, a characteristic that allows the clown-servant to manipulate economic situations of service within his play. The Vice adds the next component in the development of the proto-capitalist clown-servant because the Vice relies less on dutiful courtly service and more on the manipulation of words and their meanings. In essence, Cacurgus is a proto-capitalist who seeks domestic job security as Philogonus's traditional clown-servant. His Vice-like character possesses a proto-capitalist sense of risk seen in later dramatic clown-servants. In relation to the Vice of the early modern English stage, medieval literature places the fool in the realm of the Vice or devil. The corrosive effect of the Vice, as moral devil, on traditional order reveals early signs of proto-capitalist influence later fully developed in clown-servants.

By the mid-sixteenth century, clown-servant and the Vice become interchangeable characters, both popular on the Elizabethan stage.[15] As commodified personae, the clown-servant and Vice are composed of varying degrees of humor and mischief. Just as the jesting Vice often disguises his mischief in the humor of popular fooling, reciprocally, the clown-servant veils his fooling in Vice-like displays of mischief. If the clown-servant characters are portrayed as mischievous, then this portrayal carries with it the debilitating socioeconomic forces that the Vice brings to the stage. Thus, viewing the Vice-like qualities in Cacurgus makes clear that the clown-servant character moves further away from Somer's dutiful service to Henry VIII and in the direction of proto-capitalist enterprise.

In addition to aspects of his clown-service that *Misogonus* clearly imitates, Somer's fooling is evident in Cacurgus's interaction with other servants. This manipulation differs from the domestic leverage of the clown-servant since it occurs within the burgeoning proto-capitalist theatre. Within the relatively short span of public theatre development, Cacurgus's theatrical clown-service embodies clowns who use their wit decisively to influence bonds of service. As late feudal bonds of service give way to proto-capitalist endeavor, and as theatrical clown-servants move away from Somer's court service, clown-servants assume proto-capitalist means of exchange and earn money in addition to customary bonds of domestic service. By viewing the development of the theatrical clown-servant that begins with Will Somer and his courtly origin, both feigning dutiful servant and the proto-capitalist Vice may be seen in Cacurgus.

A part of Cacurgus's likeness to the Vice resides in his dualism concerning profit, the same economic force with which Misogonus wrestles. Both characters seek to carouse in a market of free enterprise while simultaneously connected economically to a traditional household. Misogonus enters the play and aptly characterizes the "Vice-like" qualities in Cacurgus, qualities that fit his own disposition of waste rather than his father's notions of familial wealth. Misogonus cries:

> Body of God! stand back! what monster have we here? An antic or a monk, a goblin or a fiend? Some hobby horse, I think, or some tumbling bear- If thou canst, speak and declare me the kind . . . Passion of me! it is Robin Hood! The devil take thee and all thy fond gear? (1.1.286-89, 291, 297)

Having experienced Cacurgus the clown-servant, Misogonus playfully taunts the clown by revealing his true mischievous nature. The words "goblin," "fiend," and alliance with the "devil" suggest the dual nature of the Vice, and his misbehavior under the guise of benevolence. Specifically, his reference to Cacurgus as "Robin Hood" consistently suggests questionable economic practices based on perceptions of service.[16] These terms expose Cacurgus's Vice-like attributes in a play in which many of the demonic as well as heavenly references correspond to biblical allusions with God and Satan.

In the same manner that *Misogonus* uses biblical overtones of service and order to relay positive depictions of master-servant relationships, these biblical overtones relay negative or sinful master-servant bonds in the play. Biblical references to service hierarchy are relevant to this study because these references are the philosophical foundation of late feudal order. The Bible outlines the duties of masters and servants. Cacurgus, in his false allegiance to traditional order, prospers because Philogonus adheres to his biblical responsibilities of a master, which include protecting his household, including his servants. Within the economic construct of the play's setting, the patriarchal master of the household assumes a god-like position of power over his wife, children, and servants. If biblical symmetry found between the master and his domestic servants exists between the master and his clown-servant who only pretends to be dutiful, the result is a reflection of biblical scripture that outlines the hypocrisy of the master. Furthermore, just as the traditional clown-servant reinforces the bond between master and servant, the proto-capitalist clown-servant is free to bond with money in the form of gratuities as a means of sustenance.

Cacurgus's attempt to play both sides against the middle, the philanthropic father and the misanthropic son, creates irresolvable contradictions. It is his hope that the best of both of these worlds will fall on him, the real middleman, and verbal instigator between the father and son. What Cacurgus fails to realize is that "domestic service is first and foremost a relationship," and that his dual service violates the expectations of hierarchal order (Maza 6). Within the dimensions of obligation, "Whether they [the servants] provided security or received it from their employers, they flourished by imitating behavior through associations where intimacy and loyalty were prized" (Weil 10). By imitating a traditionally loyal domestic servant, Cacurgus's unique domestic position between upper and lower classes breaks down once his status as natural dissolves.[17]

The nexus between the wit of Somer and Cacurgus is the use of their domestic service positions in the lives of other lower class citizens. These acts reveal direct intent by the clown-servants to defraud other lower class citizens deemed threatening to their domestic status. For the late- feudal clown-servant, conflict among servants may reinforce or break traditional domestic ties. For the developing clown-servant, these conflicts lead to greater economic leverage within the traditional household. In both cases, positions of domestic service give these clown-servants leverage to better their lots through foolery. For example, among Armin's many accounts of Somer are several tales in which he admonishes his peers. In Somer's encounter with a lesser fool in the Court, he resorts to tricks of a court jester, deviant strategies to undo and expel his rival servant.[18]

In the course of Somer's jests, he displays the qualities of wordplay, games of questions and answers, slapstick, and the manipulating of others to commit acts that prove to be self-defeating for his opponents. Similarly, in Cacurgus's interaction with local *testes vetulae*, the old women-witnesses, we see these characteristics as he serves Misogonus through disguise, a tactic later utilized by other dramatic clown-servants. Cacurgus exhibits the qualities of verbal persuasion and slapstick to get others to commit self-defeating acts. However, unlike Somer who outwitted others through verbal feats of logic and reason, Cacurgus is blatantly fraudulent in conversation. This change to Cacurgus's character signals that he plays more the proto-capitalist than Somer, who plays the traditional domestic servant. For example, when Somer insults the lesser fool, he begins by engaging Henry in clever verbal banter that sets up his joke:

> Will Sommers brings vp a messe of milk and a manchet, Harry saies hee lend me a spoone: Foole saies the Iester, vse thy hands, helpe hands for I haue no lands, and meant, that saying would warrant his grose feeding. I sayes Will Sommers,

> Beasts will doe so, and Beasts will bid others do,
> as they doe themselues. Will, said the King, thou
> knowst I haue none: true Harry saies he, I know
> that, therfore I askt thee, & I would (but for doing
> thee harme) thou hadst no tongue to grant that
> foole his next sute, but I must eate my creame
> some way. (46)

The witty verbal setup insures that Somer maintains Henry's approval in the face of the visiting fool. In order to disgrace and anger the visiting fool into committing a vile act against the King, Somer throws milk in his face. In the presence of the King, the visiting fool draws his dagger against Somer and is ousted from the court. Somer's slapstick, an early version of the comic pie-in-the-face routine, is the final physical accent to a jest that began with verbal wordplay. His calculated wit well-applied, Somer returns to the disposition of Henry's dutiful clown.

In an act that illustrates his move toward proto-capitalist endeavor, Cacurgus misrepresents himself as a traveling physician and astrologer to beguile Isbell and Madge:

> By profession I am a very good physician.
> Before I could, speak I had learned all arts liberal.
> I am also a very skilful soothsayer and magician.
> To speak at one word: I can do all things in general.
> There is no sickness, disease or malady,
> But I can tell only by viewing of the hand.
> For every grief I can prescribe a present remedy.
> (3.1.113-19)

Like Somer, Cacurgus reasons that the arrival of Misogonus's possible twin brother will jeopardize his economically advantageous position of service to both masters. Unlike Somer, Cacurgus resorts to unscrupulous means to gain the women's oaths of silence. He uses his verbal wit to gain favorable outcomes for himself, not for his master. Cacurgus masquerades as a dentist and touches Madge's tooth, which causes her to cry out in pain. The slapstick foreshadows comic bits of the quack dentist and the poor soul with the toothache. Rather than a pie-in-the-face, Cacurgus reinforces his words with another's pain. This slapstick upholds the physical aspects of Cacurgus's service as a transient dentist and illustrates his ability to manipulate falsity through witty words.

Cacurgus is more the proto-capitalist than Somer, a difference that points to Somer's inclusion in the domestic economy of a monarchal court and to Cacurgus's proximity to the shifting proto-capitalist economy of lordless men. Foremost, Somer's economic rhetoric is thought provoking. The act of leaving the audience mentally nonplused helps to carry the butt of the jest and Somer emerges from the dialogue unscathed, having affected the economics of his target. Somer's fooling, unlike Cacurgus's, remains within the allowed context of his clown-service to Henry. As the stage clown plays the role of Cacurgus, his fooling adds proto-capitalist endeavor to Somer's witty comic style to entertain paying audiences.

All in all, from an economic perspective, the brand name appeal of "Will Summer" helps to develop commodified personae for dramatic clowning-servants. Much like the stand-up comedians George Carlin and Leo Gallagher who convey an anti-establishment stage presence familiar to the audience,[19] so does the stage presence of William Summer infer critical commentary of domestic service economics in early modern England. Like these contemporary examples of stars with recognizable names that draw box-office profits, Tarlton and Kemp (as Will Summer) were sixteenth century celebrities who helped the theater to prosper. When Cacurgus enters, Philogonus greets his clown-servant as

"Will Summer" rather than by his proper name: "What is the matter will summer" (1.1.199). The dramatic tag of Will Summer gives a brand name to a theatrical product of service, a brand name illustrative of proper theatrical clown-service. Cacurgus answers to the title, "Will Summer," Philogonus's objectified pseudonym for his traditional servant and for their service bond. When Cacurgus later rejects this title and the duties of service that it entails, he loses his service bond.

There exists, here, a semiotic relationship between clown and message, between the character "Will Summer," the signifier, and the dramatic acts of the actor playing Will Summer, the signified. Branding dramatic characters and actors (like Tarlton and Kemp) as Will Summer illustrates proto-capitalist development of the clown-servant. Economists concerned with the semiotic relevance of brand name advertising fall into two primary camps. The first school argues that "even for goods with high visibility brand names or trademarks, objective measures of product quality drive prices . . . that brand names and the associated price premia are efficiency enhancing" (Wiggins and Raboy 377). The other school contends that subjective product differentiation factors are more important, and that brand name differentiation is a barrier that impedes consumer choice. Economists Steven Wiggins and David G. Raboy agree that empirical resolution on this issue is elusive based on the difficulty of separating subjective from objective factors (377).

Perhaps, when applied to clown character that emulate Somer's clowning style as well as the character of Summer as written, the objective qualities of the domestic clown-servant may be distinguished from subjective audience expectations of humor. In other words, one may look like a clown and act like a clown; however, in dramatic context, one must be funny to be a clown. This supposition merges objective effectiveness of "trademarks" and the subjective nature of the paying audience. First the latter, the popularity of the subjective product, the character, Will Summer, illustrates that brand names celebrate commodity. As a theatrical commodity, Summer's clown characters in plays produce humor and are subsequently tagged with the title of Will Summer. The former objective idea shows that Will Summer the character and the actor portraying Will Summer are objective brand names or trademarks that are commodified personae. This idea is the essence of marketing strategy. The star quality of actors that results from brand naming illustrates this point. Moshe Adler suggests that "the phenomenon of stars exists where consumption requires knowledge. Stardom is a market device to economize on learning costs in activities where 'the more you know the more you can enjoy'" (208). Early modern theatrical performance often feature well known actors, stars, to promote box office ticket sales. Consumers will pay to see a plays with a star, an actor whose clowning style is known. David R. Shumway views the economic appeal of "star quality" as its ability to be both identified and desired (87). The brand name Will Summer spotlights an identifiable character in plays and a recognizable style of clowning by the actor. What matters is that name branding often leads to the popularity of the clown actor and his foolery, celebrity essential to the development of the theatrical clown as a proto-capitalist. In the chronological development of the dramatic clown-servant, no actor prior to the famous Richard Tarlton assumes the full scope of Will Summer's foolery to accomplish theatrical stardom. Tarlton achieves this stardom as a full time clown on stage, in taverns, and in banquet halls (Wiles 14). Wiles points out that because of his full time clowning, "no absolute distinction can be made between the roles which he played in different environments" (16).

DERICKE, THE FAMOUS VICTORIES OF HENRY V

In the theatrical development of clown-servants, Richard Tarlton signals the next progressive dramatic step away from the late feudal domestic clown toward the proto-capitalist. Thompson posits that Tarlton began his career as a solo entertainer and grew into a player alongside the growth of public theatre (408). Tarlton fuses Will Somer's style of foolery with his own affinity for ribald jests. Tarlton is a figure renowned throughout England whose dramatic persona and ready wit, like William Somer, emerge from his dual status as lower class peasant and courtly comic. Recent discoveries show that Tarlton was apprenticed as a haberdasher to Raphe Boswell (*Haberdashers*' MS 15842/1). He was freed by Boswell on 26 September 1576, less than five months before his marriage to Thomasine Dann in Chelmsford, Essex on 11 February 1577 (*Parish Register* MS D/P94/1/2). On 27 May 1584, Tarlton was translated to the Vintners, adding support to the posthumous tradition that he kept taverns; on 4 October of that year, he paid 20*d* to become free of the Vintners by redemption, and ten days later, on 14 October, he bound an apprentice in the Vintners, Richard Haywarde (*Vintners*' MS 15211/1). Tarlton's labor history enables him to use his clown-servant appeal to bridge gaps among the classes. He is both a royal jester to Elizabeth as well as a man of the people. But as the clown-servant progresses from court to stage, a move not possible for Somer, Tarlton progresses beyond the courtly service of his early years to proto-capitalist endeavors that directly influence later stage clown-servants like Kemp and Armin. This move away from traditional service marks the spirit of Somer's foolery as the essence of Tarlton's jests. In other words, the foolery mastered by Somer that was limited to the court audiences of the early sixteenth century reaches the public stage through Tarlton. What was once the late feudal clown, restricted to royal domestic service, is now the stage clown shared by the nobles and the masses through his on-stage presence.

In addition to performing as a clown, Tarlton also participates in the proto-capitalist growth of public theater as a shareholder. In the development of early modern theater, shareholding marks another progressive step away from late feudal economics. Early touring companies who prospered by playing the provinces change into proto-capitalist companies that profit from a system of shareholding and wage laborers in the theater (Bentley 65-6). Bradbrook reports that as a shareholder in the Queen's Men in 1583, Tarlton shows his entrepreneurial spirit when he chases out of the theater "one Wynsdon [who] tried to get into the Queen's Men's performance without paying, and upset the takings" (50). Shareholding also illustrates a parallel move away from late feudal economics, as laborers give-up or take time from late feudal guild occupations to invest in the business of theater. A former haberdasher turned vintner and actor, Tarlton transfers his business savvy from business occupations to the theater. Likewise, players who were also freemen of their respective guilds and who transfer their proto-capitalist enthusiasm to the theater include John and Lawrence Dutton (weavers), Warwick's Men, 1575 and Oxford's Men 1580; James Burbage (joiner) and John Heminges (grocer), Chamberlain's Men, 1594; John Shanks (weaver), Pembroke's Men, 1597 (Knutson 22; Bentley 26, 36). This list illustrates that the progressive development of the proto-capitalist clown servant character occurs within the business of theater in the midst of its own proto-capitalist growth. Both the economic energies of paid actors and development of proto-capitalist clown characters facilitate Tarlton's rise in popularity to the point of clown stardom.

From these standpoints, Tarlton's star-quality is a direct result of the theatrical commodification of Will Somer's clown-service, a change that allows Tarlton to create characters that are more jesting Vice than dutiful clown. Tarlton is the pivotal performer between clown-servant and Vice traditions in the early modern drama of England. When qualities of the Vice combine with those of the clown-servant, the resulting character manipulates the economic actions of service in the play. Similar qualities in the clown-servant and Vice characters to illustrate the relationship between the choices of these characters and their use of comic devices to influence monetary change that affects service identities in the play. The clown-servant acquires the Vice's affinity for mischief, a quality that often proves detrimental to the economics of his adversaries. This devaluation of customary economic practices occurs when the clown-servant encourages his adversary to reconsider his own economics in terms of profits and losses.

The Famous Victories of Henry V, printed by Thomas Creede in 1598 with anonymous authorship, but acted by the Queen's Men between 1583 and 1588, offers an early glimpse into the devaluation of domestic economics. The play casts Tarlton as the clown-servant, Dericke, who practices the act of commodity consumption in order to lead John Cobler, his adversary, to commit acts of gluttony that displace him from traditional social and communal service.[20] When Dericke meets Cobler, he gets Cobler to hire him as a cobbler's apprentice. Once Dericke convinces Cobler that he would make a good apprentice even though he has no shoemaking skills, Dericke undermines Cobler's traditional belief in hard work. Dericke gets Cobler to turn against shoemaking and his small community of cobblers to join the war. As Dericke interacts with Cobler in monetary decisions, the quality of the Vice in his character convinces Cobler to reappraise his economic viewpoints. Once Dericke convinces Cobler to reappraise his economic status, Cobler must eventually forfeit his relation of service to his township in order to profit monetarily.

The Vice of the sin avarice and commodity go hand in hand since the object of the Vice is to encourage the re-evaluation of commodity. In the moralities, the Vice is the tempter who typically characterizes one sin aimed at persuading his opponent to become aware of self-interest (McRae 17-18). Originally, the Vice was the servant of the Seven Deadly Sins, and sought to entrap "Mankind" into the power of evil. This medieval grounding of the Vice in labors of service primes him to continue the effective use of service to delude his adversaries. He was a kind of agent or "middleman" for the Deadly Sins given that his reward depended on the success of his service. His attention to commodity and service persisted throughout the development of the early modern dramatic clown-servant. David Womersley notes that in Shakespeare's history play, *King John*, the bastard character connects Vice-like qualities with commentary on commodity (508).[21] In Shakespeare's *1 Henry IV*, Prince Hal refers to Falstaff as "reverend Vice" and, as mentioned earlier, Falstaff gives Vice-like commentary on the commodity of naming: "I would to God thou and I knew where a commodity of good names were to be bought" (2.4.448). Richard II believes that a name, particularly his name, the name of King, was ontologically absolute, a fundamental aspect of the self, and thereby could not possibly be a commodity. Falstaff, in regarding a good name as a commodity to be bought suggests that the so-called self is nothing.

Once the clown-servant fuses with the Vice, a character emerges that experiences domestic economics as a servant and responds to economic tensions as a trickster. The mix of clown-servant and Vice employs comic tactics that complement the quality of proto-capitalist endeavor later seen in dramatic clown-servant. In other words, the traditional clown servant of the court like Somer goes together with expectation of service in the same manner that the wit of later clown-servants complements the proto-capitalist economics for cash of late sixteenth century England. The importance of Tarlton to this observation of clown-servant development is that he experiences both the worlds of the court and the proto-capitalist theater in his lifetime, work experiences that provide a lucrative income in the fluctuating Elizabethan economy.

Tarlton's particular combination of Vice and traditional domestic servant mark him as the first in Somer's line to develop a reputation of "star" quality. The visual appeal of his clowning together with his penchant for witty repartee combine to make him a star. His stardom signals a proto-capitalist shift away from court jesting toward the business of staged performance. In the case of Richard Tarlton's stardom, Alexandra Halasz suggests that

> the layering of meanings onto his reputation suggests that celebrity, rather than being created by the media, actually participates in the development of the media and the (proto)capitalist organization of both daily life and national identity. (20)

The development of the theatre as a proto-capitalist organization accounts for Tarlton's significant influence on the commercialization of playacting. Andrew Gurr notes that Tarlton may have played to over-packed houses as early as 1575 with the Sussex's Men (*Playgoing* 174). Southworth reports that Tarlton was an active player and leading "sharer" or shareholder of the Queen's Men in court and on tour from 1583 to his death in 1588 (124-6). Southworth actively supports the theory that Tarlton straddled the worlds of court and public stage (115-16). Early in his career he was jester to Queen Elizabeth I (as early as 1565) and later a member of the Queen's Players (1583-88) (115-6). Not only did Tarlton excel as a clown performer, his popularity was significant in the dramatic development of the clown-servant character.

Tarlton's fame derived from his ability to fuse aspects of the clown servant associated with court domestics with proto-capitalist aspects of the Moral Vice to create a character equally sensitive to the humors of early modern England's landed aristocracy, the growing middle class, and the migrating peasantry. Moreover, it has been argued that Tarlton, the most famous clown in the Elizabethan era, relied on acts of "misrule" within the hierarchical structure of early modern England balanced with a sense of communal identity with the audience (Wiles 20, Hornback 41). However, his actions within the plot structure of the play and his interactions with the audience owe their theatrical lineage to the stage antics of the Moral Vice. Therefore, Tarlton's fame is the result of the forging of the role of the commodified theatrical clown-servant. Important to this study's view of the transition from late feudalism to proto-capitalism is the relevance of commodified personae to the new commercial mindset of Elizabethan playgoers. Sacks observes that commodities, the myriad of products, first found their way into English homes, then accompanied playgoers into the theatres as part of an emerging culture of consumption (152-4). This culture of consumption grows into a commercial economy that pays greatly for the luxury of theatrical performance. Tarlton's career illustrates the court comic as he moves into the theatre and his foolery becomes a mainstay of commercial drama.

By the end of the Elizabethan era, a litany of literary and artistic forms expounded Tarlton's fame. The clownish domestic found in *Misogonus* that Shakespeare later crafts into recognizable characters achieved "a kind of common currency" in Tarlton.[22] By the latter half of the sixteenth century, an anonymous poet writes that

> When Tarlton clown'd it in a pleasant vaine
> With conceits did good opinions gain
> Upon the stage, his merry humorus shop.
> Clownes knew the Clowne, by his great clownish
> slop. (Arnold 206)

From these rhyming lines, we see that Tarlton's success came from his ability to leaven haughty discourse with a pleasurable disposition, a theatrical commodity primary to Somer's earlier comic exchanges with Henry. A direct descendant of Somer's clowning, Tarlton also balanced vituperative wit and pleasant disposition in his on-stage persona. For Somer, this comedic balance occurred within the noble domestic structure of early modern society.

Tarlton plays the character, Dericke, in *The Famous Victories of Henry V* (ca. 1598). Dericke is the first clown-servant character to portray Somer's court service on stage. Dericke's role in *The Famous Victories of Henry V* reflects the commercialization of Somer's clowning legacy. In the play, Dericke illustrates a purposeful move away from late feudal hierarchy and toward a proto-capitalist means to profit. Not only does Dericke signify the individual autonomy associated with proto-capitalist endeavor, but also he extends his progressive economic practices to an established member of a pre-modern community. Dericke's influence over Cobler, the cobbler, illustrates the plausible spread of proto-capitalist thinking among a working class still tied to traditional forms of exchange. Like Cacurgus before him, Cobler's final act is his plunge into a commodified world of exchange, leaving behind his traditional domestic setting, a point that will be discussed below in greater detail.

Positioning Tarlton's portrayal of Dericke within Somer's lineage of domestic clown-service illustrates similar court origins in a play that combines the disposition of a dutiful servant with facets of proto-capitalism. Tarlton imbues

Dericke's character with sarcasm and craft. Goldsmith notes that "so complete was the confusion between the jesting Vice and the stage fool at one time that the jester Richard Tarlton was sometimes referred to as the Vice" (17). The commonality between fool and Vice frequently based on their often disputed costumes rests with Billington's report that

> the mid-sixteenth century was a period of transition, which accounts for Vices dressed as Fools and Fools arrayed as Vices. Specifically, the 1550s provide the transitional decade for the merger of the Vice and Fool characters. In the Revels' Account for 1552 and 1555, the costumes for Vices and Fools are interchangeable, specifically the wooden dagger of the Vice and the hood of the Fool. (26-8)

As Dericke, Tarlton illustrates similar perceptions of dress early in the play that account for his comic mix of clown-servant and comic Vice. The significance of Dericke's costumes forms the substance of critical analyses to distinguish clown-servants from other comics. Dericke establishes his dual role in the play. He is the clown-servant, thoroughly aware of the social and domestic issues of the play. He must also play the Vice while both fellow players and audience are made aware of Dericke's duplicity. Referring to Dericke as "plaine Clowne," Robin assumes the presence of a traditional order that Dericke will not yet upset. However, in the course of the play, Dericke not only upsets this order, but his Vice-like qualities urge his adversary to proto-capitalist actions. Dericke, like Somer, assumes the clowning style of thought provoking inquiry as his prologue to dialogue:

> Am I a clowne? sownes, maisters, Do Clownes go
> in silke apparell?
>   I am sure all we gentlemen Clownes in Kent
> scant go so Well: Sownes, you know clownes very
> well: Heare you, are you maister Constable? and
> you be, speake, For I will not take it at his hands.
> (1.2.132-127)

In Somer-like fashion, Dericke ends the jest by inverting
Robin's misperception of costume and by reapplying it
to Cobler whom he addresses wrongly yet knowingly as
"Constable." Disallowing other lower class characters to
identify him solely as clown frees Dericke within the plot to
incorporate the Vice into his character.

Goldsmith offers the following helpful list of
characteristics for the amalgamated Vice/clown-servant
that, when applied to the idea of Tarlton's theatrical
commodification, reads as a list of commercial attributes
(19). Vice and stage-fool share physical stock tricks, verbal
shifts and devices, malapropism, innuendo, stage asides,
and parody.[23] I add to Goldsmith's list of characteristics
the clown-servant's persuasive use of witty comebacks and
economic discourse to further his jests. Dericke exemplifies
the presence of Vice within the clown-servant persona. Thus,
Tarlton's comic formula for stardom combines Goldsmith's
characteristics with the economics in *Famous Victories*.

From Goldsmith's list, Tarlton excels at the physical use
of stage antics and asides (Wiles 14). The aside plays up
Tarlton's popularity to provide him with a moment to be
recognized by the audience. The stage directions say that
Dericke is "roving," a physical action that Thompson reads
in context with Dericke's entrance and exclamation: "Whoa!
Whoa, there! Whoa, there," a stage aside whereby Dericke
signals that he has been robbed and seeks assistance to
recover his stolen horse (410).[24] In this move that connects

Tarlton with the audience prior to establishing his relevance to the plot, his brief appearance has the similar effect of current motion picture cameos by known movie stars. It is not only the appearance of the familiar face in the scene, but also the actions of the actor in the context of the script that commodifies star quality. As one of Christopher B. Balme's commodified "theatre goods," Tarlton's early appearance works to advertise his brand of clowning. In addition, as Peter Thomson sees, Dericke's first brief entrance and exit are scripted occasions to feature Tarlton (410-11).

However, in the character of Dericke, Tarlton's portrayal of brand of humor merges conversational and solo asides by positioning his speech between the stage players and the audiences, an act that makes it hard for other characters to hear and understand the contexts of his lines. Taking Dericke's words as stage aside, Thompson suggests that Dericke pretends to be oblivious to the presence of other characters (410), a move that I view as a solo act. Even though other characters hear his words, they remain outside of the clownish antics between Dericke and the audience. By searching the audience for the thief, Dericke separates himself from the other characters on-stage, and the "Whoa, there" heard by the characters is not figuratively the same "Whoa, there" experienced by the audience. The players do hear Dericke conversationally, but hearing his lines without meaning supports the aside and keeps the players outside of the comic discourse. The scripted aside and multiple entrances and exits would have no doubt given the audience the opportunity to acknowledge Tarlton's presence in the show. I add to Thompson's speculation that Tarlton, once recognized by the audience, would not have passed up the chance to employ further his signature commodified improvisations. Thompson asserts that Tarlton as Dericke would have used this improvisational moment to work the audience: "On the platform stage, where an entrance at one door, a circuit of the platform, and an exit at the other stage door involves the covering of a fair distance, Tarlton . . . the master of exits and entrances . . . must have had a field day" (410). In the role of Dericke, Tarlton's momentary possession of the stage would have allowed a variety of the physical antics for which he was well known.

Further evidence that Tarlton in the role of Dericke combines clown-servant and Vice is his verbal treatment of the adversarial Theefe. According to Wiles, the role of Dericke illustrates that "in Tarlton, the Vice and rustic are fused" (12). This blend of Vice and rustic distances Tarlton's portrayal of clowns from the Vice tradition that counters "virtue and wisdom" (22-3). It moves his characters toward a tradition of service counter to "urbanity and status" (22-3). Wiles further links Tarlton's Vice-like qualities to constant "competitive" and "aggressive" battles of wit with street and tavern crowds as well as within playgoing audiences (14-5). Peter Thompson asserts that Tarlton's development of the clown persona was "subsequently exploited by playwrights in discrete episodes written for Tarlton's clown, of hopelessly outwitted rustic who suddenly turns the tables on his tormentors" (408). Dericke's character displays similar uses of witty comebacks to trump verbally Theefe, acts that ensure Theefe's incarceration and Dericke's good standing among the play's lower class laborers. Verbal repartee belonged to the repertoire of verbal wit of both the Vice and clown-servant, an aspect of language upon which Tarlton relies to win verbal jousts with his opponents. Tarlton's reputation as an improviser of verbal comebacks often in rhyming verse developed his comic persona (Thompson 408). In a dialogue with Theefe, Dericke uses the last word of Theefe's line as a prelude to his verbal wit. He manages to upset the linguistic foundations of Theefe's discourse and thereby undermines Theefe's credibility with other characters as well as the audience. Often, comebacks allow the clown-servant to invert the speaker's meaning to serve his own turn. For example, Dericke inverts Theefe's plea for leniency to suggest that he be hanged:

> Theefe: I prethie be good to me honest fellow.

> Dericke: I marry will I, ile be verie charitable to thee, For I will neuer leaue thee, til I see thee on the Gallowes. (1.2.220)

Dericke plays on the words fellow/Gallows to complete the verbal comeback and mark Theefe as Dericke's verbal opponent throughout the play. The commodified effect this word play sets in motion is a sequence of dialogue in which the audience and fellow players expect the clown-servant to finish wittily the thoughts begun by the speaker. Even when other characters side with the clown-servant's opponent, Dericke readily employs the tactic of verbal comeback to invert meaning. For instance, when Henry V (as young Hal) attempts impunity for Theefe, Dericke interjects:

Henry 5.	What, wast you butten-breech? Of my word my Lord, he did it but in iest.
Dericke.	Heare you sir, is it your mans qualitie to rob folks in … iest? In faith, he shall be hangd in earnest. (1.4.328-31)

Here, we see verbal comeback work within the license of free speech to allow Dericke to alter the words of the Prince with impunity.

Dericke's character depicts a commodified, proto-capitalist Vice/clown-servant in scenes where he uses his scripted verbal foolery to discuss John Cobler's shoe business. The economic dialogue provides Dericke with an avenue to enter into seeming friendship with Cobler only to disrupt his concern with domestic relations of service. As tempter, Dericke uses verbal devices of malapropism, innuendo, and parody to causes Cobler to re-evaluate his livelihood as a cobbler and accept Dericke's Vice-like counsel. In the same manner that morality Vices like Nichol Newfangle in the morality play *Like Will to Like* by Ulpian Fulwell (ca. 1568) attempt to upset the moral constitution of their plays through the economic practices of their victims, Dericke in *Famous Victories'* disturbs the domestic fiber of the cobbler's household through economic means. Newfangle's conversation with Collier, his newest recruit for Lucifer, begins with inquiry into Collier's recent business transactions, dealings that suggests that Collier like Cobler belongs to a business community of servants:

Newfangle.	Tell me what market thou hast made of thy coal to-day.
Collier.	To every bushel cha zold three peck; Cha beguil'd the whorsons that of me ha' bought: But to beguile me was their whole thought.
Newfangle.	But hast thou no conscience to beguiling thy neighbour?
Collier.	No, marry, so ich may gain vor my labour. It is a common trade nowadays, this is plain, To cut one another's throat vor lucre and gain. A small vau't

as the world is now brought to
pass. (314)

In these lines we see Newfangle broach the subject of profit
to gauge Collier's economic morality, a morality that exists
prior to Newfangle's Vice-like influence and is more so a
product of economic shifts in the worlds of the play and
audience. When Newfangle asks specifically about the
effects of the "market" on Collier's livelihood, he ties himself
directly to proto-capitalist change, an economic shift that I
maintain characterizes the foolery of later dramatic clown-
servants. What follows Collier's explanation of his business
practices is his pairing with Lucifer, an act that signifies
Newfangle's successful use of economic talk that focuses on
profits and losses to enter into a service bond with Collier.

Likewise in *Famous Victories*, Dericke enters into
a bond of service with Cobler through inquiry into his
economic standing as a cobbler, a relation that results
in the undermining of Cobler's household and business
legitimacy. In the tradition of the morality Vice, Dericke
functions as the agent or middleman for Sloth and Gluttony.
These are unseen demonic forces in the play that encourage
the indulgence of consumption from Dericke's adversary.
Dericke cleverly segues from a jesting Hal into the domestic
service of Cobler. In the context of the jest, when Cobler
inquires of Dericke who still pretends to be Hal, "But I
maruell what will become of thee," Dericke breaks from the
jest and answers Cobler as himself: "Ile dwell with thee and
be a Cobler" (1.5.424). Since Dericke boasts of no cobbler
skills, it is understood that he expects the service bond of an
apprenticeship and his daily sustenance from Cobler.

Their dialogue does not address whether or not Dericke
is fit for the cobbler business, but rather turns to the topic of
consumption. Cobler makes clear that even as a vocational
laborer of shoes, he lives not on "Capon once a yeare, except

it be at Christmas, at some other mans house for we Coblers be glad of a dish of rootes" (1.5.431-2). It is the image of roots in the play that reflects the real population pressures on the food supply experienced by early modern England (Holton 191). To Dericke's proposed living arrangement, Cobler replies: "With me? alasse I am not able to keepe thee, why, thou wilt eate me out of doores" (1.5.425-26). Just as the Vice is deceptive concerning his true nature, so does Dericke declare that he is not slothful and gluttonous:

> Oh John, no John, I am none of these great slouching fellowes, that deuoure these great peeces of beefe and brewes, alasse a trifle serues me, a Woodcocke, a Chicken, or a Capons legge, or any such little thing serues me. (1.5.427-30)

The sins of gluttony and sloth are significant and these behaviors highlight the consumptive acts of Dericke and Cobler later in the play. Dericke coerces Cobler to embrace military service, and in doing so, Cobler must turn his back on his household service and his shoemaking to war-profiteer with Dericke. In the tradition of the jesting Vice, Dericke uses humor to soften the disposition of his befriended rival. With Vice–like persuasion, Dericke masks his true intentions of affecting Cobler's shoe production, his commodity, with discussions of Cobler's food consumption.

   As the Vice-like clown-servant, Dericke gets Cobler to evaluate his status as the "laboring poor" and the inadequacy of his diet of roots to upset Cobler's position as a community servant in his township.[25] Cobler defends his diet not through an affinity for the taste of tubers, but by associating his reliance on roots to his poverty. On the subject of poverty and food in Tudor England, Paul Slacks notes that the plight of the "laboring poor" was most evident in Tudor England in years when high food prices made casualties inevitable. Slack points out that *Three Sermons or Homilies* (1596) distinguishes a separate sect of the working class poor from lordless beggars, a distinction that reviewed the need for food in terms other than laziness:

> Though they do labour and take pains in their vocation and trade, yet by reason of the extremity of the world, for their rents are so great, the prices of all necessaries so dear, and the hearts of men so hardened, they cannot live by their labour, nor maintain their charge, but suffer want and are poor. (28)

Slack suggests that both pre-modern and market forces coexisted in Tudor England as depicted in the marketing of Cobler's vocation within the governance of his township. Slack views a laboring Tudor poor "ashamed to beg" as a laboring poor tied to time-honored ideals of service and order in the face of economic shifts towards a market economy. In line with Slack's ideas of the laboring poor, Cobler is a "labourer" who subsists on the trade of his vocation. He is a character who attempts to maintain a customary livelihood in the midst of acute economic change.[26] The notion that Cobler "be glad" for his meager consumption of roots is the premise upon which Dericke plays the Vice. In other words, for Cobler, the image of roots signifies acceptance of his station, an acceptance that symbolizes his production and repair of shoes within the market economies of his township. As the Vice, Dericke's clown-service attempts to get Cobler to pursue profit through less reliance on old notions of service and more on proto-capitalist acts of risk. He seeks to dislocate Cobler from his humble group of root eating cobblers and their community of service.

From these perspectives, *Famous Victories* positions the labor of a cobbler and his shoe production as the commodities by which to view clear shifts from late feudal to proto-capitalist economies. I join Slack (24-6), Sweezy (43-4) and Wallerstein (247), and others who view economic factors of production and exchange within new economic markets rather than changes to political order, as significant attributes for the triumph of capitalist economy over older forms of feudal production. Changes in the bonds between nobles and serfs point to the strengthening of market forces like "rent" and "necessaries" that benefit the peasantry. In turn, noble domestic practices like large retentions of servants lessen. Importantly, Cobler makes clear that his satisfaction with roots reinforces his service to his community of cobblers as well as his expectation of service from Dericke. Dericke's admission to Cobler that his poor diet will not suffice foreshadows the insults that he hurls at Cobler's wife upon being served roots to eat.

Late in the play, Cobler's shift from community servant to proto-capitalist occurs in the form of war profiteering with Dericke. In scene 21, with the war ended, Dericke and Cobler have been scouring the battlefields to steal clothes and shoes from the dead bodies in a plan to profit by marketing them in Cobler's hometown. Ironically, as the play's jesting Vice, Dericke gets Cobler to commit the same act of theft for which he persecutes Theefe in scenes 2 and 3. In the same fashion that Theefe profits from the sale of stolen horses, so does the now corrupt Cobler hope to profit from stolen shoes, offenses that cause both characters to fear the hangman. In an act that signifies Dericke's triumph as the play's jesting Vice, Cobler behaves less like the town cobbler concerned with the traditional order and more like a market savvy shoe speculator. Dericke succeeds in getting Cobler to reevaluate his labor in relation to the actual product of shoes. Cobler becomes one of Agnew's sixteenth century English businessmen pressured into new assumptions about the "uniformity of human motivation in exchange" (2-3).

For Cobler, "uniformity" describes his business alliances with fellow cobblers and the townships that they serve. His "human motivation of exchange" is the inner dependency of his township on its members and his economic membership validated by his cobbler status. Rodney Hilton notes that one significant transition from the late Middle Ages to the early modern period is that many English towns made the shift from agrarian settlements to industrialized villages (102). Hilton sees these changes as market opportunities for rural crafts like shoemaking and views small markets of the township as capitalist preludes to industrialized factories (102-03). Yet such changes did not instantly raise skilled members of the peasantry to the ranks of wealthy merchant. Like the laboring peasants that Hilton describes, Cobler is both a laborer and a town worker once tied to ideals of community. Cobler's labor relations with other cobblers illustrate socioeconomic vestiges of nostalgia for late feudalism. Hilton's description of industrial development for the small sixteenth century English town aptly applies to Cobler's town:

> The industry which stimulated such development was usually woolen textiles, although the metal industry, especially the cutlery trades, also figured in a minority of cases. Naturally, the existence of significant concentrations of specialized producers attracted a range of service occupations, especially in food processing and clothing. In towns of this type one still finds a significant minority of peasants, the survivors of the older economy. (102-03)

As the jesting Vice, Dericke uses the awareness of these early influences of proto-capitalist market forces on production and their affects on communal relations to get Cobler to consider shoe making from the perspective of a buyer's market for his product. In other words, Cobler now views his economic status not as an active laborer in a traditional community, but as one who controls a proto-capitalist market through his accumulation of a product. It is the profit to be gained from the arms full of stolen shoes, not the act of cobbling, that Dericke exploits to redefine Cobler. The play ends abruptly and leaves the audience to wonder whether Dericke and Cobler profit from stealing shoes or are arrested and hanged for their thievery. The open ending supports speculation concerning the livelihoods the great number of unemployed Tudor laborers who turn from vocation to crime.

CONCLUSION

As a chart of the dramatic development of clown-service from Somer, the court clown-servant to Will Summer, his theatrical persona and "brand name" of stardom, this chapter observes a theatrical lineage of Shakespeare's domestic clown-servant. The chapter began with Somer, and explored his brand of clown-service for its relevance to the development of Shakespeare's clown-servants. Somer's chronological proximity to the beginning of early modern theatre in England and the subsequent appearance of his name in plays as a "brand name" or watchword for clown-servant antics make him the pivotal force behind the move from court jester to commodified public servant of the theatre. This chart of dramatic development shows a trend that begins with William Somer, jester to Henry VIII, through Cacurgus, the clown character tagged "Will Summers," in *Misogonus*, to Tarlton's portrayal of Dericke in *The Famous Victories of Henry V.* By evaluating relationships of domestic clown-service in these plays that span the chronological influence of Will Somer's style of foolery (1564-1605), I am able to view developmental characteristics central to later portrayals of domestic clown servants. Most influential of these characteristics is the overall breakdown of late feudal household governance and the subsequent economic response of proto-capitalist market economies. The development of Will Somer's clown-servant persona from court to stage occurs amid rapid economic change in early modern England. The decline of late feudalism in early modern England is not only the backdrop against which develop the theatre and the clown servant character, but also the economic impetus that spurs both dramatic literature and characters to reflect these economic tensions on stage. Somer's stage commodity, Will Summer, becomes a significant component within the burgeoning theatrical market of early modern England, an economic environment of monetary exchange for dramatic entertainment.

Perhaps radical, my notions concerning clown-servant development in this chapter suggest that the attributes of traditional dutiful clown-servant and the proto-capitalist clown-servant are not mutually exclusive characters. Clown-servants are not wholly late feudal servants or proto-capitalists. Rather, it is the scripted humor of the clown character that determines whether we experience a traditional fool, jesting Vice, or proto-capitalist clown. I further contend that qualities of the clown-servant, which uphold the tradition of the kept domestic servant, become less influential in the entertainment of the dramatic clown-servant. The theatrical clown-servant is a proto-capitalist entrepreneur who responds to economic changes yet remains a dutiful domestic servant within the noble household. Whether or not later clown-servants break their traditional bonds, they exhibit the stresses necessary to cope economically with changes to domestic bonds of service.

Ultimately, this lineage reveals a parallel trend of development in Shakespeare's clown-servant characters. In other words, Shakespeare's creation of domestic clown-servant characters begins with Somer-like clowns in *The Comedy of Errors* and *Two Gentlemen of Verona* and progressively develops into the clown-servants in *Merchant of Venice* and *Twelfth Night*, entrepreneurial forces and economic brokers of their play's monetary tensions. Remarkably, these first two of Shakespeare's comedies offer pairs of clown-servants, one more connected to traditional domestic order, and the other more the proto-capitalist, scripted clown-servants that continue the evolution of the dramatic clown-servant. Chapter 2 will allow explorations of the similar trends of late feudal to proto-capitalist development that centers on the symmetry of Shakespeare's clown-servant actors Kemp and Armin as well as on their portrayals of characters.

CHAPTER II

BONDS AND HOUSEHOLD SERVICE IN THE COMEDY OF ERRORS AND THE TWO GENTLEMEN OF VERONA

Dromio of Ephesus.	*When I desired him to come home to dinner, He ask'd me for a thousand marks in gold: "Tis dinner-time,' quoth I; 'My gold!' quoth he; 'Your meat doth burn,' quoth I; 'My gold!' quoth he: 'Will you come home?' quoth I; 'My gold!' quoth he. (The Comedy of Errors 2.1.59-64)*

Speed.	*The shepherd seeks the sheep, and not the sheep the shepherd; but I seek my master, and my master seeks not me: therefore I am no sheep.*
Proteus.	*The sheep for fodder follow the shepherd; the shepherd for food follows not the sheep: thou for wages followest thy master; thy master for wages follows not thee: therefore thou art a sheep. (The Two Gentlemen of Verona 1.1.87-93)*

The Comedy of Errors and *The Two Gentlemen of Verona* illustrate the early microcosmic development of Shakespeare's clown-servant characters, an evolution within the macrocosmic development of the dramatic clown-servant Will Summer on the early modern English stage.[1] In these plays, representations of service continue to illustrate the move away from feudal domestic hierarchy and move toward proto-capitalism. Servants played a prominent role in the transitional economy of Shakespeare's day. As Mark Thornton Burnett notes, "From apprentices learning a trade to the officials of the great noble households, servants were perhaps the most distinctive socio-economic feature of the sixteenth and seventeenth century society" (1). Charles Wells notices that "Servants are the only category of people to appear in all thirty-seven plays, a fact which, in itself, attests to their importance in Tudor society" (142)..[2] In "Pretie and Shorte Discourse of the Duetie of a Servingman" (1578), Walter Darell voices complaints about an emerging practice among the English gentry to hire personal servants that are not of gentle origins, and reports that the word "servingman" is synonymous with the servant's "kind" (qtd. in Weil 7). What Judith Weil views in Darell's complaint as the portrayal of "a static social cosmos [that] replaces dynamic characters," I read more specifically as a proto-capitalist response by both gentry and non-gentry to changes in traditional early modern domestic order. This approach by no means attempts to link capitalism to a decline in patriarchal structures. On the contrary, traditional family order continues to be the foundation upon which proto-capitalist change occurs into and beyond Shakespeare's day. Of importance, late sixteenth century England experiences change from medieval domestic identity defined by the master-servant relationship to analogous identity based on money. New economic markets directly challenged late feudal domestic arrangements by blurring the hierarchical order of service relationships. In England, early modern noble households attempted to cling to late feudal domestic order even as economic changes lead to a reduction in household staff.

CLOWN-SERVICE IS DOMESTIC SERVICE

In *Errors* and *Two Gentleman*, clown-servants are household servants or domestics. The term domestic describes the clown-servant's adherence to the household needs of the master regardless of the master's physical whereabouts. As pointed out earlier, of Shakespeare's clowns are domestic servants. Therefore, they do not serve in non-domestic capacities. A service with its roots in the domestic order of England's past, by the sixteenth century domestic service reflects attempts by English nobility and middling class households to maintain time-honored domestic relationships in the face of proto-capitalist change. In a study of domestic plays in early modern England, Vivian Comensoli points out this change:

> With the weakening of the feudal system of mutual obligation and rights, the family assumed a crucial function in the promotion of social stability and governance. Obedience to husbands, fathers and masters was considered the principal duty of women, children, and servants, and rebellion within the family was viewed as synonymous with rebellion against the state. (17)

It is from this "feudal system of mutual obligation and rights" that the domestic clown-servants of Shakespeare's comedies progressively escape. On the importance of England's early modern household and its domestic arrangements, Kari McBride notes:

> Early modern England inherited from a mythologized vision of an ideal past, an ideal currency as a traditional touchstone even as the country became decreasingly rural and agrarian and increasingly urban and mercantile. Perhaps because of the rapid changes in social, economic and political life . . . the late medieval country estate remained the symbol of good housekeeping: a moral economy wherein all classes and peoples lived in right relationship with each other and with the rest of creation. (5)

Foundational to the opening action of both *Errors* and *Two Gentlemen* is this notion that household order reflects the order of the universe. This perception of the orderly household becomes the problematic ideal that these plots seek to upset through proto-capitalist influences. It is McBride's idea of "a moral economy," the nexus between service and sustenance within these plays that proto-capitalist modes of production irreparably alter.

C. L. Barber and Richard P. Wheeler also note that in *Errors*, "Shakespeare is marvelous at conveying a sense of world that is already there" and in S. Dromio's first lines the "routine tensions" of "daily ordinary life" that run through the play are heard (68). Dramatic displays of daily ordinary life allow both these plays to explore late feudal household order from the viewpoint of the downstairs economics of the servant class. E. Dromio conveys this image of domestic life when he first encounters S. Antipholus:

> The capon burns, the pig falls from the spit,
> The clock hath strucken twelve upon the bell;
> My mistress made it one upon my cheek:
> She is so hot because the meat is cold;

The meat is cold because you come not home.
(1.2. 44-48)

The setting of *Errors* imitates the household economics of early modern London. E. Dromio's concern with household duties of food preparation, dinner plans, an angry mistress, and an overdue master parallels S. Antipholus's persistence to secure room, board, and indoor comfort. The humor of this scene exemplifies S. Antipholus and the economic concerns of an itinerant master. S. Antipholus has recently sent his clown to secure lodging and food, a dramatic act that supplies the comic setup for the misunderstanding between S. Antipholus and E. Dromio concerning money, lodgings, and dinner.

Of *Two Gentlemen*, Shakespeare's next comedy, assessments by Barry Weller and earlier critics that see a play that bears "little resemblance to men of flesh and blood" are corrected in Louise Schleiner's more recent look at the significance of service relationships in the play (Weller 344). Schleiner suggests that "at the level of plot the servant and the young master or mistress are two characters, but on another level they are a single unit of dialectic action" (302). Speed cleverly explains to Valentine: "O, that you had mine eyes; or your own eyes had the lights they were wont to have when you chid at Sir Proteus for going ungartered" (2.1.67-70)! In other words, although Valentine and Speed are "two characters," master and servant, they chastise Proteus from the same viewpoint or "eyes." However, now that Valentine has fallen in love with Madam Silvia, Speed explains that again they are two separate characters. Furthermore, Speed's verbal reasoning suggests that as "a notable lover" Valentine is more the servant of Sylvia and in turn it is Speed who plays the level-headed master. Therefore, a focus on dissolving bonds of domestic service rather than attempts to trace one or two agents of action throughout the plot allows the play to present early modern issues of London's changing domestic economics. Both plays offer a critique of fading domestic service bonds, and both plays make evident an altered moral economy within the master clown-servant bond.

But to speak of an altered moral economy is to speak of late feudal domestic relationships as illusions of order. Early modern domestic order constitutes an imaginary representation of the relation of individuals to their real conditions of existence. It is the job of the masters to create a household economy and an individual's place in it, i.e. the servants seem appropriate, reasonable, and natural.[3] Therefore, when proto-capitalist modes of production respond to this illusion of domestic order, the result is a reordering of household economics that makes murky the identifying characteristics of domestic bonds of service. Once Syracusan Antipholus experiences the Mart in *Errors*, he reasons "And here we wander in illusions," a perception that the material world is warped and not their senses of themselves (4.3.42). *Errors* begins with a clear example of paternal authority attempting to reinstitute its rule in Egeon's familial tale. Egeon is a merchant and resides in the market economy of the Grecian isles. His tale of family lost at sea during a commercial venture sounds like the later accounts of lost merchandise in *The Merchant of Venice*. The equating of human life to merchandise is befitting of Egeon's tale because what follows is the Duke's decree that places a monetary value on Egeon's life and therefore on the success of his quest. Egeon's telling of the simultaneous births of the Antipholuses to a "joyful" mother and a wealthy merchant father and the Dromios to poor peasants reinforces their master-servant paradigm within domestic service. Egeon narrates:

That very hour, and in the self-same inn,
A mean woman was delivered
Of such a burden, male twins, both alike:
Those, — for their parents were exceeding poor, —
I bought and brought up to attend my sons.
(1.1.53-57)

Egeon attempts to justify for the Duke his search to reunite a late feudal domestic economy, his illusion of the family unit in terms of the relevance of service to sustenance. Egeon's account begins the play by framing the births of the twins in economic terms. He views the births of the masters-Antipholus as "joyous" and the clown-servants' births as "a burden," economic conditions that he presents not only to justify his purchase and subsequent rearing ("I bought and brought up") of the Dromios within domestic order. But he also attempts to naturalize identities of domestic service in single name identifiers for masters and servants. All Antipholuses are masters and all Dromios are servants, names that highlight their traditional service relations and decentralize their individual identities. In his naming of masters and servants, Egeon seeks to recover relationships bonded by late feudal service from a proto-capitalist Mart.

Likewise, *Two Gentlemen* begins with an illusion of late feudal domestic order as a zone of familial security that opposes the outward venture toward "some rare noteworthy object" (1.1.13). Nonetheless, Valentine and Proteus enter into the domestic arrangements of the Milanese Duke and his court, a move that illustrates the service of Speed and Launce to their young masters. Valentine's criticism of Proteus that "Home-keeping youth have ever domestic wits" echoes the notions of Proteus's father and uncle. Concerning Proteus's in-home "cloister," Panthino, his father's manservant repeats their paternal sentiments:

> He wonder'd that your lordship
> Would suffer him to spend his youth at home,
> While other men, of slender reputation,
> Put forth their sons to seek preferment out:
> Some to the wars, to try their fortune there;
> Some to discover islands far away;
> Some to the studious universities. (1.3.4-10)

Proteus trades one delusional late feudal household for another. The Duke's court of Milan represents a large functional family unit much like the real court of Henry VIII, the domestic abode of Will Somer. Panthino's reprimand equates service and sustenance with social economic identity. In *Two Gentlemen*, the fathers rationalize their sons' quests for "fortune" beyond the confines of the home to maintain their own illusionary dominance over the household as well as to strengthen the ever-weakening domestic bonds between master and clown-servant. In these plays, proto-capitalist forms of the Mart and entrepreneurial villainy challenge paternal and late feudal domestic constructs. Paternal authority does not run counter to entrepreneurial endeavor. Rather, entrepreneurial endeavor occurs against the ever-present backdrop of fatherly order that makes proto-capitalist possible.

In *Errors* and *Two Gentleman*, the entrance of commodities into the sphere of domestic clown-service sets in motion the dismantling of identities in both the household and the markets. Aristocratic display turns into proto-capitalist consumption in E. Antipholus's failure to enter into his house and claim the marital rites of Adriana, his wife, and his subsequent turn to the Mart and its gold jewelry to obtain a prostitute of that Mart. In early modern England, conspicuous consumption is evident in the availability of non-essential goods. Natasha Korda notes that while London had long been recognized as a hub of foreign trade, a center of conspicuous consumption, the expansion of domestic industries or "projects" across England between 1560 and 1630 "set the wheels of domestic trade turning faster, encouraging the making of yet more consumer goods, spinning and ever more elaborate web of inland commerce" (Korda 17).[4]

These projects spurred expanded domestic production and consumption of a "bewildering variety" of commodities beyond the staple necessities of life, including glass, and brass wares, stockings, tobacco, tobacco pipes, and 'innumerable fashion goods for women,' including ruffs, masks, busks, muffs, fans, periwigs, bodkins, and gloves" (Korda 17). Thus, in addition to late feudal bonds of service, the masters in these plays use goods and services as conspicuous consumers to represent social status. It is commodities that, when introduced into the domestic master and clown-servant relationships, foster errors of identity.

THE SERVANTS DROMIO

In *Errors*, it is the fungibility of gold into coinage for the conspicuous consumption of the gold chain, a non-essential good, rather than fungible ore into the iron crowbar, a practical domestic good that unsettles the domestic identities of masters and clown-servants. In one of the play's most humorous scenes, it is the direct intrusion of Mart commodities into E. Antipholus's household economy that distorts these identities (2.2). *Errors* showcases the servant class and further demonstrates the interchangeability of the Dromios's clown-service. S. Dromio's domestic clown-service inside the home directly blocks E. Dromio's domestic clown-service outside the home. Therefore, E. Dromio is sent for an iron crowbar, an object with a greater household use value than exchange value either as a tool or as ore. As door-keeper, E. Dromio has lost to domestic position the emblem of his identity as clown-servant. The iron crowbar becomes an extension of that service since it will allow him to open and re-claim his post of service and his perceived identity. But Balthazar informs E. Antipholus that as a homeowner seen breaking into his own house to confront a seemingly adulterous wife would appear rash, "Herein you war against your reputation" (3.2.87). From the advice of a fellow merchant, E. Antipholus decides on the gold chain rather than the iron crowbar as a means to maintain his reputation in Ephesus. In essence, he decides to re-identify himself more as a merchant than as a householder. The gold chain is used as an anti-domestic object of the Mart that further disrupts the household and remains counter to the iron crowbar and domestic service. By giving the chain to the Courtesan rather than to Adriana, his wife, E. Antipholus redistributes household wealth back into the Mart.

The dinner party of merchant-masters and a clown-servant at the Porpentine illustrates the presence of the Mart within the household. Not only does E. Dromio return with his merchant-master for dinner as ordered, but also his service brings in tow, two additional merchants into the household. In a play that pits the modes of household economics against proto-capitalist change, the direct intrusion of the domestic abode by representatives of the Mart is blocked by S. Dromio's domestic clown-service. E. Antipholus says to Angelo, the goldsmith:

> Get you home And fetch the chain; by this I know 'tis made:
> Bring it, I pray you, to the Porpentine;
> For there's the house: that chain will I bestow—
> Be it for nothing but to spite my wife—
> Upon mine hostess there: good sir, make haste
> (3.1.114-119)

For E. Antipholus, the Porpentine substitutes for his domestic abode and his affiliation with the Courtesan replaces his domestic union with Adriana. E. Dromio shares his master's household displacement much like S. Dromio's service to S. Antipholus. Like S. Dromio, E. Dromio relates to the merchants and navigates the Mart. Both clown-servants have the ability to keep house as well as to move through the Mart, dine with the master, merchants, and the Courtesan at the Porpentine, and function as a domestic clown-servant among commercial influences.

More profound than E. Dromio's clown-service to his outcast master is S. Dromio's instant shift from clown-servant to a traveling master to the efficient and funny door-keeper of a household. It is at this point in the play that the dialogue more fully complements the theatrical appeal of clown-servant humor, a humor based on an understanding of the noble or "upstairs" livelihoods of his master, Adriana, and Luciana from his servant class or "downstairs" perspective. As S. Dromio assumes E. Dromio's post, he also acquires E. Dromio's perceived identity as clown-servant in the play's downstairs hierarchy. S. Dromio finds that he is engaged to E. Antipholus's kitchen-wench, a match that furthers the domestic order of the upstairs masters. Indirectly, the bawdy sexual banter of the servants on opposite sides of the door parodies the worst case scenario for E. Antipholus, an adulterous wife who redirects the sexual economy outside of the household. On the implications of possible adultery, Ralph Berry highlights the bawdy input of the clown-servant to hit home for E. Antipholus the possibility of his cuckoldry:

> Dromio adds to the effect with 'Your cake here is warm within' (3.1.7), 'cake' being 'woman', and his next line, 'It would make a man mad as a buck to be so bought and sold' presents his master as a male deer in rutting season, and a cuckold. The

> worst . . . has happened. Antipholus thinks so too,
> and eventually plans a sexual revenge with the
> co-operation of the Courtesan. (Berry *Awareness*
> 39-40)

Just as E. Antipholus and E. Dromio adapt to domestic exile from the household and embrace the practices of the Mart, S. Antipholus and S. Dromio shift to accommodate domestic expectations of household order. The Courtesan of the Mart and the exchange of the gold chain for her gold ring and sexual favors counter E. Antipholus's inability to enter into his home. The gold chain that Adriana hoped would bring E. Antipholus from the Mart to his domestic marriage bed becomes instead a symbol of infidelity as opposed to household integrity.

Along the lines of domestic service, the Dromios in *Errors* are interchangeable. One common responsibility of both Dromio clown-servants is to assist their masters to navigate unfamiliar markets. Errors of identity derive from the interaction of the markets (the Mart) and the late feudal domicile (the household), with the clown-servants and consumer goods. The Mart influences the first errors of identity that pertain to tasks of domestic service and the commodity of gold coins. On a grand scale, the gold coins symbolize the influence of the Mart in the social interactions in Ephesus that parallel in sum and importance the unfortunate plight of Egeon as well as reflect the existence of foreign coinage in the economy of early modern London. Wiles perceives the influx of foreign coins as a sign of London's changing economy (41). Berry notes that the appearance of foreign monies on the Elizabethan stage, references to "marks" and "ducats" in both *Errors* and *The Merchant of Venice*, reflects the influx of foreign coins into Elizabethan London. He reasons that "Marks touches off some wry levity with the Dromios. The coinage of the last two acts is ducats. It appears that 'Many foreign coins were in continual circulation in England during Elizabeth's reign', hence the coinage has a distinctly English, as well as Continental reference" (Berry *Awareness* 41). Further, Berry applies Charles de Gaulle's notion that gold's presence in the play as "universal, immutable, and impartial" identifies it as a commodity and links it by monetary exchange to the practices of the Mart (Berry *Awareness* 42).

Within the scope of the play's master-servant bonds, not only is gold a proto-capitalist symbol of the Mart, but also the gold coins objectify the expectations of obedience, the social adhesive of late feudal master-servant relationships. For S. Antipholus, the one-thousand marks become the fungible commodity whose theft seems to devalue S. Dromio's clown-service. Receiving a prearrangement of gold coins from a Syracusan merchant, S. Antipholus relies on S. Dromio's obedience to secure their room and board with the money:

> Go bear it to the Centaur, where we host,
> And stay there, Dromio, till I come to thee.
> *[Gives money.]*
> Within this hour it will be dinner-time. (1.2.9-11)

S. Dromio's answer, "Many a man would take you at your word, and go indeed, having so good a mean" (1.2.17-18), illustrates not only domestic clown-service to secure room and board, but also it foreshadows the mysterious power of gold as a commodity disruptive to the perception of service hierarchy and the identities that they suggest. On *Errors*, Shankar Raman remarks that the circulation of gold "preserves its functional identity, the value inhering in its fungibility—but only at the risk of dividing value, of substituting the copy (the image of value, money) for the original figure (gold, the metallic representation of value)"

(194). The functional identity of gold, then, is that since it has very little life sustaining or use value, its identity rests in its ability to substitute differing exchange values in various economic situations. The presence of the gold coins extends the monetary concerns of the master to the duties of the clown-servant. When the coins seem to disappear without the authority of the master, they cease to function as an extension of the master's will and reappear in the form of buying power in the hands of the servant.

When E. Dromio enters abruptly, dialogue with S. Antipholus about the missing money revolves around acts of obedient domestic service that help to navigate the master from the Mart to a domestic setting. In a scene that illustrates the interchangeability of the clown-servant Dromios and their charge to feed and shelter their masters, the error of the gold coins also clarifies the service identities of Antipholuses and Dromios. I break from Raman's reading of the play, a reading in which S. Antipholus's line, "Here comes the almanac of my true date," misperceives E. Dromio and makes evident the loss of self-identity by S. Antipholus (187-8). Rather, when gold enters into the paradigm of domestic service, complications follow concerning its purchase and intended uses. E. Antipholus will either use the gold to impress his wife or his whore, and S. Antipholus will wear the chain as an outward sign of his is misperceived socio-economic standing in Ephesus. Gold in the form of the chain as well as in the form of money reflects the proto-capitalist mentalities of the play's masters.

As a comical farce of real economic concerns, rather than a literal representation of a protagonist on an identity quest, *Errors* presents one-dimensional characters. In other words, the merchant-master remains most mindful of his money and the servant remains mindful of his obedience. As the master, S. Antipholus insists that Dromio

Stop in your wind, sir: tell me this, I pray:
Where have you left the money that I gave you?

E. Dromio replies:

O, — sixpence, that I had o' Wednesday last
To pay the saddler for my mistress' crupper?
The saddler had it, sir; I kept it not. (1.2.53-57)

Antipholus's trust of money to his clown-servant is consistent with the behavior of merchant-masters, an occurrence with which E. Dromio is too familiar. For S. Antipholus, proto-capitalist modes of the Mart in the form of the gold coins disrupt the late feudal order of domestic service. For E. Dromio, S. Antipholus's charge of gold coins to secure home-like lodgings clouds perceived social economic identities of the domestic household. Although identities are not gained and lost, perceptions are altered in the play. This scene serves to show E. Dromio as the dutiful servant of late feudal order. He is not allowed to amass personal wealth even by keeping the change from business transactions conducted in his master's name. The amount of the monetary charge is also significant since E. Dromio's lines suggest that he usually handles small amounts of money to pay skilled laborers for menial tasks like mending a broken crupper, not securing lodgings and food in a foreign town. To do so would violate the traditional bond between masters and clown-servants. Humor arises because S. Antipholus has a bond of trust with S. Dromio that allows the clown servant to handle enough money to liberate himself.

Speed's Wit

Along the same lines of domestic service, Speed and Launce of *Two Gentlemen* are less interchangeable than the Dromios, and it is the entrepreneurial speech of Speed that continues to illustrate the dissolution of late feudal master-servant identities. Unlike *The Comedy of Errors, The Two Gentlemen of Verona* separates the twin portrayal of traditional and proto-capitalist clown-servants into two twin-like clown-servants within disparate developmental phases of clown-service. In Speed, Shakespeare transforms the clown-servant to a witty proto-capitalist. His banter with Master Proteus early in the play attests to his interchangeability with Proteus's clown-servant Launce in station, yet Speed's economics are more progressive than Launce's. Speed earns his own money in addition to the rewards of his customary service. Word play between Proteus and Speed reflects economic changes to domestic service relationships in Shakespeare's London. Their use of a shepherd/sheep metaphor to debate the economic symbiosis of master-servant bonds calls into question the identities of Speed and Valentine in relation to their master-servant union. Ralph Berry states: "Often as in the dialogue between Luciana and Julia, Speed and Valentine, the servants hold a clear advantage over the master and mistress" (*Social Class* 18). To Proteus's assertion that Speed is the "sheep" and his master, Valentine, the "shepherd," Elizabeth Rivlin asserts that "Speed's response, 'Why then my horns are his horns,' stresses the inseparability of the master's and servant's interest and effectively demotes Valentine to the status of sheep, or worse, a cuckold" (1.1.78) (110).

In addition to Rivlin's view of the "master and servant [as] interchangeable referents" (110), Speed's final remarks voice a declaration of economic autonomy representative of the effects of nascent capitalism on early modern bonds of domestic service. Speed exhibits the signs of early modern servant individuality that Paul Delany identifies as more fully developed in the eighteenth- and nineteenth-centuries: "Where the feudal ethic had exalted service to a superior as the most honorable of human bonds, the bourgeois era regarded it as an intrinsic violation of individual dignity"

(434). While Speed's act does demote Valentine as master, it more so promotes the clown-servant to the mentality of the noble. Clearly, Speed retorts:

> The shepherd seeks the sheep, and not the sheep
> the shepherd; but I seek my master, and my master
> seeks not me: Therefore I am no sheep. (1.1.87-9)

He attempts to deny his sheep-likeness "by a circumstance" of logical word play, a clown's game to denounce aspects of a late feudal hierarchy that tie him to Valentine. Proteus's seeming verbal checkmate that makes Speed cry "baa" in witty surrender further reinforces the point concerning identity and proto-capitalist modes of exchange. Speed's "baa" is a witty fore-cry to his "sheep-like" response to employment by Proteus without monetary compensation. Without the exchange of money, all that Proteus and masters alike will gain from new economic clown-servants like Speed is a compensatory "baa." Now that Speed has reduced the servitude to the level of animals, references to "mutton" will soon follow.

Proteus's final verbal volley makes apparent the differing domestic service aspects of obedience and reward found in *Two Gentlemen*. Proteus uses the tie between sustenance as food and wages as money to highlight the domestic relationship of room and board to domestic service. Like a sheep to a shepherd, Proteus posits, Speed follows and serves his master for food and shelter, the same expectations that propel the sheep. Proteus says:

> The sheep for fodder follow the shepherd; the
> shepherd for food follows not the sheep: thou
> for wages followest thy master; thy master for
> wages follows not thee: therefore thou art a sheep.
> (1.1.90-3)

Unlike late feudal domestic service relationships in *Errors* that subsist on wage-less bonds, proto-capitalist conditions in *Two Gentlemen* portray traditional master-servant bonds that include monetary exchange for services rendered. The coexistence of dominant and emergent forms of domestic service economies reflects economic change evident in London's early modern domestic economy. Proteus soon learns that although his reason may succeed in verbal matters, the final checkmate belongs to Speed since Proteus's (and Julia's) failure to compensate him properly for postal services renders Proteus's messages undelivered. In this denial, Speed sees himself as his own cash earning man, defined rather by his choice to follow and serve than by traditional early modern social codes in which service is exchanged for sustenance. Thus, Speed presents a viable breakdown in late feudal expectations of service. This scene also illustrates a breakdown of late feudal expectations of dutiful service regardless of payment. Proteus expects Speed's obedience in the matter of delivering his messages. The scene shows that at no point of Speed's services does Proteus anticipate the need to pay him to get the job done. It is Speed who teaches Proteus that money has become a part of traditional service, a point that Proteus still fails to get following the "shepherd/ sheep" exchange.

More clever than Proteus, Speed continues Proteus's sheep metaphor to illustrate the nature of his proto-capitalist identity concerning domestic tasks and the monetary costs of obedience. Speed suggests that his identity resides in his economic relation to Valentine as a cash-earner to an employer not as a sheep to a shepherd. The sheep-metaphor resonates with late feudal order: Speed continues:

> Ay sir: I, a lost mutton, gave your letter to her, a laced mutton, and she, a laced mutton, gave me, a lost mutton, nothing for my labour. (1.1.90-93)

Speed uses cooked meat as the commodity to explain the link between labor and pay, a clown-servant's assessment of his own proto-capitalist identity later heard from Launcelot Gobbo in *The Merchant of Venice*. Mutton represents a further step in commodifying the sheep into food that Speed likens to his own further commodification from domestic clown-servant to cash-earner for hire.[5] Just as the mutton must be paid for to be eaten and enjoyed, so must Speed's clown-service be paid for to be employed.

Now as an earner of cash payments, Speed further highlights the identities of master and servant as interchangeable signifiers, as described by Rivlin. In the development of Shakespeare's clown-servants, Speed experiences a dual identity as a late feudal and proto-capitalist servant. As a cash-earner, Speed makes money and alters the perception of his late feudal clown-service to Valentine. Speed also joins the ranks of his masters since he now may choose with impunity whether or not to complete a designated task. Rather than relay Julia's reaction to the letter as evidence of his good service, Speed retorts wittily: "Open your purse, that the money and the matter maybe both at once delivered" (1.1.28-29). Proteus does not beat Speed for his disobedience, an act reserved for his primary master Valentine.

In light of the interchangeability of the clown-servants as domestic laborers, their differences also attest to their proto-capitalist development along attenuated lines of domestic service. It is important to observe hierarchal aspects of domestic clown-service and how dissimilarities in the services of the Dromios and of Speed and Launce derive from the disparities in their masters. These differences prompt questions as to whether or not there are characteristics in the portrayal of masters that influence the demeanors of the clown-servants. Is there some individuality in S. Antipholus and Valentine as masters, some attribute of their treatment of S. Dromio and Speed that magnifies their wit in their clown-service? Why are S. Dromio and Speed the proto-capitalist clown-servants to E. Dromio and Launce, the traditional late feudal clown-servant?

LIKE CLOWN-SERVANT, LIKE MASTER

In these comedies, the pairing of proto-capitalist clown-servants to itinerant masters and traditional late feudal clown-servants to domestic masters continues to illustrate the development of Shakespeare's clown-servant proto-capitalists within the early modern economic progression from late feudal to proto-capitalist modes of exchange. The proto-capitalist responsibilities of S. Dromio move him closer to personal autonomy than do the household responsibilities of E. Dromio. In *Errors*, the interaction of traditional forms of domestic economics and new forms of commercial exchange obscure identities of a house-holding master-merchant and a proto-capitalist master, and their working relationships with domestic clown-servants. Money and the Mart create a formula that tests the bonds of the masters and clown-servants and causes the questioning of identities that are defined by service relationships. It is the exposure of these service relationships to the economics of the Mart that leads to errors in perception. Within this exposure, the identities of clown-servants reflect the social economics of their masters. Just as the domestic mode of authority displayed by E. Antipholus characterizes the traditional clown-service of E. Dromio, so does the proto-capitalist behavior of S. Antipholus characterize the proto-capitalist acts of S. Dromio. Thus, together the Ephesian master and clown-servant signify the attempt of early modern English households to maintain a traditional late feudal domestic structure of authority. On the other hand, the relationship between the Syracusan master and clown-servant expresses the struggles of new Londoners to survive in an unstable economy. McBride describes the relevance of *Errors* to the social economy of its time:

> Like Antipholus, who arrives with only a bag of gold and a head full of stories about a 'town full of cozenage' (1.2.1-8), these young men [of 16th and early 17th England] left their childhood towns for the greater economic opportunities afforded by London and regularly arrived in the city with great expectations, some trepidation and few connections. (84-85)

Against the backdrop of a changing English economy, the pairings of market-minded masters to progressive clown-servant like S. Antipholus to S. Dromio illustrates the development of the proto-capitalist clown-servant in Shakespeare's plays. This is not to say that the traditional clown with ties to late feudal domestic order disappears from Shakespeare's comedies. His dull humor is reduced to clown-like characters, such as Dogberry in *Much Ado About Nothing*, that survive as buffoons and simpletons rather than influence significantly the economics of the plot.

In *Two Gentlemen*, noticeable dissimilarities in the masters Valentine and Proteus and in their approaches to studying abroad mark dissimilarities in the characterizations of their clown-servants. From these dissimilarities, the pairings of masters and servants continue to show a recognizable degree of emulation by clown-servant of their masters. Rivlin argues the following point:

> Specifically, servants and masters in *Two Gentlemen* share an imitative bond that consolidates broader concerns about the role of imitation in constructing social identity. The servant acts as his master's proxy, an iterative function, but one

> that allows him to exploit the space between will
> and its function. The imitative relationship of
> servant and master is thus informed by difference
> as well as similitude. (105)

In other words, Shakespeare's plays pair like masters with like servants to illustrate shifting identities that stem from growing tensions among members of the domestic hierarchy. Nonetheless, the differences in class and station between masters and domestic clown-servants make possible movement away from traditional forms of service bonds. I posit that Speed, with his affinity for proto-capitalist enterprise imitates Valentine. He is a clown-servant who functions within Rivlin's "space between will and its function" (105). In the same manner, modern business people create a consumer zone, an atmosphere of buying and selling, as they sell their services for what they "will" earn in relation to the actual acquisition or "fruition" of those earnings.[6] Speed creates a consumer zone that wills his services to generate profit above and beyond expected acts of service. He uses the repetitive function of service to diversify his monetary earning through labor for money, acts allowed by Valentine's reaction to domestic difficulties within the Duke's court. Valentine breaks from the Duke, a symbol of late feudal authority, to mark his rejection of traditional social grooming. On the other hand, Proteus relies on the illusory late feudal advantages of obedience to his superior, the Duke, in return for his acceptance. Likewise, his clown-servant Launce looks ahead to the milkmaid and his own lower class imitation of Proteus's attempt at domestic order.

The first of Shakespeare's comic proto-capitalist clown-servants, Syracusan Dromio of *Errors*, initiates the practice of offering economic advice to a social superior. His verbal ability inverts the late feudal notion seen in Will Somer's bond with Henry VIII described in Chapter 1, a master-servant bond founded on the premise that the words of the traditional clown-servant are divinely inspired. Unlike King Henry VIII, S. Antipholus is more the merchant-master than a royal householder. His clown-servant offers wise advice that mirrors the master's proto-capitalist attitude more than his traditional social status as a householder. Unlike E. Dromio, who offers no advice to E. Antipholus and whose service bond resides in a system of verbal commands and repeated complaints, S. Dromio often breaks his subservience to voice his economic opinions in the presence of his superiors. To the domestic bond between proto-capitalist master and clown-servant, S. Dromio adds the service of advisor. An attribute that later allows the clown-servant the autonomous break from the master, the advisory role of the clown-servant grooms him for economic self-sufficiency.

In S. Dromio's reference to "the bald pate of father Time" (2.2.69), money is the underlying topic of the witticism. Although S. Dromio relates father Time's baldness to the idea that all things occur in their time, the real topics of debate are the subjects of service in terms of consumerism and the purchase of hair. To natural hair loss, S. Antipholus leads S. Dromio with the query: "May he not do it by fine and recovery?" (2.2.73). In other words, he asks whether or not a man may buy more hair, a question that attempts to gauge the resourcefulness of money.[7] It is money and S. Antipholus's misperception of S. Dromio's clown-service through the Mart with the gold to secure room and board that facilitates this witty exchange. In the logic of the jest, S. Dromio asserts a relationship between the scarcity of hair and the abundance of wit. According to S. Dromio's viewpoint, a man of wit or of an astute business sense relieves himself of attributes that create losses in profit: "The one, to save the money that he spends in trimming; the other, that at dinner they should not drop in his porridge" (2.2.96-98).

Keeping his argumentative focus on monetary exchange, S. Antipholus attempts to extract a pith of business savvy from S. Dromio and questions whether or not "hairy men [are] plain dealers without wit" (2.2.85-86). E. Dromio's bawdy comeback suggests that even the "plain dealer" will lose his hair, perhaps by venereal disease at the purchase of sex. S. Dromio's final retort reveals that his jest progresses along the lines of commentary on service relationships and not time management. Therefore, S. Dromio's words "Thus I mend it: Time himself is bald and therefore to the world's end will have bald followers" (2.2.105-106), convey a self-identifying statement of his own service relationship with S. Antipholus. He is the bald/witty lifetime advisor to his master.

S. Dromio's notions of proto-capitalism are further seen in his reluctance to convert to domestic order, an act that mirrors his master's warning about Ephesian women and his overall desire to leave Ephesus at the earliest possibility. Although the Dromios are interchangeable domestic servants, their identities differ according to the economic roles of their masters. The play fosters two key interconnected acts that emphasize these differences between traditional and progressive clowns: the rejection of household arrangements with Adriana and the kitchen wench by S. Antipholus and S. Dromio respectively. Unlike E. Dromio who readily accepts marriage to another domestic servant, S. Dromio seeks to avoid marriage to E. Antipholus's kitchen wench, a match that would earn his place in the downstairs household economies of Ephesus. As Shakespeare's plays move away from the portrayal of traditional clown-servant, they often position clown-servants within domestic home-lives that mirror the domestic home-life secured by the master.[8] The scene in which S. Dromio wittily outlines the physical geography of the kitchen wench follows S. Antipholus's rejection of Adriana's claim to him as husband. S. Dromio remarks: "As from a bear a man would run for life, So fly I from her that would be my wife" (3.2.153-4). S. Antipholus's recent attempt to woo Luciana into pleasure's bed rather than into a contract of marriage adds overtones of bachelorhood. Likewise, S. Antipholus rejects all marital advances, and even his possibly legitimate attraction to Luciana is treated as the allures of a siren song.

Similarly in *Two Gentlemen*, Speed marks the next step in Shakespeare's development of the proto-capitalist clown-servant. The service bond between Speed and Valentine demonstrates the pairing of a proto-capitalist clown-servant to an itinerant master, an imitative service relationship that nonetheless points to the dissolving identities of masters and their clown-servants. Central to the early development of Shakespeare's proto-capitalist clown-servant is the economic adaptability of the master and his clown-servant to waning contracts of late feudal service. Three of Shakespeare's four early comedies (*Two Gentlemen*, *Taming of the Shrew*, and *Love's Labor's Lost*) are directly concerned with clown-servants and masters. The thematic of Speed's clown-service highlights the relevance of changing service ideals, weakened bonds that reflect the economic priorities of early modern London. In Speed, Shakespeare presents the first clown-servant who profits by expanding the economic parameters of his domestic service. As an imitative clown-servant and master, Speed's commercial approach to service foreshadows Valentine's break from the virtues of hard work and obedience and his subsequent embrace of a proto-capitalist form of exchange in the play.

Like S. Dromio, Speed uses his verbal ability to advise his master, Valentine, in matters of service and identity. Based on Speed's constant imitation of his master's character, he has made it a responsibility of his service to point out the change in Valentine's service and in the identifying social posture of that service. Silvia's first word to Valentine is

"Servant" (2.4.1)! Since Valentine assumes the character of a servant, an economic identity familiar to Speed, Speed takes the opportunity to advise his master accordingly. In other words, since Speed is the clown-servant who aspires to be like his master, he is very aware when his master assumes qualities of the clown-servant. For example, in Act 2, scene 1 at the Duke's palace in Milan, Speed begins comic routine of the hailing clown-servant, an act that not only signals the emergence of a head-strong domestic but also that of a servile master. Speed acts out a misperception of service, a comic routine later replayed between Shylock and Gobbo in *The Merchant of Venice* illustrative of an inversion of service as well as a break in their service bond. To Speed's hail of "Madam Silvia! Madam Silvia," Valentine replies "How now, sirrah? Why, sir, who bade you call her? Well, you'll still be too forward?" (2.1.6, 7-9). With this quality of the emergent proto-capitalist, Speed must be "too forward" to advise Valentine concerning his recent submissive behavior. Speed's "too forward" advisement is a reflection of Valentine's assessment concerning Proteus's courtship. Dialogue between Valentine and Speed points to the accurate mimicking of the master by the advising clown-servant. Therefore, Speed notes changes in Valentine's character. When Valentine is with Silvia, he resembles Proteus whose home-keeping makes him a servant of courtly love and ties him to Verona. Speed prefers a master who endeavors to travel abroad and profit rather than stay at home to woo.

Speed's knowledge of his master by special marks continues allusions to marks of service and identity from *Errors*, marks that distinguish householders from the merchant-minded. In particular, Speed echoes S. Dromio's reference to his own identifying marks that signify his domestic obligation of service to marry E. Antipholus's kitchen wench whom he asserts "laid claim to me, call'd me Dromio; swore I was assured to her; told me what privy marks

I had about me" (3.2.139-141). For S. Dromio, the domestic union with the kitchen wench is just as out of character for the merchant-minded as S. Antipholus's illusory marriage to Adriana. Like S. Antipholus, S. Dromio avoids the domestic qualities of marriage. Speed marks changes in Valentine that make him less like his master:

> Marry, by these special marks: first, you have learned, like Sir Proteus, to wreathe your arms, like a malecontent; to relish a love-song, like a robin-redbreast; to walk alone, like one that had the pestilence; to sigh, like a school-boy that had lost his A B C; to weep, like a young wench that had buried her grandam; to fast, like one that takes diet; to watch like one that fears robbing; to speak puling, like a beggar at Hallowmas. (2.1.17-25)

Speed's observation of his master first likens Valentine to Proteus, a master that Speed has verbally matched. The importance of Speed's observation is that it casts Valentine in a group of superiors that he is able to outwit, as further evidence of dissolving service relations between master and clown servant. Now that Valentine shares Proteus's occupation as a "home-keeping youth," neither of their "homely wit" is a match for Speed's jests (1.1 2). Valentine acts out Speed's terms "wreathe," "malecontent," "walk alone," "sigh," "weep," and "speak puling," words that all amount to identifying marks of sorrow (2.1.18-24). Speed's comment suggests that on previous occasions, Valentine was only sad "for want of money" (2.1.28). When he was in possession of money, he was happily content. Valentine must eventually cast off these behaviors to regain his business savvy and masterly authority.

By rightfully noting changes in Valentine's marks of character, Speed positions himself to play the sagacious advisor to a master who misperceives domestic arrangements of service. The significance of this position is that it highlights Speed's verbal victories of outwitting two male masters early in the play, an act that further establishes the credibility of his new economic practices. In addition to these economic practices, an interaction among Speed, Valentine, and Madam Sylvia illustrates Speed's knowledge of traditional service arrangements. If we view Valentine's pursuit of Sylvia in relation to his relationship of service with Speed, it becomes clear that Speed's presence reemphasizes service expectations rather than the mutual attraction between Valentine and Sylvia. Speed's aside begins the verbal wit characteristic of the dramatic clown, and he concludes by noting Valentine's misevaluation of service:

> O jest unseen, inscrutable, invisible,
> As a nose on a man's face, or a weathercock on a steeple!
> My master sues to her, and she hath taught her suitor,
> He being her pupil, to become her tutor. (2.1.131-134)

Speed's first lines do not readily inform Valentine of his misperception, but rather convey that a "jest" has been played of which he and Sylvia alone possess the knowledge. This act not only allows the clown-servant to mimic upper class characters with impunity, but also it signals a brief inversion in which Valentine is reduced to her "tutor" or servant.[9] Speed's advice helps Valentine to understand arrangements of service in relation to his wooing. Speed muses: 'O excellent device! was there ever heard a better, that my master, being scribe, to himself should write the letter?" (2.1.35-36). In other words, Speed makes known that Valentine's mastership of his affections for Sylvia have made him a servant both to

Sylvia and to himself. Valentine accepts the advice of his clown-servant. As the play progresses, Valentine must better understand aspects of service with the help of Speed's advice to profit in the proto-capitalist modes of exchange that he encounters in the forest.

In the forest scene of act four, Speed advises, "Master, be one of them; it's an honourable kind of thievery" (4.1.39-40) and Valentine accepts a proto-capitalist alternative to the late feudal society. Rivlin points to this as one of the "places in the play where servant/master mimesis opens the elite subject to heterogeneous social positions and undercuts its naturalized claims to authority and dominance" (121). The forest scene's "servant/master mimesis" is achieved through Speed's social appraisal and offering of economic advice that sheepishly leads the master safely into a new market economy (121). The forest of *Two Gentlemen* is not to be confused with the theoretical Eden or "green world" as a naturally oppositional setting to the court as seen in later Shakespeare's comedies.[10] Unlike the green world that emphasizes nature's ability to transform displaced people, like the Forest of Arden in *Midsummer Night's Dream* or the influence of pastoral celebration in *The Winter's Tale*, the green world of *Two Gentlemen* serves as a background for displaced gentlemen and their practice of thievery. Rather than a green world of nature's power or pastoral life, the forest of Valentine and Speed serves to cloak their exile.

Valentine's forest is more reflective of the criminal redistribution of wealth and the practices of the unemployed and opportunistic villains, rather than of humble pastoralists. The forest, like the Mart, becomes the social economic leveler of its play. Like the escapades of highway robbery shared by Falstaff and Prince Hal in *Henry IV Part I*, the highway robberies in *Two Gentlemen* represent attempts by outcasts to redistribute wealth. Their thievery represents members of society who function outside of the play's feudal economics yet have the ability to enforce their own economy. Yet unlike the sixteenth century portrayal of Falstaff and the Prince, Valentine's band of thieves depicts the criminal reaction of the unemployed to profound changes in the early modern London economy. The Third Outlaw wants Valentine to

> Know, then, that some of us are gentlemen,
> Such as the fury of ungovern'd youth
> Thrust from the company of awful men:
> Myself was from Verona banished
> For practising to steal away a lady,
> An heir, and near allied unto the Duke. (4.1.44-49)

The Third Outlaw makes the distinction between masterless vagrants and gentlemen, a point that reinforces Woodbridge's unmasking of "the common belief that vagrants were organized in highly disciplined societies" (6). The Third Outlaw's point is not that vagrants are organized since they are organized, acting under a leader. Rather, he points out that he and his men are not vagabonds at all. They are gentlemen who have been exiled wrongly from the kingdom. His explanation suggests that even as robbers, they are men of genteel character and wish to be accepted for their past nobility rather than rejected for their present crimes. They incorporate physical abuse to commit highway robbery. Whether in the forest or at court, masters practice physical abuse to maintain their servants.

The cycle of verbal commands and physical abuse reveals the strain involved as the householder attempts to maintain domestic discipline in the midst of changing household economics. Ephesian Dromio, the clown-servant traditional of *Errors*, plays a character exposed to the kind of physical, slap-stick humor that is significantly decreased as the plays develop the verbal wit of the economically astute clown-servant. This is not to say that later clown-servants make monetary exchanges that absolve them completely from threats or physical abuse at the hands of their masters. Nor is it to infer that the abuse of servants is an integral component of uncivil sixteenth century English domestic arrangements. However, it does suggest that new commercial forms present in the market economics of the Mart illustrate a re-ordering of traditional domestic associations. In other words, the Mart confounds the domestic identities of master and clown-servant and calls into question their perceived social economic identities.[11]

It is when these mimetic identities of master and clown-servant are locked out of their late feudal home and prevented from obtaining its economic benefits that the Mart escalates the occurrences of misperceived identities.[12] E. Antipholus says: "Since my doors fail to entertain me, I'll knock elsewhere, to see if they'll disdain me" (3.1.120-121). It should be noted that his doors fail him because his household mistakes S. Antipholus for E. Antipholus. E. Antipholus forgoes his first decision to break down the door to his home and decides instead to spite Adriana through commercial means. He says to Angelo, the goldsmith:

> Get you home
> And fetch the chain; by this I know 'tis made:
> Bring it, I pray you, to the Porpentine;
> For there's the house: that chain will I bestow –
> Be it for nothing but to spite my wife –
> Upon mine hostess there: good sir, make haste.
> (3.1.114-19)

Harmonious household economics requires that the exchanges of the Mart must profit the household and reinforce late feudal domestic order. Problems arise in the course of the play as market exchanges supersede household economics and the relationships of service that characterize it. For example, when E. Antipholus commands E. Dromio, "go thou and buy a rope's end," he sends him among the Mart's crowd of merchants for an instrument of further domestic abuse. E. Dromio's failure to secure a rope attenuates his bond with E. Antipholus and signals that the exchanges of the Mart supersede the needs of the household.

Likewise, Adriana accepts that it is business outside of the home that detains E. Antipholus. Still, she expects to receive the gold chain, profit from the Mart that reinforces their domestic union (2.1.105). When profitable exchanges of the Mart do not reinforce domestic order, they alter the structure of the hierarchy of service upon which the household functions. When domestic servants complete tasks at the behest of their masters, their obedience reinforces the subservient relationship of clown-servant domestic to master.

Unlike S. Dromio, who advises his master, E. Dromio serves under the constant threat of beatings, acts that reflect the traditional power relationship of master and clown-servant. Ronald R. Macdonald suggests that "even at the very onset Ephesian Dromio's orderly causal scenario looks not so much like a neutral description of the way things indisputably work, as it does like an attempt to impose order on a world increasingly resistant to such orderings" (7). By physically abusing E. Dromio, E. Antipholus and the upstairs members of his household impose late feudal order even as the Mart presents alternatives that resist their domestic arrangements. E. Dromio is beaten distinctly four times in the play to S. Dromio's one time, and E. Dromio receives threats of beating at least four times to S. Dromio's one time.[13] If we return to Rivlin's theory of servant/master mimesis, the "naturalized claims to authority and dominance" are comparable to E. Antipholus's perceived identity as householder within the economic society of the Ephesian Mart (121). Thus, since we continue to find representative traits of the master in the servant as well as traits of the servant in the master, what does E. Dromio's act of following E. Antipholus and subsequent physical abuse say about the waning bond between household masters and traditional clown-servant in the wake of domestic economic changes present in the Mart? Important to this query is E. Dromio's self-identification as an unfairly treated traditional clown-servant who follows the instructions of his master in matters of commercial exchange.

E. Dromio enters the play through discourse that self-identifies him as a follower who is expected to conduct the business of his master without any economic self-interest. The household limits of E. Antipholus's household economics prevent E. Dromio from participating in market exchanges. It is E. Dromio's lack of economic autonomy that points to the breakdown of his feudal master/clown-servant bond with E. Antipholus. Lalita Pandit suggests that E. Dromio "consoles himself with the thought that his name never made it easy for him to get any credit in town (meaning both loan-money, and praise), but it got him much blame (for not doing things right)" (94). E. Dromio's lack of credit in the Mart stems from his identity as a household domestic servant. It is not that he cannot get credit in the Mart, but rather that he can only get it for his master upon E. Antipholus's reputation as a local home owner and business man. For example, when questioned by S. Antipholus about the gold coins for room and board, E. Dromio explains that the saddler kept the money left over from the exchange for the crupper. E. Dromio's job is to follow orders with an exact payment for goods rendered, not to be credited with extensions of payments through credit-based exchanges. Unlike Speed of *Two Gentlemen*, E. Dromio is prohibited from earning money to accumulate profit, and he attributes any excesses of commercial exchange to the business cycle of the Mart. He implicates the "saddler" as the conductor of any additional monetary transactions concerning monies left over from his task to secure a crupper. Although E. Dromio does not personally imitate the business sense of his master, he does mirror E. Antipholus's frustration concerning his masterly identity.

When E. Dromio imitates his master, he mirrors Antipholus's frustration with the breakdown of his social economic status as master, householder, and merchant of the Ephesian Mart. The breakdown of identity occurs because E. Antipholus interprets the insubordination of his traditional clown-servant as a direct threat to his household authority. He sees in E. Dromio the qualities of being "too forward," qualities later seen in Speed that signal early signs of economic autonomy and the further dissolution of the service bond between clown-servant and master. E. Antipholus's response is to revert to late feudal aspects of ownership that allow the physical abuse of servants. E. Dromio mirrors his master's frustrations with stagnant domestic identities, constructed in terms of inferiors and superiors. Of particular interest is Dromio's response to a lifetime of exchanging service for beatings. He exclaims: "I have served him from the hour of my nativity to this instant, and have nothing at his hands for my service but blows" (4.4.30-31). From the perspective of service economics, E. Dromio's reference to having "nothing at his hands for my service" points out that he functions in a system of familial acceptance and maintenance in return for service without payment of money. His "nothing" directly signals that he is restricted from possessing capital in any form, not even the change from the purchase of the crupper. Fearing a future disability from this physical abuse, he also fears his ejection from E. Antipholus's traditional domestic order: "I bear it on my shoulders as a beggar wont her brat; and, I think, when he hath lamed me, I shall beg with it from door to door" (4.4.37-39).

LAUNCE, STARRING WILLIAM KEMP

In *Two Gentlemen*, Launce's role as the traditional late feudal clown-servant who follows his master illustrates not only the influence of William Kemp to the further development of Shakespeare's clown-servants on the Elizabethan stage, but also the dramatic waning of the late feudal clown-servant and further development of proto-capitalists. Like Somer, Kemp is a significant nexus between the real actor playing a clown and the clown of the scripted play. Kemp's celebrity, his star quality mentioned in the previous chapter stems from the reality that he was a clown both on and off the stage. Unlike other actors, Kemp was a clown at court, on the stage, on the street, and in the tavern. His real life jigging was not just a character-type that he portrayed, like a juggler or acrobat; it was his skill and further, his identity. Noteworthy, the incorporation of jigging clown-servants like Kemp into scripted plays shows further evidence of the transition from late feudal to proto-capitalist modes of exchange along domestic lines of service. Like the connection of Somer to the early dramatic characters that reflect Somer's style of clowning, Kemp's career encompasses both real court service and real jigging as well as playing fictitious characters on stage. His life as both real and pretend clowns makes him central to the study of the transition from late feudal to proto-capitalist clowning of the early modern theater. Incorporated into the centralized growth of London theaters in the late sixteenth century, Kemp was familiar with both the nomadic life of the touring company and the great playhouses of the city. Greenblatt rationalizes that

> The rise of the public theatres in a city with a rapidly expanding population hungry for amusement gave at least some of these companies the opportunity to have a lucrative home base where they would do most of their performing. They would still go

out on the road from time to time, but the wagon with the costumes and props, the scrambling to find a place to perform, the fraught negotiations with the local authorities would no longer occupy the center of their professional lives. (*Will* 188)

It must be considered that on one front, Kemp's theatrical endeavors with the Chamberlain's Men point to the capitalist ambitions of early modern English theatre. Kemp brings to the stage identity of Shakespeare's clown-servant the star quality of a brand name clown actor. As a scripted actor, Kemp hereafter centralizes the clown-servant; Shakespeare does not return to verse-speaking clown-servants like the Dromios without a larger-than-life stage presence. The scripting of Launce seems to accommodate directly Kemp's addition to the Chamberlain's Men (Wiles 73). On another front, his clowning technique points back to a simplistic tarltonesque style of physical buffoonery still very popular with later sixteenth century theatergoers (73-4). Kemp begins the characterization of clown-servants whose actions in their plays are spotlight moments that occur within the context of the plots, yet still show signs of physical humor and slap-stick buffoonery. It is when Shakespeare's capital endeavors as a working clown-actor merge with his honed style of clown-servant buffoonery that his plays begin to construct clown-servants that make use of Kemp's talents.

In the lineage of Will Somer's witty clown-service and as the direct descendent of Tarlton's Vice-like physical humor slapstick, Kemp also acted out the concerns of late feudal order through humorous monologues seemingly detached from the play. Having mastered Tarlton's style of jigging clown and ballad-making, Kemp performs as a domestic clown-servant. "Singing Simkin," the only extant copy of Kemp's jig in print, shows evidence of comic routines later seen in Shakespeare's portrayal of the clown-servant, routines that must have entered Shakespeare's repertoire through Kemp's influence.[14] Gurr points out that

> 'Singing Simkin' is a rhyming farce for four players, a housewife, the clown, who appears as the housewife's first lover, a soldier her second lover, whose arrival causes the clown to hide in a chest, and the old husband who is told when he enters that the soldier is hunting for a thief. The wife and husband persuade the soldier to leave, and let Simkin out of the chest. The husband leaves, Simkin makes up to the wife, the husband catches him at it, and wife and husband together beat the clown off the stage. (*Stage* 114)

Interestingly, Shakespeare's early comedy is full of domestic moments that feature clown-servants and bawdy humor accompanying the jeopardized marital fidelity of other characters. Kemp was already a well-established clown when he met and began to work with Shakespeare's company, and the bawdy humor illustrated in the above passages carries over from his jig into Shakespeare's creation of the Dromios, Launcelot Gobbo, and Falstaff. In agreement with Clifford Leech, David Wiles shows that "the part of Launce 'was doubtless Kemp's,' and dates around the time of the Chamberlain's company" (73). This supposition is predicated upon Leech's findings that the existing text of *Two Gentlemen* is a reworking, and that the character of Launce was not a part of the original script (xxi-xxxv). According to Wiles, "When Kemp and Shakespeare became fellows, equal sharers in the new company, one of Shakespeare's first acts was to take an old play and construct a part in it for Kemp based on Kemp's routines or 'merriments'" (73).

From Kemp's jig, Shakespeare's early comedies weave seemingly detached moments of action into a greater overall integration of the clown-servant character into the play-proper, an act that coincides with the decline of the jig and the rise of playacting during Shakespeare's time. C. R. Baskervill notes the author's claims of the tract *Mar-Martine*: "These tinkers termes, and barbers jesters first *Tarleton* on the stage. Then *Martin* in his bookes of lies, hath put in every page" (102). These lines point to the growth of scripted performance centered on the antics of the clown character whose amusement is linked directly to the growth of early modern London theatre. One may assume that Shakespeare's later seeming animosity in *Hamlet* (3.2.38-45) toward extempore clowning would result in its absence from his plays. However, as Wiles points out, the opposite occurs and Shakespeare's early clowns integrate their showmanship into Shakespeare's clown characters. Although extempore clowning does seem to disappear by *2 Henry IV*, it flourishes through Kemp's character portrayals in Shakespeare's early plays. Wiles states:

> From the view of Kemp, the role of Launce marks a transition: in later roles for the Chamberlain's, the clown becomes increasingly integrated with the narrative. From the point of view of Shakespeare, new possibilities are established: Shakespeare is now writing for an actor whose art is rooted in minstrelsy, and who therefore knows how to dominate a stage without support from plot mechanics. This enables Shakespeare to turn aside from models provided by the Vice and classical slave, and to create a dramatic structure based on the alteration of different modes of performance. (73-4)

With Kemp, the clown-servant assumes the spotlight. This is precisely the case in Launce's scenes with Crab.

Shakespeare's early comedies direct the clown through dialogue within the parameters of the script, even between speaking clown and speechless dog. In other words, the much discussed caution later in *Hamlet* that only clowns speak lines set down for them may or may not be aimed at Kemp. Hamlet's warning may apply to Kemp since Kemp leaves Shakespeare's company at the height of its success. He returns to full time jigging with promises of financial gain not sure box office profits. Nonetheless, Hamlet's warning does identify the trend in early Shakespeare's comedies to feature clown-servants with Kemp-like showmanship yet also to limit humorous plot deviations more akin to jigging than drama. The reality that Shakespeare's plays do not totally abandon spotlighting on the clown shows the popularity of the clown-character. Although the jig does not totally disappear from early modern entertainment, it is absent from Shakespeare's plays.

From these perspectives, Kemp, as Launce, stages a clown that continues the pairing of traditional clown-servants to domestic masters in ways that illustrate social economic nostalgia in the midst of changing household economics. Kemp's role as clown-servant domestic in *Two Gentlemen* presents his domestic wit and economic state as a traditional clown. Rivlin states that

> In his historic relationship with his dog/servant, Launce both recreates and parodies the servant's mimetically derived control over his master. The monologues function in dual fashion: they reinforce the dynamics of mimetic service elsewhere in the play, and they reduce the relation of servant and master to an absurd, animalistic one. (115)

In this regard, Kemp's work as Shakespeare's traditional

clown-servant is pivotal to the continued development of the proto-capitalist domestic clown-servant. In Launce's two scenes most concerned with issues of late feudal service economics, Kemp uses the familiar role of the displaced domestic servant to entertain the audience. The first scene (2.3) is Launce's account of the familial reaction to his departure to serve Proteus abroad. Important to this scene, Kemp, like Tarlton before him, is allowed to work solo (save for Crab his dog). This feature builds on the star quality and audience interaction characteristic of the clown-servant actor. In addition to jigging, Wiles notes that "Kemp was a solo comedian" (33), a theatrical model that, like the jig, allows the actor to interact with the audience outside of the plot. But as the integration of the domestic clown-servant into the plot favored witty dialogue over physical buffoonery, Kemp's dutiful service is used to introduce the youthful Speed and his fresh economic concerns that become the voice of later proto-capitalist clown-servants.

The second scene (3.1) displays this use of dialogue between Launce and Speed. In the same manner that E. Dromio's domestic livelihood promotes his union with the kitchen wench, so Launce attempts to secure traditional domestic arrangements with the milkmaid to secure his place in the hierarchy of domestic service. Launce's use of simple dialogue also occurs with Crab his dog. Crab, unlike Speed, cannot match verbal wits with Launce, a quality of the clown/dog relationship that gives Launce (Kemp) the whole stage for buffoonery. It is safe to reason the buffoonery follows because scripted dialogue is the dramatic construct that keeps Kemp's entertainment within the parameters of the play and prevents his clowning from turning to jigging.

Kemp's portrayal of the clown-servant domestic Launce with Crab, his "cruel-hearted cur" is the exception to the old theatrical adage that cautions actors not to work with children or animals (2.3.9). Like Tarlton before him, famous for his jests with the Queen's dog, Kemp brings to the stage the late feudal service bond between animal and traditional clown servants. The appearance of Launce and Crab alone on stage in Act 2, scene 3 not only illustrates the breakdown of the late feudal master-servant bond by mirroring in the servant the character of the master, but it also affords Kemp the opportunity for popular humorous improvisations while directly addressing the audience. Although dialogue between actor and dog may seem detached from the dialogue of the play-proper, it is by no means separate from the play's treatment of late feudal service. According to Berry, Kemp's direct address to the audience "subverts the autonomy of the play world" (*Awareness* 1-2). In the role of clown-servant Kemp, like Tarlton, was able to bridge the worlds of the stage and the audience. Robert Weimann identifies Launce as a figure that moves between the Elizabethan reality of a clown confronting a theatre audience and the dramatic actions of a character relating to other characters:

> The real performance of the actor and the imaginative role of the servant interact, and they achieve a new and very subtle kind of unity. Within this unity, the character's relations to the playworld begin to dominate, but the comic ease and flexibility of these relations are still enriched by some traditional connexion between the clowning actor and the laughing spectator. (40)

It is the subversion of the "play world" which allows the play to make direct parallels with the world of the audience, including changes to the domestic economies of late sixteenth century London. As the character with the most direct lines to the audience, the language of clown-servant actor best conveys aspects of domestic service consistent with the play world and the world of Elizabethan economy.

Although Launce's language differs from that of Proteus, Kemp's depiction of Launce continues the mirroring of late feudal master and servants seen in the bond between E. Antipholus and E. Dromio. Like earlier clown-servant descendants of Will Somer, Kemp and Crab jest from positions of late feudal servitude, familiar comic postures that prime audiences for Kemp's improvisation of the script. Kemp's improvisations and the seeming detachment of his scene with Crab from the rest of the play allow him "to take liberties with the action" and manipulate simple props like his shoes and staff to garner laughter from audiences (Billington 49). An examination of Launce's lines illustrates their difference from the poetic iambic pentameter of other characters. In the role of Launce, Kemp may deviate from the script without altering the jest of the scene:

> This shoe is my father: no, this left shoe is my father. No, no, this left shoe is my mother. nay, that cannot be so neither: yes, it is so, it is so— it hath the worser sole. This shoe, with the hole in it, is my mother, and this my father; a vengeance on't! there 'tis: now, sit, this staff is my sister, for, look you, she is as white as a lily and as small as a wand. this hat is Nan, our maid: I am the dog: no, the dog is himself, and I am the dog--Oh! the dog is me, and I am myself; ay, so, so. (2.3.13-23)

The loose construction of Launce's lines would allow Kemp to entertain the audience in mood and tone unhampered by formal poetic meter. Unlike E. Dromio in *Errors* who speaks in iambic pentameter and rhyming couplets, Kemp adds to Launce's words a visual component in a manner similar to current prop-comics in order to extract base laughter from his audiences. Edgar I. Fripp notes that Kemp mixed words with the customary bawdy gesture of laying his leg over his staff to insure roars of laughter from audiences (284). Like E. Dromio, Launce's acts reflect the sentiments of his master. Kemp's freedom with the language provides a humorous mimicking of Proteus's remorseful farewell to his life of home keeping. If we accept that Crab is both companion and servant to Launce in the same manner as Launce to Proteus, then his disobedience, especially in domestic situations, signals the reflection of master-servant identities. Crab's portrayal relates to Launce's own tense late feudal relationships with Proteus. Important to this viewpoint and to the highlight of the term "cur" is Shakespeare's specific casting and references to dogs in his drama.[15]

In contrast to other dogs of Shakespeare's drama that are defined by their efficient services to their master, Crab's currish disposition to late feudal service reflects that Launce, like his master Proteus, "is a kind of knave" (3.1.262). As a dog without pedigree, Crab is not endowed with the canine instincts of a purebred dog, like the hunting dogs. For example, in *The Taming of the Shrew*, another of Shakespeare's comedies, a Lord and his First Huntsman/ servant debate the services of the Lord's hunting dogs:

> Huntsman, I charge thee, tender well my hounds—
> Brach Merriman, the poor cur is emboss'd;
> And couple Clowder with the deep—mouth'd brach.
> Saw'st thou not, boy, how Silver made it good
> At the hedge-corner, in the coldest fault?
> I would not lose the dog for twenty pound.

The First Huntsman replies:

> Why, Belman is as good as he, my lord; (Int.1.15-
> 21)

As the servant whose duty it is to care for the dogs, the First Huntsman boasts the service of the dogs from his position as their immediate master. The First Huntsman sees in the dog Belman reflections of his own service to the Lord as well as qualities of the Lord in the same manner that Launce sees qualities of both himself and Proteus in Crab's crassness. Belman displays qualities of obedience and diligence for the sake of the master, prized character traits in any servant, human or canine.[16] For Launce, even the qualities of his future wife are likened to the praise of the pedigreed qualities of a "water spaniel" (2.1.270). In other words, his future domestic arrangements will not be with a currish milkmaid.

To view Crab as an extension of service between master and traditional clown is to better understand the breakdown of the service bond between Launce and Proteus, a relationship that no longer subsists on threats or acts of physical beatings. In the same manner that E. Dromio endures beatings by E. Antipholus, Launce suffers whippings for his dog-servant Crab. Like the Dromios and Speed, Launce is a servant who reflects characteristics of his master. As the master of Crab, Launce's suffering of the dog's punishments may fuse their emotional friendship, but at the same time it dissolves the subservient relationship of beast to man. As Launce explains, it is he, Crab's master, who endures the beatings for the servant guilty of domestic abuses like the theft of a capon's leg from the dinner table or urination in the dinner-chamber. Launce makes clear his masterly intercession on the servant Crab's behalf in terms of servant/master inversion:

'Friend,' quoth I, 'you mean to whip the dog?'
'Ay, marry, do I,' quoth he. 'You do him the more

wrong,' quoth I; 'twas I did the thing you wot of.'
He makes me no more ado, but whips me out of
the chamber. How many masters would do this
for his servant? Nay, I'll be sworn, I have sat in
the stocks for puddings he hath stolen, otherwise
he had been executed; I have stood on the pillory
for geese he hath killed, otherwise he had suffered
for't. (4.4.24-33)

Crab's offenses violate domestic decorum for servants, the
late feudal pillars upon which rest the master/clown-servant
relationship. John Timpane notes the sequence of mirroring of
servants and masters as Launce plays the cur with his master
Proteus by outwitting and overstaging him only to mirror
Proteus's folly (198). In other words, as traditional clown-
servant, Launce's inefficient services as follower, messenger,
and later gift-giver, undermine Proteus's masterhood, yet
Crab's inefficient similar canine services undermine Launce
more successfully, since Lance is physically beaten for his
dog-servant.

Launce's engagement to the milkmaid mimics "Proteus's
folly," his pursuit of a wife and household both at home
and at the Duke's palace. These acts signal an understood
continuation of late feudal home-life for the clown-servants
at the ends of their plays, acts previously witnessed in
their masters. For examples, E. Dromio (*Errors*) seeks
domestic arrangements with the kitchen wench, Launce
(*Two Gentlemen*) will settle with the milkmaid. For Launce,
his paper that lists a "cate-log of her condition" ties his
future household to domestic concerns. Muriel St. Clara
Byrne makes note that Launce's reading of his slip of paper
verbalizes what Launce thinks and speaks. He values his
future service and wife in terms of domestic service and
service-oriented economics. His letter states that among
her "many nameless virtues" (3.1.311), she can fetch and

carry, milk, brew, sew, knit, wash and scour, and spin. Set down among "her vices" (3.1.315), she has a sweet mouth yet sour breath, talks in her sleep and is slow in speech, is proud, has no teeth, and drinks liquor. Among the faults are that "she hath more hair than wit, and more faults than hairs, and more wealth than faults" (3.1.345-346). He makes allowances for her hygiene, appearance, and disposition. It is her service abilities that are important to Launce.

CONCLUSION

To sum, Shakespeare's comic clown-servants develop from portrayals of traditional late feudal domestic servants to proto-capitalist domestic servants. This chapter shows the evolution of clown-servant actor from the clowning of the real court fool Will Somer to the stage comedy of William Kemp. Chapter 2 has traced the evolution of the dramatic clown-servant domestic in Shakespeare's early comedies, *Errors* and *Two Gentlemen*. Key to the development of the clown-servant in Shakespeare's comedies is the clown's place of domestic servitude in early modern drama. In roles of household service, the clown expresses economic tensions on stage that reflect economic concerns in Tudor England. Amid this change in clown-servant characterization, it is late feudal servitude that continues to afford clown-servant domestics greater leverage to express the socio-economic tensions of their plays. An evaluation of late feudal servitude points to both the attenuating master and clown-servant domestic bonds in the plays and the move away from traditional domestic arrangements of service in early modern English households.

Central to understanding Shakespeare's clown-servant characters and their economic contributions is their common social identity as domestic servants. Rather than suggest that service identities in *Errors* and in *Two Gentlemen* are lost then subsequently found, these identities are blurred, altered, or abandoned for proto-capitalist modes of exchange in the rise of non-essential goods. It is from the dramatic vantage point of domestic servitude that clown-servant characters reflect changes in master/servant household economics both of the stage and in Elizabethan society. In the Dromios of *Errors* and Speed and Launce in *Two Gentlemen*, Shakespeare's plays illustrate the progressive dissolution of the master and clown-servant bond by proto-capitalist forces in the play.

An important observation is the significant difference in clown-servant portrayals that illustrates differences in master and clown-servant characterizations: disparities in characterization relate to the dramatic roles of traditional clowns and proto-capitalist clowns. The pairing of these traditional clown-servant to domestic masters and proto-capitalist clown-servants to itinerant masters paints a picture of early modern economic progression from late feudal to proto-capitalist modes of exchange. This trend of economic development in the plays shows how proto-capitalist alternatives break the cycle of late feudal mastership. When Shakespeare creates Launce of *Two Gentlemen*, he ends the portrayal of the late feudal clown-servant whose service bonds act to reinforce traditional forms of late feudal order. In the next chapter, we meet Launcelot Gobbo, the clown-servant of *Merchant of Venice*, as he breaks the strictures of traditional order.

Finally, the acting career of William Kemp and his portrayal of Launce shows how Shakespeare's first clown-servant actor continues in the tradition of Will Summer. Kemp's clown-servant portrayal further illustrates Shakespeare's clown-servant development from the perspective of the theatre and the audience. The next chapter moves away from the clown-servants who maintain strong ties to late feudal domestic service and evaluates the wit-driven proto-capitalism of Launcelot Gobbo in *The*

Merchant of Venice. The clowning servitude of William Kemp illustrates the continued development of the proto-capitalist clown-servant. Characterized by progressive economics, the clown-servant becomes even further integrated into the household economics in the play and continues to reflect tensions and changes in household Tudor economics. Examining Launcelot Gobbo's influences in *The Merchant of Venice* illustrates Shakespeare's next steps away from the late feudal clown-servant toward a more money-minded clown-servant.

CHAPTER III

LAUNCELOT GOBBO: ECONOMIC CRITICISM AND THE MERCHANT OF VENICE

Launcelot Gobbo.   *The fiend is at mine elbow and tempts
                      me saying to me 'Gobbo, Launcelot
                      Gobbo, good Launcelot,' or 'good Gobbo,'
                      or good Launcelot Gobbo, use your legs,
                      take the start, run away. My conscience
                      says 'No; take heed,' honest Launcelot;
                      take heed, honest Gobbo, or, as aforesaid,
                      'honest Launcelot Gobbo; do not run;
                      scorn running with thy heels' . . . The
                      fiend gives the more friendly counsel:
                      I will run, fiend; my heels are at your
                      command; I will run. (2.2.1-9, 27-9)*

In *The Merchant of Venice*, further observation into
Shakespeare's development of the clown-servant reveals a
character more engrossed in the economic tensions of the play
than the clown-servant characters in *The Comedy of Errors*
and *Two Gentlemen of Verona*. Launcelot Gobbo portrays
both traditional and proto-capitalist characterizations
through his socioeconomic consciousness and service.
The Merchant of Venice offers a dramatic look at shifting
modes of socioeconomics that the clown-servant character
continues to moderate in domestic settings. The play presents

Launcelot Gobbo, the next holistic clown-servant character of Shakespeare's comedies. Like Syracusan Dromio in *The Comedy of Errors* and Speed of *The Two Gentlemen of Verona*, Launcelot Gobbo continues Shakespeare's move away from clown servants motivated by customary late feudal bonds of affiliation and toward progressive clown-servants aware of their own socioeconomic profitability. It is precisely the play's economic tensions of merchant class wealth within old aristocratic forms of social order that continue to illustrate the move of Shakespeare's clowns away from feudal order.[1]

A merchant class setting allows *The Merchant of Venice* to serve as a dramatic midpoint between the traditional noble household economics of Shakespeare's earlier clown-servants and the progressive earning of cash payments by *Twelfth Night's* clown-servant, Feste. To illustrate merchant class wealth in relation to the upper and lower classes, late sixteenth-century London society may be neatly split into three stations: the gentry (nobles), who have a landed or investment income and live "without the mechanism of employment; a merchant (middle) class, who work but do not depend upon their hands," living as they do by the profits of capital and by the employment of others, "either in trade or manufactures" and those "others"–"the mere labouring people who depend upon their hands" (Earle 143). *The Merchant of Venice* deals only with the merchant and servant classes and depicts one clown-servant in the homes of merchants rather than multiple clown-servants of noble households as in *The Comedy of Errors* and *Two Gentlemen of Verona*.

In this play, which relocates the significant rise of the merchant class and its proto-capitalist influence in early modern England to Italy, the clown-servant Launcelot Gobbo represents perspectives of servant-class workers in changing Tudor domestic economics. Ronald R. Macdonald contends that "Venice is, to put it bluntly, a bourgeois capitalist republic based on trade and profit from economic exchange, the buying cheap of luxury items in one place and the selling of them dear in another" (58).[2]   By observing how the clown-servant functions in this society, the play illustrates the development of the domestic clown-servant as he continues to serve in traditional households like those in *The Comedy of Errors* and *The Two Gentleman of Verona* but for proto-capitalist masters in *The Merchant of Venice*. Focus on the clown-servant helps to place the merchant class in the transition from late feudalism to proto-capitalism. The clown-servant's adaptations of proto-capitalist practices to traditional domestic arrangements reflect changes to households in Tudor England, like reductions in the size household staffs. Although *The Merchant of Venice* is set in Renaissance Italy, its issues reflect the economic growing pains of the early modern English home. Concerning economic household discontinuity, Jonathan Barry points out that "the period 1550-1780 has been portrayed as one of crisis and rupture between two periods in which association created civic and bourgeois identity" (97). Particularly in London, emergent economic identities point to the rise of the middle or merchant class and its influence on early modern household service. One clown-servant, Launcelot Gobbo, reflects the continuation of the traditional clown-servant in his "conscience," the dominance of the proto-capitalist clown-servant in his "fiend," and their relevance to socioeconomic relationships within the play.

Launcelot's opening soliloquy (2.2.) presents the dueling spheres of his consciousness that challenge the domestic arrangements of service in the play. Launcelot's conscience is the advocate of dutiful domestic service. It reflects what early modern England would have called a feudal order based on service. As Stephen Greenblatt has observed, "The hallmark of power and wealth in the sixteenth century was to be waited on by others" (*Will*

29-30). As one of the others who waits and serves, Launcelot seeks an advantageous position of service to those with new money and old ways. His conscience is the knowledgeable voice of a household servant affixed to Shylock whose altered economics reflect his insistence on profit from his domestic servant. A proponent of traditional service bonds, the conscience may not simply choose to change masters. The conscience is a signifier of the inflexible components of traditional service that view wives, children, and servants as properties of the patriarch. Jan Lawson Hinely observes in *The Merchant of Venice* that the conscience not only represents Launcelot's sense of duty, his service bond between servant and master (218), but also that the conscience depicts feudal service bonds as the play's overall objects of the mockery (220).

In contrast, the advice of the fiend voices urgency toward what may seem an irrational business sense. Launcelot's opening scene not only grounds him in the fiend's socioeconomics of risks, but also it points to his move away from traditional domestic order that would limit his mobility. For Launcelot, risk breaks his traditional dependence on Shylock's form of household economics, a proto-capitalist move in itself. Further, risk also causes him to accept a revised form of traditional service to Bassanio. Launcelot's pre-determination to act upon the advice of the fiend clearly casts him as the proto-capitalist clown-servant. In the play, the economic principle of risk in relation to profit is the tie that binds proto-capitalist masters and servants.

LAUNCELOT'S FIENDISH ECONOMICS

First, we observe in the "the conscience" its resistance to risk and change. Launcelot first appears immediately following the bond agreement between Shylock and Antonio in a comic version of the play's central bond motif (Fortin 261). In a decision-making moment, Launcelot considers whether to dissolve the master-servant bond with Shylock to risk employment with Bassanio, a prodigal master of unsure wealth. Launcelot's conscience is the voice of a domestic servant who clings to his master-servant bond with Shylock. By advising Launcelot to remain in Shylock's service, the conscience illustrates its acceptance of Shylock's household as a workplace with both traditional arrangements of domestic service and Shylock's own philosophy of profitable service. Launcelot says:

> Certainly my conscience will serve me to run from this Jew my master. The fiend is at mine elbow and tempts me saying to me 'Gobbo, Launcelot Gobbo, good Launcelot,' or 'good Gobbo,' or 'good Launcelot Gobbo, use your legs, take the start, run away.' My conscience says 'No; take heed, honest Launcelot; take heed, honest Gobbo,' or, as aforesaid, 'honest Launcelot Gobbo; do not run; scorn running with thy heels.' (2.2 1-9)

Launcelot's conscience reasons that traditional arrangements of service define a good servant as an obedient servant unwilling to risk change since obedience reinforces late feudal domestic order. The conscience represents the dutiful servant. Without the quality of duty, the hierarchy would be unable to enforce codes that distinguish good behavior from bad. This philosophy insures the maintenance of traditional service. In other words, the conscience resists sanctioning the servant's rebellion against the master and urges Launcelot to remain the ever-faithful domestic servant. In order to get Launcelot to self-identify as good and dutiful, and continue service to Shylock, the conscience refers to him six times as "honest" (2.2.6, 7, 8,13-14, 14, 15). Befitting the play's socioeconomics, the term "honest" for the clown suggests a domestic whose service harkens to household order rather than proto-capitalist endeavor. Feudal ethic dictates that just as citizens owe allegiance to their King and may not openly declare service to another ruling monarch--that is, their duty is to serve one master and not to change regardless of his reign--domestic servants are expected to give dutiful service to the masters of their households without change. Launcelot's conscience represents a traditional domestic servant of the emergent merchant class, the Shylocks, Bassanios, and Antonios made wealthy by Venetian proto-capitalist venture. The "honest" servant is the servant who knows her or his place within traditional order and labors for the social benefit of the master, rather than the servant who takes on proto-capitalist enterprises by changing masters for personal gain. Economic forces that benefit the merchant-class thus determine honesty or goodness for the merchant characters.

Launcelot Gobbo enters the play immersed in thought concerning his labor status, an act that begins the play's transformation of consciousness on an economic plane.[3] Steven R. Mentz among others misreads Launcelot's soliloquy as introspective debate.[4] But a re-examination of these lines from a socioeconomic perspective of domestic order shows clearly that Launcelot is in the middle of self-chastisement, not debate. His decision to act has already been made. What remains is a careful browbeating of his conscience for disagreeing with his previously arrived-at decision: "Certainly my conscience will serve me to run from this Jew my master . . . Certainly the Jew is the very devil incarnal; and my conscience is but a kind of hard conscience, to offer to counsel me to stay with the Jew" (2.2.1-2, 26-29). It is his conscience that fails to support his decision to run, and Launcelot admits that the fiend, being "the devil himself," counsels him to flee Shylock, who, himself embodies the devil. Shakespeare's attractive imagery suggests two opposing angels perched on Launcelot's shoulders, the good angel or the conscience offering virtuous counsel, and the fiend tempting him toward mischief. Launcelot experiences opportunity for self-interest as fiendish mischief, a point that illustrates that he is not yet comfortable with an ideology of self-interest and that risk plays a significant part in changing masters.

Reflective of an economy in transition is the bond between masters and servants. Launcelot describes his opportunity to leave as a temptation because choices of employment that blend his self interest for food and clothes with traditional household service are not yet fully acceptable in an ideology in transition. The fiend or bad angel encourages Launcelot to go against the idea that one cannot change one's master, a notion that challenges traditional domestic arrangements. Key to this transition is understanding that the ideologies of master and servants are mimetic. Although Launcelot chooses to follow the advice of the fiend, later actions indicate that there are no distinct winners or losers within Launcelot's consciousness, only dueling socioeconomic features. Launcelot does not wholly abandon the notions of his conscience since his service to Bassanio illustrates both late feudal and proto-capitalist bonds of service. In fact, it is his conscience that ties him to domestic servitude, the labor environment that allows the fiend to comment wittily on the play's economics. Neither does the proto-capitalist clown replace the traditional clown nor does the fiend replace the conscience. Nonetheless, the fiend does achieve a proto-capitalist consciousness that motivates the clown-servant towards employment that allows him to exercise his verbal wit of rather than service in dutiful silence. The fiend represents Launcelot's self-interest evident in his explicit motive to get better food and clothing. It is his proto-capitalist endeavor for personal prosperity that leads to more freedom of wit.

The existence of dueling forces in the play reinforces the

notion of economic transition in English society. Unlike the angel metaphor, in which the unpersuasive angel disappears and leaves the other in triumphant command, the conscience and fiend continue their dual governance of Launcelot's socioeconomics throughout the play. Launcelot's fiend signifies a progressive economic mindset, progressive in the sense that the fiend urges change yet must reside within the world of domestic servitude maintained by the conscience. According to David Bevington, when Launcelot says to his father that he will leave Shylock's service, he expresses running away in terms of the card game primero for its final wager: "Well, well: but for mine own part, as I have set up my rest to run away, so I will not rest till I have run some ground" (2.2.99). Bevington notes that the phrase "set up my rest" means "determined, risked all; a metaphor from the card game *primero*, in which a final wager is made" (268).[5] In Hamlet's expression of paralysis in his soliloquy "To be or not to be," there is an implication that the most people are cowards who avoid hazard. Hamlet's use of the term "coward" in his line "Thus conscience doth make cowards of us all" not only refers to people who fear the unknown and prefer to endure hardship that they seem to understand and thereby they choose to remain in oppressive situations. But also, it refers to the ability of the conscience to create a "coward" by prolonging the decision-making process. Through the act of overanalyzing, the conscience delays actions. This delay enervates the impetus to act. It takes the risky act of one's inner fiend to leave fixed situations to prosper from change. Launcelot's conscience illustrates Hamlet's form of cowardice because he would rather serve under Shylock's oppression than flee and risk employment to a new master.

For Launcelot as for Hamlet, the consciences would rather that they bear ills, ills for Launcelot that amount to a weary life of grunting and sweating under Shylock's roof than risk change. From the perspective of a clown-servant, Hamlet's reference to "enterprises of great pith and moment" aptly describes Launcelot's chance to leave Shylock's employment for service to Bassanio. Steven R. Mentz points out that "Launcelot displays a preference for motion over stasis that establishes his symbolic connection to economic exchange" (181), economic exchange akin to the fiend, as discussed below, who aims "to keep the economy in circulation" (181). The inaction of the conscience keeps things the way that they are, keeps bonds between clown-servants and masters in check, and keeps Shylock's blend of traditional practices of domestic service and new approaches to wealth intact. Launcelot resolves to act by running to Bassanio, forsaking domestic service to Shylock's home. The motion of the fiend advocates and facilitates economic change and attenuates the bond between Launcelot and Shylock. As seen in *The Merchant of Venice*, characters' abilities to endure and prosper from hazards drive the actions of the play. Two characters with disparate approaches to their prosperity and to their servant are Shylock and Bassanio.

Shylock and Bassanio have disparate approaches to Launcelot's domestic service, actions of the clown-servant that represent the dutiful conscience. When Bassanio meets Launcelot, we learn that he not only has an interest in Launcelot's service, but that he also somehow secures the clown's service from Shylock pending Launcelot's agreement. Bassanio tells Launcelot that

> I know thee well; thou hast obtain'd thy suit:
> Shylock thy master spoke with me this day,
> And hath preferr'd thee, if it be preferment
> To leave a rich Jew's service, to become
> The follower of so poor a gentleman. (2.2.136-40)

Bassanio's lines refer to actions that do not occur in the

play. In Act 1 scene 3, the only allusion to Launcelot is by Shylock who says that he has left his house in the fearful guard of an unthrifty knave (1.3.173-3). The play does not reveal how the topic of Shylock's domestic servant and of his transfer into Bassanio's service make their way into the tense verbal exchange concerning the loan of money and a man's flesh as bond. The scene works to advance the play's economics by uniting Launcelot and Bassanio, two of the play's proto-capitalist risk-takers who establish a traditional master and clown-servant bond. Unlike Shylock, Bassanio sees Launcelot as an asset to his service staff. Bassanio readily accepts Launcelot into his service because Bassanio is without his own funds and arguably a prodigal.[6] He employs Launcelot with the future hopes of marrying Portia and securing his own economy and servant staff. For Launcelot, the "simple line of life" that he will garner from employment to Bassanio is preferable to Shylock's inaccessible riches (Bevington 268). When Bassanio questions Launcelot concerning his "preferment to leave the rich Jew's service" (2.2.138-9), Launcelot merely frames his answer in the proverb "The old proverb is very well parted between my master Shylock and you, sir: you have the grace of God, sir, and he hath enough" (2.2.141-43). Launcelot plays on the proverb that instructs: "He who has the grace of God has enough" (Bevington 268). A bold move out-of-line with the expectations of customary domestic servitude, Launcelot's act of changing masters constitutes a challenge to traditional order. However, Launcelot's move from Shylock to Bassanio is a lateral change of employment that lands Launcelot firmly within a similar traditional household setting. As the clown-servant in yet another household, Launcelot and the feudal ethics of his conscience begin to govern his domestic responsibilities.

Likewise, the move of Launcelot's conscience from Shylock's home does not liberate Launcelot from traditional expectations of clown-service. Although John Drakakis refers to Launcelot's move as an "escape from captivity" (40), the clown-servant's proto-capitalist change of employment does not suggest that late feudal forms of service offer a lesser degree of freedom than proto-capitalist endeavor. Macdonald reasons that

> It may seem at first glance that the transition to capitalism sweeps away the notion of hierarchy entirely, that the putative equality of opportunity to venture and to gain or lose by venturing puts all on an equal footing. But little reflection will reveal that societies always create differences between persons and persons. (58)

Social hierarchy remains visible in both the households of proto-capitalists Shylock and Bassanio. Their households do not make gentlemen from servants. Far from parody, the class climbing of their servants, the merchants in the play rely on traditional hierarchical distinctions to subjugate the servant class. Launcelot's proto-capitalist experiences cannot gain him access to the merchant class. However, subservience is not without benefits. Launcelot's domestic service makes him an extension of Bassanio's home. He wears the livery of Bassanio's house, a public symbol of his master and clown-servant bond with Bassanio. He eats in Bassanio's home in return for service. As Bassanio prospers, so does Launcelot prosper, and as Bassanio fails, so does Launcelot experience economic hardship. Thus, the notion that Launcelot's move is risky suggests that he stands to lose, at the very least, the food and shelter, which were the benefits of Shylock's household. Even after the risk has been taken, Launcelot remains in domestic service. Any freedom that Bassanio's household seems to offer Launcelot is merely the freedom to do his job as clown-servant. Bassanio's domestic arrangement allows Launcelot to serve and to clown, the two primary characteristics of his occupation. In Belmont, Launcelot's work illustrates the clown service indicative of all of Shakespeare's clowns. He jests wittily with his superiors, prepares their dinner, and delivers their messages.

The dialogue immediately following the soliloquy gives dramatic clues as to the nature of Shylock's employment and Launcelot's material expectations. Shylock seeks economic acceptance on the Rialto. Macdonald asks, "If the Jew is really 'the very devil incarnation' (2.2.27-28), as vulgar as clown Launcelot Gobbo characterizes him, why is he not thrust from the Venetian's midst?" (57). Macdonald's answer is simple; "merchant adventures need moneylenders" (57). As he observes, "In a capitalist republic like Shakespeare's Venice, differences will be defined not according to who owns land and who does not, but according to who has accumulated a greater amount of money, who less" (58). It is within this economy that Shylock envisions his excellence, his sense of aristocracy. For Shylock's self interest, to be a "good man" is to be financially "sufficient" (1.3.16-17). Therefore, when the clown-servant proves to be the opposite of profitable, Shylock agrees to discontinue Launcelot's employment. Just as Launcelot's conscience urges him to stay in Shylock's household order, Shylock's self-interest urges his insistence on a profitable servant. For Shylock, household economics relies on profit, not just domestic service:

> The patch is kind enough, but a huge feeder,
> Snail-slow in profit, and he sleeps by day,
> More than the wildcat. Drones hive not with me;
> Therefore, I part with him, and part with him
> To one that would have him waste
> His borrowed purse. (2.5. 47-52)

Shylock's reaction may appear merely as "sour grapes" since

his clown-servant has allied with his enemies. However, in the matter of worker efficiency, Shylock is warranted in his complaints. Even by modern standards, a domestic servant who consumes great amounts of household foods, sleeps on the job, works slowly, and is wasteful would surely face termination.

Shylock's description of clown-service differs from Will Somer's (Henry VIII's fool) court service and the dramatic clown-servants that follow. In Shylock's material world, it is not enough to be merely "a kind patch," quick with word play and jests. Shylock wants his clown-servant to be frugal, a worker bee for his hive, not a clown-servant maintained out of responsibility to the peasantry and from a desire to be entertained. Shylock's view that Launcelot should be drone-like combined with his later complaints about hungry servants suggests that Launcelot's accusations of malnourishment are creditable.

Launcelot's complaints to Lorenzo about insufficient food and hungry servants echo his complaints about food in Shylock's employment earlier in the play. Shylock's allusion to Jacob's shepherding represents domestic service in the same manner as animal husbandry. For Shylock, Launcelot is but one of the sheep, a raw product of profit. Shylock uses animal references not only to discount Launcelot's verbal wit, but also to move him downward in social hierarchy. For example, when Shylock refers to Launcelot as "a huge feeder" who is "snail-slow in profit" he complains that Launcelot is too high-maintenance a servant since his upkeep outweighs his profitability. He literally measures Launcelot's productivity in worker bee denominations, in drone-terms; he is worth as much as he produces. "Drones hive not with me," states Shylock (2.5.49). For Shylock, Launcelot is a lazy bee that wastes its honey in search of a hive.

Shylock's proto-capitalist view of service as gaining the most work for the least cost leads to Launcelot's similarly self-interested decision, voiced by his fiend. Launcelot's fiend is both a decision making voice of a proto-capitalist clown-servant, a part of Launcelot's conscious mind, and an exterior influential entity representative of merchant class hegemony. Launcelot's fiend retains characteristics of the moral Vice. Just as Vice-like characteristics moved portrayals of the mid-sixteenth century clown-servant further away from the traditional domestic with ties to late feudal domestic order (i.e., Cacurgus, Will Summer, and Derrick, cf. Ch.1), so does Launcelot ally with his fiend and move Shakespeare's clown-servant toward the proto-capitalist. Like a ghoulish animated image in a funhouse mirror, the fiend reflects mischievous counsel as quite distinct from the seemingly sound judgments of the conscience; however, the fiend is as much a part of Launcelot's psyche as is the conscience. The fiend projects a blend of Launcelot's materialistic desires through a class-consciousness of Venetian society. In addition to the influence of the Vice figure, Launcelot's use of "fiend" to describe a proto-capitalist temptation to move from one master to another suggests serious anxieties implicit not only in the move but in the ideology that would support it. The Satanic or fiendish attributions will reappear in the demonic imagery associated with Iago, who serves Othello only "to serve my turn upon him" (1.1.44).

So, why does Launcelot's fiend desire to run from one master to another, from old to new? The dialogue immediately following the soliloquy gives dramatic clues as to the nature of Shylock's employment and Launcelot's material expectations. Launcelot's exclamations, "I am famished in his service, you may tell every finger with my ribs," (2.2.101-2) and ". . . Master Bassanio, who gives rare new liveries," (2.2.104-5)—suggest that he wants more food and new clothes. Camille Slights suggests that "Like Jessica, Launcelot feels guilty about leaving Shylock, but his reasons are that Bassanio sets a more generous table and gives new liveries (2.2.101-5); Jessica's resolution to escape . . . contrasts favorably with Launcelot's decision to deny his conscience for materialistic reasons" (362). David Bevington notes that Launcelot also measures his "simple coming-in" or "income" in terms of eleven wives and nine maids, a considerable increase in domestic servant benefits from Shylock's household (268). Launcelot remarks: "Go to, here's a simple line of life. Here's a small trifle of wives! Alas, fifteen wives is nothing. Eleven widows and nine maids is a simple coming-in for one man" (2.2.151-54). At the behest of the fiend, Launcelot's decision to run in pursuit of a new master constitutes proto-capitalist motivation on Launcelot's part. The fiend operates on risks and the advocacy of risky behavior. Above all, the decision of the fiend sets the risky economic standard by which other characters negotiate monetary difficulties.

RISK: 'WHO CHOOSETH ME MUST GIVE AND HAZARD ALL HE HATH.'

An old gambler's quip explains that when the risks outweigh the gains, the act in question is rash and should be abandoned or revised. With Mentz's economic view of risk, I weigh Launcelot's fiend and the decision to run to Bassanio's service. Risk and the arbitrary nature of monetary exchange are parts of Launcelot's decision to run. Mentz claims that

> Launcelot's speech, however, points out the limits of rational choice theory. His decision appears to be wholly arbitrary. Both fiend and conscience 'counsel well', and there is a devil on either side of the equation. There seem no firm criteria for resolving this dispute, beyond Launcelot's desire for change. (182)

More drives Launcelot than merely the need for change. The fiend's run from Shylock and pursuit of Bassanio, his self-induction into the markets of service and exchange is not arbitrary. However, in agreement with Mentz, the "extra-ideological nature of transactions themselves" (180), the very markets of service and exchange that Launcelot seeks to join are arbitrary. Risk, then, is the primary factor that Launcelot and others apply to seemingly irrational economic decisions to acquire profitable outcomes.[7] Risk is the fiend's force that Launcelot accepts; and thereafter, risk is the impetus of other characters making monetary decisions. In the play, the term risk applies to the play's use of the word "hazard," as a verb that point to degrees of probability in economic acts or in failures to act. Rather than focus on loss as the play's motivational call to action, risk in *The Merchant of Venice* calls characters to prioritize gain or profitability. This section also observes Launcelot as an earner of cash. A socioeconomic reading of the play shows that as a cash-earner Launcelot exemplifies the conflicts experienced by a domestic servant in the shifting economics of early modern England.

Launcelot's physical movement away from Shylock's fixed bond of service into Bassanio's employment provides the added possibility to earn cash gratuities within traditional arrangements of domestic service. In this arrangement, Launcelot resembles Tudor players. Alwin Thaler notes that payments to real Tudor traveling actors in gratuities allowed towns and patrons to avoid legal restrictions on paying wages to play actors (143). Gratuities provide a method of payment that does not conflict with the rules of formal labor arrangement signified by wage earning (143). In the play, Launcelot's gratuities from Lorenzo and Jessica do not jeopardize his primary form of traditional domestic service yet offer an economic incentive for additional work and pay.

Launcelot receives cash payment once from Jessica (2.3.4) and once from Lorenzo (2.4.19).

Risk moves Launcelot one step closer to becoming a proto-capitalist, and he profits as an earner of gratuities as well as a domestic servant. He receives gratuities as coins for delivering messages. Unlike Speed in the previous chapter or Feste in the following chapter (*Twelfth Night*), Launcelot does not accent moments of monetary exchange with witty comments. His verbal wit is a result of his liberation from Shylock and new dual work status for Bassanio as household servant and earner of gratuities. As an earner of gratuities like Speed and Feste, Launcelot serves Bassanio who gives him greater control of his socioeconomic condition than service to Shylock. His dual work status allows him to comment later (3.5) on the socioeconomics of Venice (England). Frederick Turner evaluates Launcelot for "Shakespeare's conclusions" regarding the commercialization of work (71). Turner points out that Launcelot accepts a better offer of employment from Bassanio, one that he prefers over working for Shylock:

> The message is that in such normal circumstance, though we give up some personal rights in accepting a wage, the voluntary nature of work contracts sufficiently preserves the freedom of the individual that we value as defining the person. For this freedom to be possible, there must be a plurality of employers, in competition with each other for the services of the employed. If there is only one possible employer, then we are not free. (71-2)

Launcelot changes one employer, Shylock, for Bassanio, and later (temporarily) for Jessica, and Lorenzo. His change of employers illustrates his freedom to earn gratuities. Jessica first pays him for past service in Shylock's house: "Our house is hell, and thou a merry devil, Didst rob it of some taste of tediousness. But fare thee well, there is a ducat for thee" (2.3.3-4). Launcelot also receives cash tips from Jessica (2.3) and Lorenzo (2.4) for delivering his letters. For Launcelot's "fiend," cash tips are outward signs of economic security for the servant-class. For his conscience, cash represents economic security within the decorum of household service. A description of his consciousness remains central to understanding Launcelot's economic position between feudalism and proto-capitalism. Thus, Launcelot's mobility is limited to bettering his economic situation within the bounds of his class and station. Something in his consciousness, in his self-conceptualization as a servant, allows him to join the proto-capitalist characters through obligations of service.

As Launcelot earns cash, he represents Bassanio's investment in proto-capitalist wealth. Like the Venetian public in *The Merchant of Venice*, Shakespeare's economics-minded audiences are well aware of the merchant-class tendency to imitate noble customs. The economics of early modern England may be described as an "Elizabethan revival . . . an 'imaginative refeudalization' of culture . . . to reaffirm the primogenitive and due birth and to clothe the image of dynamic power in the costumes of chivalry" (Ferguson 68). Similar to many Elizabethan servants in the audience-pits, Launcelot's class remains late feudal, even though, like some of them, he serves a merchant instead of a titled noble.

So, though Launcelot continues in domestic service, his new employment seems less oppressive than Shylock's. In the casket game, the risk awards Portia to the suitor who chooses correctly and lives of bachelorhood for those suitors who choose incorrectly. The play's unseen master-merchant, Portia's father, leaves three caskets as an economic puzzle that jumbles perspectives of risks and gains, his own ideas of good and bad business hidden in the correct choice. In the midst of merchant class society in Belmont, Portia's father makes winning her a game engaging attitudes towards financial gain. Portia's wealth is a "lott'ry," and Morocco, the suitor who has chosen the gold chest, fails the test. Following the scene of Morocco's choice, we, the audience, know how Portia's father viewed the consumer who is fooled by veneer, the suitor who chooses the gold chest because he desires to attain what is desired by others. Only the silver and lead caskets remain for us. But Aragon, like Morocco and later Bassanio has three choices. Only the silver and lead caskets remain for us. The economics of risk applies to the proper casket choice. For Portia's father, to win all, one must be willing to risk all. From this perspective, the risk of the casket choice does not outweigh the gain of Portia as a wife, but rather the risk of all equals Portia who, by her father's estimation, is worth all. Nerissa, another of the play's servants, explains that the will of Portia's father combines merchant-class philosophy of risk with his daughter: "therefore the lott'ry he hath devis'd in these three chests gold, silver, and lead, whereof who chooses his meaning chooses you" (1.2.30-31). Portia's suitors must assume her father's proto-capitalist mind in order to win her hand in marriage. Risk, for her father, is an all or nothing game.

At stake is the future ability of the suitors to woo in the name of marriage. According to this rule, Morocco and Aragon become eternal bachelors. They do not forfeit their wealth, but their ability to create households. In addition to an astute business sense, Portia's father must have valued the husband's ability to form a household or he would not have made it such an extreme condition of the casket game. Samuel Ajzenstat suggests that "Portia's golden existence in Belmont requires, at least as her father sees it, that she and her wealth be handed over to a man (or manager) whose main qualification is to be wised-up enough to the hypocrisies of others so that he can survive his forays into Venice" (271). Likewise, Portia's father must have valued the household to manage Portia's wealth. His game suggests that it is not enough for a merchant to be wealthy. He or she must create a household wherein proto-capitalist wealth is properly managed. In this sense, the casket game represents the place of the traditional household in a proto-capitalist society. It is proto-capitalist not only because customary order remains foundational to mercantilism, but also because capitalist endeavor has not yet trumped late feudal economic practices. The theme of fatherly economics in male dominated households runs throughout the play.

In a play with a plethora of fatherly business philosophies, Launcelot and his economics of risk appear in them all. Shakespeare presents us with three sets of commodified offspring in the Gobbos, father/Portia, and Shylock/Jessica. In his chapter on Renaissance drama, Andrew McRae notes that "Certainly, parents who view their children as servants or commodities are not hard to find in the period's drama" (60). He goes on to highlight Shylock's commodification of Jessica, seeing little difference between his daughter and the money that she takes. The same commodification happens to Portia. Specifically, within the context of Portia's betrothal, the play inserts the proto-capitalist ideology. In a proto-capitalist sense, the last act of Portia's father, the rich, benevolent, "ever virtuous" merchant, is to commodify his daughter, his most prized possession through a game of fortune.

In contrast to the tragic Lear— a king who disrupts feudal order by allocating living inheritances to his daughters—and his fool who chastises him for his paternal folly, the posthumous authority of Portia's father reifies merchant-class savvy as well as secures her fortune in a tightly wound set of proto-capitalist circumstances. Launcelot's risk of domestic employment resides in what the play terms "hazard," the financial posturing necessary to obtain her proto-capitalist fortune. Engle notes that "In a play about economic, erotic, social, and religious venturing, circulation, climbing, and conversion, however, finally only the lead casket, with its injunction to give and 'hazard', stands for, or enables, the variety of the kinds of exchange that the play presents" ("Money" 92). At the point that the Prince of Aragon enters the play, we are well aware of the risk-based rules that govern the play's business interactions. The inscription on the silver casket says, "Who chooseth me shall get as much as he deserves" (2.9.35). In other words, when Aragon chooses the silver casket and receives the fool's head and witty message, it is no surprise that the fool's head illustrates insights on risk.

A careful reading of the fool's scroll will reveal the problematic of risk. The fool's head depicts a Vice-like image, a recognizable picture of a fool. For Aragon, pride, one of the Seven Deadly Sins, is the sin that results in the choice of the silver casket and the vituperative fool's head. Once Aragon wrongly selects the silver casket, the fool's head points out his poor judgment. Foolishly, Aragon gambles on his merit and just deserts in a casket game of risk. The enclosed fool's scroll reads:

> The fire seven times tried this:
> Seven times tried that judgment is,
> That did never choose amiss. (2.9.63-66)

The fool's message begins in line 63 with a biblical caution from Psalm 12 against vain hypocrites who put themselves above the poor and the needy.[8] Psalm 12:6 states: "The words of the Lord are pure words: as silver tried in a furnace of earth, purified seven times" (King James Version). The words of the silver casket are as cautionary the words of the Psalm. The fool's head, like Launcelot, toys with biblical verses to outwit his opponents. The fool's head jibes at Aragon's system of merit. In the course of the play, Aragon's merit is only self-serving. Because Aragon is not willing to chose the lead casket and risk or "hazard" all, his viewpoint ensures failure. Without risk, Aragon's vain merit becomes his "shadow" in line 66 and his narcissistic lover.

Although critics comment on the fool's head of the silver casket, little attention is paid to parallels in economic language between the clown-servant and the message of the fool's head. Rather, focus centers on Prince Aragon's reasoning that leads him to the choice of silver.[9] As a Prince, seemingly Aragon would fall back on notions of aristocratic lineage through noble birth. But, this is not Shakespeare's Spanish Prince. Aragon practices a system of merit that attempts to minimize consumer risk. He sees himself as a connoisseur, a Prince whose good taste should take precedence over market factors like risk. By petitioning "fortune" for assistance, Aragon appears at first to be a player of economic risks. "Fortune now to my heart's hope" (2.9.19-20) is a clue that Aragon may possess somewhat of an entrepreneurial mind, the kind of merchant's mind admired by Portia's father. However, as a consumer, he is more the epitome of the "preferred customer" who feels that his accumulated wealth, a show of who he is and what he is, makes him deserving of the best business deals. In other words, Aragon acts like the proverbial "Mr. Big Shot" whose ego makes his socioeconomic presence enough to gain an advantage in any situation. In Aragon's ideal world, merit, not games of chance, determines human prosperity. If so, Aragon would be a Prince who need not fear the economic risks of monetary games. Aragon contemplates a system of merit to distinguish the socioeconomics of class:

> O, that estates, degrees and offices
> Were not derived corruptly, and that clear honour
> Were purchased by the merit of the wearer!
> How many then should cover that stand bare!

How many be commanded that command!
(2.9.41-49)

Aragon claims that degrees are often "derived corruptly," possibly through illegitimate births and regicide. He imagines a system of merit as preferable. It would redistribute wealth, service, "cover," and "command" in a way that would advance worthy peasantry and would humble unworthy members of the aristocracy. Aragon, despite his avowals, nonetheless gambles in the casket game. What better than the image of the fool's head to countercheck Aragon's egotism?

Clown's Wit as
Proto-Capitalist Mode of Exchange

In *The Merchant of Venice*, the clown-servant develops an autonomous voice of wit and stands with one foot in traditional service arrangements and other in proto-capitalist endeavor. Launcelot's act of changing masters maintains his traditional domestic service. Service to Bassanio shows that Launcelot is still a domestic servant with the traditional occupational. With his new service secure, he begins to voice wit as well as receive cash gratuities for acts of service. For example, during Launcelot's tearful departure from Jessica, her remarks reveal that he has been, at times, a clown to her. She says:

> I am sorry thou wilt leave my father so.
> Our house is hell, and thou, a merry devil,
> Didst rob it of some taste of tediousness.
> But fare thee well; there is a ducat for thee. [*Gives money*] (2.3.1-4)

Jessica's description of Launcelot as "a merry devil" points to the proto-capitalist "fiend" who tempts him toward self-interest. Jessica's gratuity to Launcelot is the first tip that the clown receives in the play and may be read from at least two perspectives, both of which point to the act as proto-capitalist advancement for Launcelot. On the one hand, Jessica offers Launcelot a small cash gratuity for previous verbal wit in addition to the amenities that he has received in Shylock's service. Launcelot's decision to leave Shylock for Bassanio has already begun to pay off in money, a thing that he does not get from Shylock. Jessica feels indebted to Launcelot for being her clown even though Shylock, his master does not benefit from Launcelot's wit. Jessica's "there is money for thee" marks a final act of her kindness in return for Launcelot's prior jests. For Launcelot, the cash tip and a secure domestic placement of service connect his verbal wit to prosperity. The tip gives him an incentive to express his foolery for those whom he serves. From this point in the play forward, Launcelot portrays the clown-servant whose wit is central to his interactions with his superiors. Launcelot's decision to move is a proto-capitalist act, and the verbal wit that emerges from this move becomes the product use to gain gratuity. On the other hand, Jessica's gratuity may be read as a pre payment for delivering her message to Bassanio. As Launcelot's departs from Shylock, he plays Jessica's and Lorenzo's messenger to assist with their elopement. If Jessica is indeed paying Launcelot for his postal services, the payment seems to be a reward for jesting. She still pays him for his verbal dexterity. Launcelot proves a reliable post, and Jessica and Lorenzo are the only characters to tip Launcelot, acts that accompany expressions of his wit. It follows that Jessica and Lorenzo are the only characters with whom Launcelot's engages in battles of verbal wit. Although Bassanio and Launcelot share a traditional master and clown servant bond, he also shares a bond with Jessica and Lorenzo based on cash. Cash gratuity for both wit and posts are proto-capitalist modes of exchange that Launcelot does not experience in Shylock's service. Since Shylock does not value Launcelot's wit, he forfeits additional clown services to his domestic demands.

Launcelot's verbal ability, so discounted by Shylock, becomes in Bassanio's service, part of the dialogue characteristic of traditional (what would in England be called late feudal) relationships between master and clown-servant. By silencing Launcelot's fiend, Shylock mutes traditional clown-service. For example, Shylock rebukes Launcelot for hailing Jessica and protests: "Who bids thee call? I do not bid thee call" (2.5.7). Launcelot replies: "Your worship was wont to tell me that I could do nothing without bidding" (2.5.8-11). Like his decision to leave Shylock, Launcelot's verbal wit anticipates later clown servants who use language as a talent of self-profit rather than as an extension of the wealth and prestige of their masters. His lack of the traditional clown-servant voice in Shylock's employment characterizes Shylock's strict household order and his expectations of work and profit not word play. We do not hear the signature verbal humor of the clown while in Shylock's service. Launcelot is muted in his service and offers no economic commentary. The play illustrates that Shylock not only controls Launcelot's right to speak: "who bid thee call" but also that he is very distrustful of Launcelot speaking alone with Jessica. Launcelot's mere whisper to Jessica (2.5.41-4) sparks Shylock's distrust of his language and is enough for him to suspect the clown of mischief. In the line, "What says the fool of Hagar's offspring, ha?" Shylock demeans Launcelot's language because he does not value Launcelot as a verbal "fool" (2.5.45). Launcelot does not get the opportunity to be a wisecracking clown to his master until he is in Bassanio's household, and his wit cannot be valued by his employer until he has an employer who values wit. Even though Launcelot develops a personal voice, he does not achieve proto-capitalist autonomy.

In Bassanio's home, Launcelot is free for the first time in the play to voice wit characteristic of previous master and clown-servant bonds. Although more the proto-capitalist clown-servant than the Dromios, Speed, and Launce, Launcelot, the "wit-snapper" (3.5.47), also falls neatly into household arrangements of service. In Bassanio's service, Launcelot does not seek to run away or use his voice to undermine Bassanio's household economics. With Bassanio, Launcelot's verbal wit complements traditional master and clown-servant bonds. Like Proteus in *Two Gentlemen of Verona*, Lorenzo commands his friend's clown-servant to assume duties of domestic service. Launcelot gets to twist Lorenzo's simple order of "Go in sirrah; bid them prepare for dinner" into word play and answers "That is done sir. They have all stomachs" (3. 5. 45-46). Lorenzo's "them" refers to the household servants, the domestic staff to which Launcelot belongs.

If Launcelot is to move closer to proto-capitalist self-awareness, he must begin to control his newly perceived commodity, his verbal wit. Launcelot's service must incorporate enough socioeconomic flexibility to represent his own labor interests. On one hand, when Shylock mutes Launcelot, the autonomous voice of the servant, he reduces Launcelot to slavish servitude. Without his clowning character, Launcelot is no more than an ordinary household servant, with little to offer his master in the way of witty discourse. On the other hand, when Launcelot's service to Bassanio is seen in the greater developmental trend of Shakespeare's clowns from late feudalist to proto-capitalist, his awareness of verbal wit as a quality that is valued by his master and rewarded with monetary gratuities moves Shakespeare's clown-servant closer to freelance endeavors.

Launcelot's fiend does not achieve lasting proto-capitalist autonomy in the course of the play. The fiend is the voice that urges the clown to make a proto-capitalist move. But once in

Belmont, the fiend ceases to be a voice of proto-capitalism and instead becomes a part of Launcelot's wit that carves out his domestic place in Bassanio's late feudal household order. The fiend returns to the comforts of traditional order. The acts of Launcelot's fiend point to the question of whether or not it is possible to disobey or abandon a feudal master without being a proto-capitalist. Shakespeare's plays feature disobedient servants whose acts are not proto-capitalist. For example, in *Taming of the Shrew*, Petruchio complains of the recent mutiny of his domestic servants: "Where be these knaves? What, no man at door to hold my stirrup nor to take my horse! Where is Nathaniel, Gregory, Philip? . . . You logger-headed and unpolish'd grooms! What, no attendance? no regard? no duty? Where is the foolish knave I sent before?" (4.1.108-16). In *As You Like It*, Oliver deems Adam to be disobedient for his service to Orlando and dismisses Adam after a lifetime of faithful service: "Get you with him, you old dog" (1.1.78). Adam replies: "Is 'old dog' my reward? Most true, I have lost my teeth in your service. God be with my old master! He would not have spoke such a word" (1.1.80-2). The acts of these servants are not proto-capitalist acts and they remain as feudal servant throughout their plays. Nonetheless, these acts do shake the foundations of the feudal household orders of their masters and call into question the practices of traditional domestic order. Launcelot's disobedience at the behest of the fiend is a proto-capitalist act in the course of the play that does not absolve Launcelot from late feudal domestics or give to the fiend a continued sense of entrepreneurship.

In 3.5, Launcelot continues to verbalize through unfettered wit the play's economics. He comments on the economic ramifications of Jessica's conversion on the commonwealth. Now that Launcelot's conscience secures a position of service with Bassanio, his fiend voices economic criticism. For Launcelot, the question of how Jessica, a Jew who converts to Christianity, will consume (in relation to Portia) is answered in the play's allusion to a commodities market. Launcelot jocularly complains:

> We were Christians enow before; e'en as many as could well live, one by another. This making Christians will raise the price of hogs: if we grow all to be pork-eaters, we shall not shortly have a rasher on the coals for money. (3.5. 19-24)

Bruce Boehrer suggests that Launcelot's statement, "instinctively conceives of Jessica as nonproductive, as economic dead weight, and it does so despite the existence of a long-standing cultural tradition that insists on housewife's importance as a producer of commodities for domestic consumption" (Boehrer *Pet* 158). In defense of Launcelot's servant class perspective, one need not search Launcelot for knowledge of Jessica's blatant waste of her father's household wealth. Launcelot has a pre-history of life and service with Jessica, so his observance of her economic non-productivity is more a forecast of her domestic inadequacies based on past interactions rather than a general overall critique of female domestic inability. Boehrer continues: "Launcelot Gobbo not only fails to think of her as an economic producer; he thinks of her instead specifically as a consumer, one more mouth to feed, a woman whose new-found status as an eater of pork simply creates additional demand for already-limited resources" (*Pet* 159). Jessica does not seek acceptance as a Jew, nor does she speak for other non-Venetian women like Launcelot's Moor who reside outside of Venetian male authority. Launcelot's Moor does not appear as a character in the play and Lorenzo refers to her in relation to Launcelot's unseen sexual practices. Rather, she seems to take pleasure in her own conversion as a kind of free pass into Venetian social hierarchy. Launcelot uses references to pork to comment on Jessica's conversion and its effect on economy in the play.

A closer look at Launcelot's reference to "rasher" and "money" illustrates the economic relevance of the proto-capitalist clown-servant. Bacon, like flesh and blood, becomes a commodity, a representation of changing aspects of monetary exchange in early modern England. Launcelot's speech reflects on the London economy and its developing markets of exchange that commodify bacon in terms of stock trading in sow bellies. His lines concerning a rise in the price of bacon point to the overall fluidity of economic exchange in the play as well as in early modern England. Mentz's view is that Launcelot's comments about Christians becoming pork-eaters forecasts market gluts (184-85). Launcelot singles out, with reason, one part or cut of meat from the hog (the belly) to make a point about emerging capitalism in addition to market surplus. "Rasher" not only refers to bacon, but several uniform slices of bacon. The term "rasher," (fr. *rash* to cut ME *rashen* ca.1592) refers to a thin slice of bacon or a portion consisting of several slices (Simpson and Weiner 200). Perhaps early modern market demands for "breakfast meats" or "lunchables" shares an intersection with an established system of barter and an incipient system based on capital. Launcelot speculates on the possibility of an exchange rate based on bacon sales; but greater still, to English audiences, Launcelot's passage signals a proto-capitalist shift in Elizabethan England. This is not to say that people would use bacon instead of coins. In monetary terms, bacon is money within its market. Perhaps Launcelot the ambitious pork-eater will fatten his previously gaunt ribs on non-kosher meats.

Launcelot's employment to Bassanio seems to fill Launcelot with a new sense of social inclusion. In his line, "We were Christians," Launcelot's uses of the pronoun "we" shows that he counts himself among the Christian merchants in the play. For example, when Launcelot delivers the news of Antonio's "horn" of plenty, Launcelot's clownish mirth reveals his stake in proto-capitalist bounty. Launcelot self identifies with his new employer and his position of service in a merchant class household. Nonetheless, Launcelot's position as a non-possessor of liquid capital limits him to the care of his employers and the hazards of their financial dexterity. Launcelot attempts to serve and profit. His financial market remains domestic service in that his capital is restricted to necessary allowances. It is Launcelot's hope that domestic service in his new market (Bassanio-Portia) will outperform the economic conditions of his former employment.

In this effort, Launcelot jabs at Jessica and Lorenzo for their marriage. Janet Adelman argues that Launcelot's charge is that in marrying Jessica, Lorenzo is damaging the commonwealth by converting Jews to Christians (22). The comic exchange between Lorenzo and Launcelot plays on the subjects of sex, race, and the economics of the commonwealth. Lorenzo's verbal joust with Launcelot is in defense of Jessica.[10] The nature of his verbal retort follows these subjects and presents a pattern that helps to understand Launcelot's complex Moor/more reference.

In defense of Jessica, Lorenzo replies that Launcelot has impregnated a black woman, a retort meant to trump Launcelot's unpleasantness (Japtok and Schleiner 167). Lorenzo, likewise, addresses sex, race, and the economics of the commonwealth in his insult of Launcelot:

> *Lorenzo.*   I shall answer that better to the commonwealth than you can the getting up of the negro's belly: the Moor is with child by you, Launcelot.

| Launcelot. | It is much that the Moor should be more than reason: but if she be less than an honest woman, she is indeed more than I took her for. (3.5.29-37) |

Critical speculation concerning Launcelot's meaning of Moor/more varies. John Russell Brown dismisses Lorenzo's remark as a prompt for Launcelot's pun: "Perhaps it was introduced simply for the sake of the elaborate pun on Moor/ more" (note to 3.5.35-6). But, the bitterness of Lorenzo's verbal comeback is that it insults Launcelot's conscience, the part of him that values traditional domestic service. That Launcelot leaves a woman pregnant and unwed is more fiend than conscience. According to Joptok and Schleiner, the pun plays on Elizabethan beliefs about syphilis: "the notion reported by Sassonia to be current in Venice, that intercourse with a black virgin would cure the syphilitic, might supply the logic or deep structure to Lorenzo's comeback, after he learns that Launcelot has insulted Jessica and him" (168).[11] To make sense of Launcelot's pun, it must be taken in the sexual/racial/economic context in which it was meant. Just how does a Moor get into Belmont (Joptok and Schleiner 22)? The play provides two possibilities. She may arrive by the same means as Morocco. Just as Morocco enters Venice as a symbol of negative otherness, a foreign face of wasteful extravagance on the commonwealth, Launcelot's Moor, like Jessica, reflects a waste on the commonwealth. Joptok and Schleiner suggest that "in terms of race, Portia's negative reaction to Morocco and to "all of his complexion" would find its counterpoint in Launcelot's veiled defense when he is charged with impregnating a black woman or 'Moor'" (169).

Alternatively, Launcelot's Moor may fit into Shylock's

reference to slavery as "a purchased slave" (4.1.90). This viewpoint seems more acceptable. Shylock makes a point that is uncontested by the Venetian court, a point that puts Launcelot's pun on the Moor and Venetian mercy in their proper perspectives. Shylock cites Venetian law as it works in the play and would apply to an enslaved Moor:

> You have among you many a purchased slave,
> Which, like your asses and your dogs and mules,
> You use in abject and in slavish parts,
> Because you bought them: shall I say to you,
> Let them be free, marry them to your heirs?
> (4.1.90-5)

Venice, like England, is a place where people are commodities. Portia's very verdict illustrates that being Venetian makes one, in a legal sense, more human than non-Venetians. In a play where bonds outweigh humanity, where Jews are dogs, servants are drones, and slaves are comparable in value to asses, dogs, and mules, Launcelot and his Moor are no more destroyers of the commonwealth than Shylock is an attempted murderer. If it is indeed "much" or a significant thing that the "Moor should be more," that is, that this black slave should be accepted as a "woman" and share in the economics of Venice, then the "reason," the Venetian rationale for her enslavement makes "her less than an honest woman" (3.5.38-40). Unmistakably, Launcelot knows that he has impregnated a member of society with questionable humanity. This meaning makes sense of his counter check of Lorenzo on the topic of strains on the commonwealth. In other words, it is the voice of Venetian hypocrisy (i.e. racism) that calls for mercy for some and disenfranchisement for others deemed strains on the commonwealth. Launcelot is damnable because he has impregnated a foreign black woman not a Venetian (and more damnable if he refuses to marry her) in the same way the Antonio is saved not because he is guiltless, but because he is a special (privileged) member of society. Rather than yield to Lorenzo's point about the Moor, Launcelot continues his foolery by punning Lorenzo's on words.

As with Shakespeare's earlier clown-servants, verbal wit acts to loosen service bonds and give the clown-servant greater economic advantage within waning domestic arrangements of the play. Launcelot begins with the familiar challenging of the clown's wits by his master's friend. Ending his economic commentary on the commonwealth with Jessica, Launcelot concludes, "converting Jews to Christians will raise the price of pork" (3.5.33-4). Lorenzo plays the substitute master who attempts to create a new master and clown-servant bond and thereby assert his socioeconomic class hierarchy. Rather than follow Lorenzo's orders to instruct the household servants to prepare for dinner, Launcelot delays and purposely misinterprets Lorenzo's words to begin a dialogue of punning. Thomas Moisan suggests that Launcelot's disobedience serves to render social distinctions of class hierarchy problematic:

> On the one hand, his [Launcelot's] disobedience reminds us of the frailty of Lorenzo's claim to authority in a household where, after all, he is only the designated, temporary master—and 'master' over Launcelot, who, after all, is not his servant; on the other hand, Launcelot's resistance exposes the tenacity of the need to affirm social distinctions when their features have been blurred. (284)

Although Moisan points out Lorenzo's need to affirm blurred features of social distinctions, the play's overall mimetic structure is still at work. Launcelot and Lorenzo exchange affirmation of service in their temporary master and clown-servant relationship. Their brief interaction gives each man a sample of the economics of service in Bassanio's household. Launcelot resorts to verbal word play, a form of verbal disobedience that seeks to make the master aware of his economic responsibilities of the bond, a characterization that progresses with the development of the proto-capitalist clown-servant. The point is not that Lorenzo misunderstands the verbal wit. On the contrary, he understands verbal wit and carries on witty discourse with Launcelot. The point is that as a master, he attempts to frame their witty retorts to advance their own masterly concerns. Launcelot makes clear the needs of the servant in the order of the masters. Lorenzo is a master unaware of the needs of the domestic staff. He receives Launcelot's verbal wit. At the end of the scene, the clown-servant appears less subordinate to his substitute master, the results of developed proto-capitalist awareness of his service identity. The awareness is proto-capitalist since Launcelot labors verbally to increase self-profitability in the forms of food and clothing. Lorenzo comments on the effective use of wordplay:

> O dear discretion, how his words are suited!
> The fool hath planted in his memory
> An army of good words; and I do know
> A many fools, that stand in better place,
> Garnish'd like him, that for a tricksy word
> Defy the matter. (3.5.62-66)

David Bevington defines "discretion" as discrimination. From this definition, Lorenzo's "O dear discretion" (3.5.62) implies that he must be more specific in his commands to Launcelot and perhaps to all servants.

Launcelot interprets Lorenzo's commands literally. For example, Launcelot answers Lorenzo's orders to "prepare for dinner" with "They all have stomachs" (3.5.44- 46).

Launcelot's punning shows not only that the servants possess the internal organ necessary to hold food, i.e. the stomach, but also that the servants have appetites (they are just as hungry as the masters). Launcelot continues punning and corrects Lorenzo's terminology from "prepare" to "cover" because in their preparation for dinner, the servants specifically cover the table. Again, Lorenzo's orders lack specificity. He orders Launcelot not the servants to "cover," an error that allows Launcelot continues his verbal wit: "Not so, sir neither I know my duty" (3.5.52). Launcelot takes "cover" to mean the literal covering of the head with a hat, an act not allowed the servant. By punning on Lorenzo's words and toying with meaning, Launcelot's word play not only stalls Lorenzo's orders, but also confuses Lorenzo so that Launcelot has the final interpretation of the orders. The clown concludes:

> For the table, sir, it shall be serv'd in; for the meat,
> sir, it shall be cover'd; for your coming in to dinner,
> sir, why, let it be as humours and conceits shall
> govern. *Exit Clown*. (3.5.58-60)

Lorenzo's "O dear discretion" (3.5.62) is an exclamation that reflects his shift in emphasis from his order to the words of the clown. In Shakespeare's plays, wisdom is not limited to traditional clown-servants like E. Dromio and Launce of Chapter 2. Proto-capitalists like S. Dromio (*Errors*), Speed (*Two Gentlemen*), Launcelot and Feste (*Twelfth Night*) of the next chapter display wisdom as a characteristic of their word manipulation.

Conclusion

Launcelot Gobbo in *The Merchant of Venice* advances the dramatic clown-servant along the developmental plane from late feudalism to proto-capitalism. First, Launcelot's character splits, then unifies. Conscience and fiend components of his total consciousness, his decision-making abilities, are central to the play as economics. Launcelot's conceptualization of good business reflects a proto-capitalist shift not only in his individual consciousness, but also in the consciousnesses of other characters. Microscopically, a socioeconomic reading of Launcelot explains *The Merchant of Venice's* preoccupation with labor, cash capital, and financial markets, themes that critics often reduce to the usual usury versus philanthropy binary. A socioeconomic approach removes foci from this dichotomy and refocuses them on master/servant bonds and forces that promote and undermine profitability. Macroscopically, a socioeconomic reading of Launcelot parallels the emergence of proto-capitalism of the Venetian and English Renaissances. The staged economic tensions of Venice correspond to the proto-capitalist pressures of Elizabethan England.

My overall observation of the clown-servant Launcelot Gobbo has shown that rather than a minor character whose actions are of little significance to the plot, Launcelot's role is central to the economic tensions of the play. This chapter concludes that Launcelot's final wager points to a proto-capitalist in the making. Launcelot says: "Well, well: but, for mine own part, as I have set up my rest to run away, so I will not rest till I have run some ground" (2.2.98-100). Launcelot words "set up my rest" signal the final wager or risk to change masters. Launcelot's gamble on employer may be likened to Shylock's proto-capitalist risk or gamble of two thousand ducats against Antonio, Antonio's gamble on his argosies, and Bassanio's gamble on Portia's caskets. His fiscal knowledge and the ability to use verbal wit to better his economic situation proves him to be a more accomplished proto-capitalist clown-servant than the comics E. Dromio and Speed before him.

Finally, once Launcelot secures his place of domestic

service in Bassanio and Portia's home, he assumes the economic wit of a domestic clown-servant. Launcelot's commentary is the socioeconomic voice of the play, and his economic perspectives are found among characters who share his proto-capitalist approach to service. In addition, characters that do not share Launcelot's economics suffer financially like Shylock or fail in games of chance like Aragon. Overall, critical analysis of Launcelot Gobbo, the clown-servant character, allows economic observation into Shakespeare's development of the proto-capitalist clown-servant. Thoroughly engrossed in the economic tensions of *The Merchant of Venice,* Launcelot Gobbo illustrates the play's economic tensions of merchant class wealth within old aristocratic forms of social order.

CHAPTER IV

FESTE: FROM TRADITIONAL DOMESTIC SERVICE TO PROTO-CAPITALIST EXCHANGE IN TWELFTH NIGHT

Cucullus non facit monachum.[1]

In *Twelfth Night*, Feste is Shakespeare's most accomplished proto-capitalist clown-servant. Feste's representation of a character who hinges between two noble households and their economic fluctuations is pivotal to understanding the play's foundational service relationships and class economics.[2] The proto-capitalism of clown-service and exchange go hand in hand and point to changes in the service industry and the domestic responsibilities of the clown-servant. Feste is a transitional character in a play about transition. His song lyrics "Youth's a stuff will not endure" and "With hey, ho, the wind and the rain, for the rain it raineth every day" illustrate a thematic of the play, transitions in the human experience (2.3.39-52, 5.1.386-405). Feste represents the laborer in transition. He works both as a servant in a late feudal household and as an entrepreneurial salesman of songs and wit. He is a proto-capitalist, not a traditional servant depending solely on ties of service to the nobility for survival. He also is not a capitalist. Feste does not readily employ his earnings in financial or industrial enterprises. As a proto-capitalist, Feste takes steps away from late feudal dependence and toward cash income, changes that lead to future capitalism. Feste makes his blend of old and new forms of economics work. At the end of the play, Feste is still a servant of the nobility but with a cash income. He has successfully maintained his proto-capitalist methods of earning money in the face of Olivia's expressed displeasure and Malvolio's insistence on late feudal household decorum. Viewing Feste as a proto-capitalist also presents a useful reflection of the transition from late feudalism to proto-capitalism outside of the play. Cash payments to servants play a significant role in changing arrangements between masters and servants. Feste's economic practices reflect proto-capitalist change in Elizabethan England. As servants wearing the livery signifying a patronage system and also as entrepreneurs selling entertainment for box office receipts, actors fully exemplified the transitional stage between feudal and proto-capitalist economies. Residing in Olivia's household as her servant and entertaining for gratuities, Feste is, in a sense, in the position of the actors themselves.

Feste's blend of proto-capitalist and late feudal approaches to clown-service allows him to profit from the upper class through both traditional and entrepreneurial means of exchange. Analysis of Feste's economics has focused mainly on his entrepreneurial spirit. Thad Jenkins Logan says that "Feste is a professional . . . [and] Festivity is work for him" (229). Jenkins sees festivity as Feste's "trade," an uninspiring labor for the clown that only enervates him without satisfaction (229). Karin Coddon outright calls him a "protocapitalist 'service professional'" (317). Coddon sees Feste's cash income as a reminder that unlike the exchange of duty for sustenance in the antique world, Feste labors for cash and the independent buying power that it allows (317). Feste's financial insights give him a perspective not available to the melancholy Duke, the mourning Madonna, the love-smitten page, the conniving cousin, as well as the rest of the characters. If Feste's traditional clown-service illustrates his loose tie to customary domestic order in Olivia's house, his proto-capitalist modes of exchange with Sir Toby Belch, Sir Andrew Aguecheek, and the Duke show his quest for profit as a (pre) capitalist. Olivia does not pay Feste because he is in a feudal relationship with her, working as her servant for board and room. The payments that he receives from other characters become in the play coins passed as props signifying his progressive economics. His use of verbal wit more than any other of Shakespeare's clown-servants reflects the fluidity of money, as he employs tactics of labor like freelancing to subsidize the board and room provided by Olivia. In this way, Feste's ingenuity of wit allows him to profit from the value of his songs and jests by the means of entrepreneurial exchange.[3]

Feste is key to this economic transition because he works both in the feudal system of service in Olivia's house and in Illyria's more cash-oriented proto-capitalist system of festive entertainment-for-sale. Mary Ellen Lamb suggests that in the feudal ideal of service, servants freely exchanged labor for protection with nobles, and honor was the theoretical glue of static master and servant relationships (5). Lamb goes on to explain that in a later wage-labor system, value varies, and workers could market their services to the employer who paid the most money (5). Although Feste is not a wage-laborer in the sense that he works for a previously negotiated price to be paid upon the completion of his work, he does receive consistent cash profits, measurable income in the form of coins. Feste also markets his services to his choice of employers for money. He appears conveniently in the presence of Sir Toby, Sir Andrew, and Duke Orsino at times when they desire entertainment. Sir Toby and Sir Andrew pay Feste in sixpence coins for songs and jests.

The Duke, Viola, and Sebastian pay in gold. Lamb's idea of proto-capitalist labor is at the crux of this chapter:

> Within the proto-capitalist system, labor was to be produced by individuals motivated by ambition rather than by subjects motivated by loyalty. The rise of capitalist ideology of profit, with the constant rise of individual ambition, induced a crisis in the ideology of service. (Lamb 6)

In this sense, by manipulating words for monetary profit, Feste controls one aspect of household production. As Olivia's fool, his songs and jests are her property, provided as a service in return for board and room. However, when he markets his entertainment outside of Olivia's house, or even to other persons in Olivia's house, the act constitutes the earning of cash profits and Feste's songs and jests become his talents from which to prosper.

Feste's wit accompanies his songs and jests and earns him cash dividends. His access to both the household of Olivia and the Duke places him in an advantageous position to serve and criticize the nobility for a profit. On more than one occasion, his privileged dual service illustrates his claim to belong to neither household. He manipulates words, and for him "a sentence is but a chev'ril glove to a good wit. How quickly the wrong side may be turned outward" (3.1.12-3). Even though Feste roams to earn cash profits for his foolery, clearly his domestic service is to Olivia's house. He does not receive payment from Olivia for his services. Once her father's fool, the aged clown servant now jests for the mistress Olivia as later does Lavatch in *All's Well That Ends Well*.[4] Yet, to Viola's query of "Art thou not the Lady Olivia's fool" (3.1.31), he answers "No, indeed, sir. The Lady Olivia has no folly" (3.1.32). Then as Viola attempts to link his personage to the Duke's household, Feste voices his economic flexibility through his philosophy of foolery:

> Foolery, sir, does walk about the orb like the sun, it shines every where. I would be sorry, sir, but the fool should be as oft with your master as with my mistress: I think I saw your wisdom there. (3.1.38-41)

Feste's entertainment indicates perpetual servitude to many masters. Although he is able to control some aspects of his entertainment, he must play for his superiors. Whether Feste sings or applies verbal wit, the aristocratic hierarchy remains in place. No matter how proto-capitalist his endeavors, he remains a clown-servant. Yet, Feste breaks from his fixed service in Olivia's household by determining when and for whom he works. Like Launcelot's break from Shylock, Feste's break from Olivia's economy also constitutes an entrepreneurial act on the part of the clown-servant. Feste risks dismissal by Olivia to employ his talents for personal profit. In so doing, Feste's entertainment indicates perpetual servitude to many masters, in a sense, through exerting his own choices. Rather than late feudal parameters to Feste's work, proto-capitalist freelancing necessitates that he control some aspect of his income. He controls his entertainment and creates, for himself, income based on labor. Feste's economy has no predetermined work schedule to dictate that he be present to entertain Sir Toby, Sir Andrew, or Duke Orsino upon request. There is no mention in the play that these characters may punish Feste if he does not entertain them. The only mention of dire consequences concerning Feste's employment practices refers to Olivia's displeasure. Her displeasure is understandable because she is the household head whom Feste serves. Feste does serve many masters, yet the extension of his entertainment through entrepreneurial not late feudal means illustrates small steps toward capitalism. In other words, Olivia does not share Feste's service with other nobles like Valentine with Speed to Proteus (*Two Gentlemen*) or Bassanio with Launcelot to Lorenzo (*Merchant*). It is Feste who markets his own talents to other nobles and at the same time maintains domestic arrangements with Olivia.

Feste's appearance in six scenes all revolve around some form of proto-capitalist income earning. These six scenes stage his freelance singing and/or jesting for cash payment, and one, his revenge in response to another servant's attempt to have him dismissed from Olivia's service.[5] Feste's economic acts define him as a developed proto-capitalist clown-servant who masterfully labors for monetary profit in the face of jeopardizing his position of domestic service. Feste is a vassal to wit and its ability to produce income outside of his mistress and clown-servant bond with Olivia. Unlike other characters who gain stability through traditional means like inheritance and marriage, Feste serves both for the benefits of domestic association and for cash.

Entrepreneurial Feste

When Feste enters the play in Act 1 scene 5, his absence causes Maria's concern for his continued employment. This absence leads to the question of what Feste does when he is away from Olivia's house. Act 1 scene 5 illustrates the expectations of Feste's service held by Olivia and the servants of her household. Feste's job is to serve in Olivia's household. He is her clown and servant. Any unauthorized absence by Feste constitutes a breech of their late feudal domestic arrangement, a breech that marks the servant as dishonest. Early in the play, Olivia's labeling of Feste's absence as dishonest provides the means by which to view his subsequent absence from her house. Olivia's gentlewoman, Maria, remarks to Feste that "My Lady will hang thee for thy absence" (1.5.3). Olivia's initial decision to dismiss Feste reflects contemporary policies that were not, however, uniformly implemented. At the time of the play's production, concerning servants of the Royal House of the 1590s, Robert C. Braddock states: "The only reason their wages were stopped was for excessive absences, and even that rule was probably not strictly enforced" (33). Since Feste does not receive a wage, his absence jeopardizes his domestic arrangement. Feste's freelancing broaches the topic of his cash profits and his considerable dishonesty. From a socioeconomic perspective, he distinguishes himself as an economically progressive character functioning within a pre-modern expectation of domestic order. Olivia, much like the Tudor nobles, is less inclined to discipline her servants for excessive absences and would much rather benefit from her clown-servant's ability to lift her mourning spirit.

The dialogue between Olivia and Feste points directly to Feste's infractions and their resolution. Olivia states: "Go to, y' a dry fool. I'll no more of you. Besides, you grow dishonest" (1.5.38-9). To Olivia's claim that Feste is "dry" or "dull, " and "dishonest" Feste replies, "Two faults, madonna, that drink and good counsel will mend" (1.5.40-1). The pun on a drink as thirst quenching and drink as a form of alcoholic beverage of festivity are means to satisfy any dullness in his wit. "Good counsel" is restitution for his "dishonesty." Feste's good counsel that follows is the outwitting of his mistress through verbal punning. Feste's "dishonest" actions then point to the absence of his verbal wit from Olivia's disposal. By showing Olivia that he can still do his job by outwitting her in word games, he restores her faith in their late feudal arrangements of service.

Contemporary practice explains why Feste's absence from this funeral was particularly foolhardy. Often the ceremonial internment of a loved one upsets the delicate socioeconomic balance of the household. Kate Mertes sees the death of the patriarch as a transitional period in the domestic arrangements of service, a period of insecurity for servants who are unsure of their job security as the household changed hands (156). Feste's excessive absence jeopardizes his employment during an interval of change when Olivia's command to "Take away the fool" may spell the permanent termination of his services. Olivia's charge that Feste's grows "dishonest" points to his neglected household responsibilities. Mertes states that

> Household members organized and participated in their masters' funerals, arranging for the procession, burial, and largesse, and also for the wake afterwards, usually following the instructions of the will. Servants normally took part in the procession, following after the chief mourners and in some cases carrying or leading the body. . . Through the funeral ritual servants were able to express their grief, perform a last act of service for their dead lord, and perhaps, by their privileged position in the ceremony, identify themselves with the chief mourners . . . At a time of insecurity such identification may have had career as well as psychological benefits for servants and masters. (Mertes 156)

Feste's failure to participate in the traditional funeral rites for Olivia's brother suggests that Feste is neglecting significant traditional household duties. His absence illustrates that he spends his time as he sees fit, even when his actions run counter to expectations of his service within a noble household.

Although Feste's awareness of the limits of his ability to fool in the face of so natural a dilemma as mourning death urges him to call on the help of powers beyond his own abilities, he relies on the corruption of words in the form of contrived puns to impress Olivia:

> *Feste.* Wit, an't be thy will, put me into good fooling! Those wits that think they have thee do very oft prove fools, and that I am sure I lack thee may pass for a wise man . . . —'Better to be a witty fool than a foolish wit.' (1.5.29-31)

Feste seems to acknowledge that wit is inspirational. Ronald Macdonald argues that for Feste,

> The finest wit is only in part the product of studied artifice, for it has an aleatory component as well, and involves a willingness to surrender the self to what we would now call the work of the unconscious. Feste knows that wit is not something he can reliably deploy at need, for it must be wooed, evoked, prayed to. (84-5)

In the same manner that Will Somer's qualities of mirth accompany his jests to lift King Henry VIII out of his depression following the death of his wives, so does Feste possess an ability to connive jests to enliven Olivia (see Ch 1.). Feste's reply to Olivia's chastisement of "Take the fool away" is "Do you hear, fellows? Take away the lady" (3.5.36-7). Feste's manipulation of language inverts mistress and clown-servant identities in comic form. This act not only sets the play's tone for comic inversion, but also establishes Feste's credibility as an able clown-servant proto-capitalist.

Olivia allows the opportunity to engage her clown-servant in a battle of verbal wit. To Feste's request of "Good madonna, give me leave to prove you a fool," Olivia answers, "Can you do it? . . . Make your proof" (1.5.54-6, 58). Feste proceeds on a comic course to test Olivia's religious faith and to prove, his mistress, Olivia a fool:

Clown.	Good madonna, why mournest thou?
Olivia.	Good fool, for my brother's death.
Clown.	I think his soul is in hell, madonna.
Olivia.	I know his soul is in heaven, fool.
Clown.	The more fool, madonna, to mourn for your brother's soul being in heaven. Take away the fool, gentlemen. (1.5.63-69)

Having proven himself no "dry fool," Feste's wit serves Olivia to self evaluate and observe the folly of her reason. In this process, as Karen Greif notes, Feste displays a comic cynicism for his superiors (67). The rigors of his profession have not dulled his wit. Feste's jests are full of classical, aesthetic, geographic, and historical allusions that enliven his jests and outwit his listeners. Rather than apologize to Olivia or beg his job, Feste exhibits his ability to manipulate language, which, in fact, is his job. In the same manner, Feste does not vow to cease the freelancing that illustrates his disconnectedness from Olivia's feudal household economy. Yet, Olivia replies, "What think you of this fool, Malvolio? Doth he not mend" (1.5.70-1), a signal that she accepts the services of her clown-servant. Olivia drops the subject of Feste's absence and accepts the truant clown. Feste placates Olivia and continues in her employment, an act that reestablishes their traditional mistress/clown-servant bond with continued flexibility for Feste to labor and earn income outside of its parameters.

Feste's dual economy, traditional and proto-capitalist, leads to a tense socioeconomic interaction with Malvolio. His clash with Malvolio illustrates the frictions among the servants that characterize the play's downstairs plot. Once Feste impresses Olivia with his wit, she turns to Malvolio for his professional opinion of Feste's work. On one level, Malvolio insults Feste, *ad hominem*. His dislike for Feste as a person is evident. It is Feste's blatant disregard for domestic order that infuriates Malvolio, perhaps because it resembles his own even more ambitious desires, revealed in a later act, to tear down the hierarchy of Olivia's household by becoming her husband and a count. Their competition within Olivia's household leads to their mutual aversion. Malvolio insults Feste's professional dexterity. His references to Feste as "barren rascal," "out of his guard," and "no better than the fools' zanies" (1.5.81, 83, 86) suggest Feste's uselessness to Olivia and her household as well as infer the need to terminate Feste's employment. Malvolio's stewardship and his demand that other characters yield to his power over domestic order target him for the brunt of social economic change within *Twelfth Night's* shifting economy. Malvolio faces the wrath of an incensed clown-servant. Feste indirectly warns Malvolio of his vengeance and that with the help of Sir Toby, together, they will bring "a speedy infirmity for the better increasing of your [Malvolio's] folly" (1.5.67-69). R.P. Draper's work on Shakespeare's comedies reads this line as generally belonging to the Christian notion that infirmity can have beneficial effects; however, he factors in Feste's anger and resentment to suggest that Malvolio's comic spirit is in need of a psychological jolt (151-52). Where Draper sees Malvolio as a social outsider because of his lack of a sense of humor in relation to Feste, this chapter suggests that Malvolio lacks humor because of his anxiety for *Twelfth Night's* visibly waning domestic order, an order that he would like to maintain, paradoxically after he escapes its confines to find the place he believes he inherently deserves—at the top.

Moonlighting

Feste's back-to-back appearances in Act 2.3 and Act 2.4 add proto-capitalist dimensions of moonlighting to freelance economics in *Twelfth Night*. Fooling as a talent that Feste exchanges for money has either been examined within the context of begging or omitted altogether. Robert Hillis Goldsmith acknowledges that Feste demands payment in cash, a "capitalist act"; yet for Goldsmith, "Feste is an inveterate beggar" (54). C.L. Barber states that "what Feste chiefly does is sing and beg," and connects his wit and songs to personal feelings of liberty rather than to an entrepreneurial sense of enterprise (253). Yet, viewed collectively, Act 2 scenes 3 and 4 show Feste's initiative to work two jobs in a single span of time for cash profit. Feste uses his exclusive access to both Olivia's house and Orsino's palace to peddle his wares. In Olivia's house, he entertains Sir Toby and Sir Andrew late into the night. In the following scene, Feste is present at Duke Orsino's palace the next day.

Moonlighting refers to a person holding two or more jobs, or participating in a secondary labor market (Shishko and Rostker 298). Following his late night revelry with Sir Toby, Sir Andrew, and Maria (2.3), Feste is present at Duke Orsino's palace the next day. Liminal space between the scenes suggest that while Maria and Malvolio retire to bed, and while Toby and Andrew continue their festivities, Feste is en route to the Duke's palace, traveling through the night to his second job. Feste travels literally through moonlight to "moonlight." Both these aspects of moonlighting apply to Feste since he has multiple employers and operates within shifting markets. A query central to *Twelfth Night's* economics is why does Feste moonlight? An understanding of changes in service relationships sheds some insight on this question. Households were the basic economic unit, markets with inherent competitive economic implications (Muldrew *Economy* 149). In the early sixteenth century, aristocratic houses preferred male serving men to female domestics as much as twenty to one, in a medieval system in which male service to male nobles reinforced feudal order. However, from 1550-1600 a general shift occurred toward female servants who, unlike their politically representative male counterparts, were wholly concerned with domestic duties (McBride 8-9). The houses in *Twelfth Night* correspond to this late medieval trend in household economics. Orsino's more feudal palace runs on medieval bonds between men, an order that, paradoxically, Feste recognizes and exploits for his entrepreneurial practice. Olivia's less organized matriarchal household allows Feste some freedom to expand his proto-capitalist tendencies. In this regard, Feste's proto-capitalism plays in the social history of late medieval England. In *Twelfth Night*, Feste possesses knowledge of both economic orders and oscillates between variations of a court fool and domestic fool. His knowledge of each household and its social expectations allow him to tailor his clowning to profit from both houses.

In the third scene of Act 2 where Feste joins Sir Toby and Sir Andrew, the clown-servant helps to establish the atmosphere of festivity at Olivia's house through monetary exchange for entertainment. The play presents for the first time the complex mingling of upstairs and downstairs household communities and the dissolution of hierarchical barriers through the distribution of ale and songs. Feste trades his songs for coins. Both Sir Toby and Sir Andrew compensate Feste for his songs prior to his singing, an act that points not only to the proto-capitalism of Feste's labors, but also to the class descent of Toby and Andrew to make merry with the servants. Feste's act is proto-capitalist because he reverses the order of gratuity to insure a favorable transaction. As noblemen, like Orsino, Toby and Andrew may command Feste to entertain. If he refuses by requiring prepayment, they may threaten to jeopardize his employment status with Olivia. By paying him in advance, they allow Feste to match the value of entertainment that follows with the amount of prepaid money. Therefore, festivity in *Twelfth Night* constitutes festive interplay between upper and lower classes, two socioeconomic groups not merely balancing household decorum and celebratory anarchy. But also through an economic lens, the festive interplay between the classes satisfies the demands of alternative economic systems. This social interaction between servants and nobles points to the economic significance of the festivity to both groups.

This chaotic festivity breaks down class hierarchy, at least temporarily. Together with Sir Toby and Sir Andrew, the aristocrats, Feste becomes one of the three asses rather than merely a servant paid to sing. Feste's allusion to the picture, "We Three," a known portrayal of two asses of which the viewer makes the third suggests that he will add his foolery to their pre-established asininity. Elizabeth Freund suggests that Feste's allusion to a familiar piece of Renaissance visual art is an instructive paradigm rather than a particularly subtle witticism:

> 'We Three' is a picture of three asses in which the beholder of the picture makes up the third. Presumably taking his que from Andrew ("here comes the fool"), Feste's jest identifies the company as consisting of two more fools who, as in the picture of 'We Three', are conned into reading

the representation ("fool" or "ass") as a reflection of themselves. Toby catches and responds to the allusion by genially embracing the fraternity of foolery or asshood. (475)

Feste's pun on "we three" is the clown-servant's reply to Andrew's assertion of "Here comes the fool i' faith" (2.3.15). In other words, Feste jests through his allusion to art that the real "fools," Toby and Andrew, are already assembled and his presence merely completes the set. With his ability to outwit his social superiors with the fluid tool of exchange, he primes the selling of songs. As the scene progresses, his wit and songs merge into his complete show of entertainment. In many ways, Feste's performance may be likened to a play-within-a play since he is a player playing a player, and his on stage play-acting represents the overall relationship between player and patron, the business of theatre. Like the monetary relationship between actor and patron, Feste creates an atmosphere of profitable entertainment in which he controls the tempo of the cash payment and the songs.

Feste's participation in the merriment dissolves temporarily the subordinating lines of class. As one of the three asses, Feste is prepaid, a transaction that secures his active place in the merriment with Toby, Andrew, and Maria. For example, the alternate singing of the lines by Feste and Toby from the song "Corydon's Farewell to Phyllis" illustrates their festivity on an even social plane:

Sir Toby Belch. [*Sings*]	'Farewell, dear heart, since I must needs be gone.'. .
Clown. [*Sings*]	'His eyes do show his days are almost done.' . . .
Sir Toby Belch. [*Sings*]	'But I will never die.'
Clown [*Sings*].	Sir Toby, there you lie. . . .

Sir Toby Belch. [Sings]	'Shall I bid him go?'
Clown. [Sings]	'What an if you do?'
Sir Toby Belch. [Sings]	'Shall I bid him go, and spare not?'
Clown. [Sings]	'O no, no, no, no, you dare not.' (2.3.102-112)

Feste and Toby share a song of protest against Malvolio who has entered the room to shut down the revelry. Participating willingly without further cash payment, the clown-servant joins the aristocrats equally to berate Malvolio for interrupting the pleasure of their merriment, and Malvolio retreats, helpless to counter their verbal assaults. Unlike Feste's rendition of "O Mistress Mine," a song that is the direct result of prepayment, his participation in "Corydon's Farewell to Phyllis" occurs as an extension of the prepaid entertainment. This social mix of classes, nobles and servant, points to merrymaking that results from the exchange of entertainment for coins. Thus for Feste, displays of verbal wit and the singing of songs are the talents that he markets, the fluid tool of exchange like the money that he accepts.

In *Twelfth Night*, the reigning nobility absorbs the costs of festivity. From a traditional viewpoint, Olivia's house not only affords the wine, songs, and carousing of both its nobles and servants, but also it provides the open household setting necessary to experience merriment. Thad Jenkins Logan comments that

> The wealth and social position of the characters are important in several ways and should be established clearly in production; besides setting the action in a framework of aristocratic values, pleasures, and mores, they contribute a great deal to the sense of liberation and license. Characters

are, in part, free to pursue 'what they will' because they can afford to do so. (225)

Whether at Olivia's estate or at the Duke's, Feste's economic leverage is made possible by the economic freedom of the aristocrats. Although Orsino also pays Feste to sing, the moment is not charged with the same festive energies as his social interactions at Olivia's house.

Feste's wit is his talent of exchange that links the classes. Feste, the entertainer for the late night party at Olivia's house, much like paid actors of Elizabethan theatre, has been paid and the revelers, like the audience, expect a certain return on their investment in entertainment. Clearly, the crux of Malvolio's interruption threatens to discredit and short-change the revelers of their paid entertainment, for the songs and jests are instead understood by the revelers in terms of festive pleasures, "cakes and ale" (2.2.115). In the same manner that Elizabethan theatergoing represented social disorder to its governmental opponents, so does Feste's foolery violate Malvolio's idea of a domestic order, which (as steward or as Olivia's husband) he controls. In other words, the conflict posed by the festivity of Feste, Maria, Toby, and Andrew to Malvolio's ascetic governance parallels the relationship between Elizabethan theatre and the government. Coddon suggests that

If Malvolio like such antitheatrical polemicists as Phillip Stubbes, disapproves of festive misrule in principle, the government's regulation of the theatre testifies to its own anxieties about the drama's potential to produce (reproduce) fictions contesting Tudor and Stuart official ideologies. The theatre, like the 'all licens'd fool', was to an extent authorized to enact a degree of insubordination, apparently on the thought that it would thus function as a sort of safety valve for discontent that might otherwise seek less indirect forms of expression. (311)

In Olivia's home that serves as a microcosmic representation of London's domestic economics, Feste's clown-service reflects on Elizabethan theatre.

Feste's Knotting Song?

In Act 2 scene 4, Duke Orsino commands, "Ay, prithee sing" (2.4.50), and Feste receives his cash payment once Orsino hears the song, an exchange with the Duke that shows signs of Feste's proto-capitalist endeavor within the confines of late feudal authority. There is a notable shift in modes of economic exchange from Toby and Andrew to Duke Orsino. Rather than an investment in revelry consistent with Toby and Andrew's pre-payment for Feste's songs and jests, Orsino purchases Feste's entertainment in a more traditional form of master/servant exchange. Coddon notes that the transition from 2.3 to 2.4 shifts from "holiday" to "historical" action (318). Although Feste's proto-capitalist entertainment practices propel him to return to the Duke's palace, the Duke's request for his return for a command performance comes from a traditional perspective. Orsino commands: "Give me some music. Now, good morrow, friends. Now, good Cesario, but that piece of song. That old antique song we heard last night" (2.4. 1-3). Once Curio informs Orsino that it is Feste's song that he desires, Orsino orders: "Seek him out, and play the tune awhile" (2.4.14). However, *Twelfth Night* portrays waning traditional servitude, and once Feste arrives, his choice of songs illustrates that noble commands do not necessarily ensure that one gets that for which one orders and pays. Orsino's authority is not enough to control the choice of Feste's product, his song.

Significant discrepancy exists between the song that

Orsino commands and the song that Feste sings, evidence that Orsino's self-indulgence in musical aesthetics clouds his understanding of the working poor. Clearly, in an earlier interaction with Cesario, Orsino attempts to assert aristocracy through music appreciation. In anticipation of Feste's song, Orsino describes the song that he heard on the previous night as a simple work song, a knotting song used by spinners and weavers to keep time with their sewing. He calls Feste, and explains to Viola (as Cesario):

> O, fellow, come, the song we had last night.
> Mark it, Cesario; it is old and plain,
> The spinsters and the knitters in the sun,
> And the free maids that weave their thread with bones,
> Do use to chant it. (2.4.42-46)

However, it is evident that he does not get a knotting song. Gerald Porter reads in Orsino's description of bonelace weavers, "evidence that the practice of women's accompanying their lacemaking with songs was one of long habit" (39).

The difference between the art song, "Come away, come away death," that Feste sings and knotting songs sung by weavers is clear. Porter's seminal study of lacemaking songs or "tells" offers a complete example of rhyme and meter as well as the actual act of lacemaking:

> Up in the morning before it is light,
> Done all her work before it is bright,
> Down at her pillor she sits so complete
> Like a lacemaker, working so neat,
> With fingers so lissom, and bobbins so small,
> While the poor servant girl goes down the hall
> With holes in her stockings and rags on her back.
> I'll be a lacemaker, if ever so slack.

I'll tourn over timber sticks, Put in my pin of wire,
My wire pin is in
I'm one the higher. (43-4)

Porter notes that the short catchy rhymes of the tells helped the women to concentrate and remain awake during long weaving sessions, and the movement of the bobbins or bones was timed by the cheerful modulation of the tune (43-4). Possibly, on the one hand, Orsino may be so musically inept that he misinterprets a soulful art song for a lively knotting song. His noble-mindedness of what maids might sing as they work may cause him to see aesthetic beauty in the lyrics and to associate the seeming simplicity and forthrightness of their work with the simple lives of lace makers. However, as Porter notes, although lace was aesthetically fashionable, lacemaking in sixteenth century London was neither simple nor pretty: "What was considered the height of bourgeois respectability to wear depended directly on the work of the most powerless and exploitable sections of the community, old women, children, and young girls" (Porter 39). His account emphasizes the plight of young female servants clothed in holey rags. Edward Baines makes note of the disproportionate pay for a product in high demand. Baines considers that yarn shortages should have, yet did not lead to an increase in wages for textile workers whose numbers declined during the Tudor period" (22). Perhaps his missed assessment of the lives of poor workers as simple and carefree foreshadows Viola's (as Cesario)'s erroneous assumption in the following act that Feste, the clown-servant, "art a merry fellow and car'st for nothing" (3.1.26-7).

Clearly, Orsino does not get a knotting song in Feste's "Come Away Death." Feste has apparently substituted a totally different song to serve his own foolery. Feste is primarily a clown who serves, and although his singing is, in itself, an act of service, it is not without the influence of his clownish wit. John Hollander notes that the "O Come Away Death" is a kind of "languorous ayre." Hollander observes, "It is aimed at Orsino in the very extravagance of his complaint. It is his own song, really, if we imagine him suddenly dying of love, being just as ceremoniously elaborate in his funeral instructions as he has been in his suit of Olivia" (238). Orsino's frustrations are made apparent by his emotions, in a moodiness that Feste chides through wit.

Following his song, Feste concludes his attack on Orsino with a sarcastic benediction, a last allusion to sewing that chides the Duke's emotional moodiness. His consistent reference to textiles not only allows him to hurl one closing insult at Orsino, an insult with eye-opening implications for the Duke if he gets the fool's meaning. But also, the textile allusions keep the socioeconomic implication of master/servant relationships within reach of Feste's humor, aspects of service that Orsino's melancholy causes him to misunderstand. In his parting words, Feste describes a rich man of fickle disposition who, if his servants could speak their minds and impose their wills, would be banished to an ocean of lonely opportunity. Feste says:

> Now the melancholy god protect thee, and the tailor make thy doublet of changeable taffeta, for thy mind is a very opal. I would have men of such constancy put to sea that their business might be everything, and their intent everywhere; for that's it that always makes a good voyage of nothing. Farewell. (2.4.73-78)

Feste insults Orsino's lack of artistic knowledge concerning music, industry, and the socioeconomics that drive England's laboring class and its textile markets. In taffeta and opal,

Feste chooses iridescent products that lack consistency and change as the sun shines.

In essence, Orsino is a weak suitor because he is out of touch with his own desire for status. For Barbara Everett, Feste says what he sees:

> Thy mind is a very opal, an art-image of an exquisite jewel... An Elizabethan love-sonnet, that intensely courtly mode, will use jewel imagery in a way that reminds us that the woman is beautiful *and* that the love involved is, as it were, expensive, estimable, an index of the lover's standing and power. (206)

When viewed as products of proto-capitalist endeavor, Feste's allusion to the sea makes evident the economic connection between textiles like taffeta and lace and men put to sea in business of trade. Feste's sea-metaphor reduces Orsino to the level of merchant or sailor.

Perhaps, in taffeta and opal resides the pith of Feste's jest, his solar walk around the "orb," with the ability to affect Orsino's "opal mind" like the sun. His effect on the Duke is that as clown-servant, he provides other characters with different perspectives for seeing themselves, usually, like Henry VIII's Will Somer, from the perspectives of servants. He is in constant tune with the voices of the laboring poor, the voices of the knotting women and free maids. Like Shakespeare's clown-servants before him, Feste cares about the kitchen wench and the maid servant (E. Dromio), the sheep that follow their masters (Speed and Launce), and the stomachs of the domestic servants (Launcelot). Through his fooling, he shares the often painful socioeconomic realities of traditional master/servant relationships with his superiors, holding to their faces mirrors for the upper class to discern their own human insensitivities. For Orsino's mirror, Feste shows disparities between the product and its producers. In Feste's substitution of an art song, Orsino may see that the aesthetic qualities of the finished lace, the objects of his admiration, bear little resemblance to the lower class working poor who produced it. Orsino is aware enough to know that the clown-servants had the license of free speech to criticize his behavior and responds by what Barbara Everett calls, "ripostes of offended aesthetic dignity" (207): "There's for thy pains," followed by reversed-status order to depart, "Give me now leave, to leave thee" (2.4.72). Having seen a glimpse of himself in the clown-servant's mirror, Orsino resumes his suit of Olivia in his self-same delusional way, using the services of Cesario. When Feste and Orsino next meet (5.1), the Duke illustrates that Feste has moved him a step closer to self-awareness by tailoring his economic interaction to Feste's corrective use of unbridled truth. Orsino realizes not only that Feste's clown-servant wit entertains, but also that his wit challenges the conscience of the listener to self-assess with regard to its assessments of others.[6]

Orsino seems to wise-up to Feste's marketing of foolery as he sees the clown-servant less as a vassal and more as a huckster. Illyria's economic crossroads do not afford Orsino's dukedom the weight necessary to employ Feste as its vassal. His rhetorical question points to his foreknowledge of Feste's employment status[7]:

Duke.	Belong you to the Lady Olivia, friends?"
Clown.	Ay, sir, we are some of her trappings.
Duke.	I know thee well.

Clown.	Truly sir, the better for my foes and the worse for my friends.
Duke.	Just the contrary; the better for thy friends.
Clown.	No, sir, the worse.
Duke.	How can that be.
Clown.	Marry, sir, they praise me and make an ass of me. Now my foes tell me plainly I am an ass; so that my foes, sir, I profit in knowledge of myself, and by my friends I am abus'ed. (5.1.7-18)

Feste's inversion of "friends" and "foes" (5.1.10) echoes Feste's professional dislike for Viola (as Cesario), an inversion that points not only to the inversion of authority during times of festivity, but also to economic disparities between masters and servants that accompany the move away from late feudal domestic order. On one level, Orsino sees Feste through the same late feudal lens whereby he sees Viola (as Cesario), as a means to the end of achieving access to Olivia's house and affection. If Feste and the others "belong" to Olivia, then by possessing them and their seeming friendship, Orsino may possess their mistress. On an economic level, Feste's service, unlike Viola's (as Cesario) wageless vassalage, aims to profit from Orsino's wealth. However, this time (unlike 2.4), Orsino is in-the-know and quickly makes sense of Feste's clown humor. He seems more prepared for Feste's wit for cash (5.1) and is better able to counter the clown-servants puzzling allusions to "friends" and "enemies." Orsino realizes that above all Feste's earnings rely on truthful assessments of others. On this occasion when the Duke tips Feste, there is a sense that Orsino also tips himself as a personal reward for growing in the wisdom of the fool. He begins to understand service and its relevance whether in courtship or in entertainment. In return for the Duke's patronage, Feste attempts to pass on the lesson that, like the clown-servant, Orsino will profit from knowledge of himself (5.1.17). To Feste's wit, Orsino's response of, "Why, this is excellent" (5.1.22), signals that he now understands the wit of the clown-servant. In his re-assessment of "friend" and "foe," Orsino is in accord with the dual appeal of Feste's jests, to chastise and enlighten. However, coins not compliments will soften Feste's wit to fit the Duke's fresh disposition.

Feste's choice of words and the Duke's actions show that neither character fully accepts the other's economics. Nonetheless, Feste continues to insult the Duke's conventional approach to service even in the midst of the Orsino's benevolence: "But that it would be double-dealing, sir, I would you could make it another" (5.1.26-7). The term "double-dealing" both alludes to the doubling of action, committing the same act twice (i.e. tipping) or (in line with Feste's earlier insults of the Duke in 2.4), two-facedness, duplicity, and hypocrisy (Draper 156, Bevington 420). Feste cleverly adds a socioeconomic twist to his jest.

Even though the Duke develops a minute trust for Feste's freelance business sense, enough so that he hires Feste as his messenger, he is still reluctant to invest in the rapid movement of money for services. After paying Feste for his word-play on "double-dealing," an act that shows that Orsino takes himself less seriously than earlier in the play, he responds: "You can fool no more money out of me at this throw" (5.1.37-8). His allusion to dice as a money-game of risk and chance points to his greater awareness of the relevance that money plays in the lives of the servant class. However, he still will not pre-pay Feste like Toby and Andrew, two nobles with a more developed sense of progressive economics than Orsino. When it comes to unpaid messengers, Feste's unwillingness to serve without pay is reminiscent of Speed's unwillingness to deliver Proteus's letter in *Two Gentlemen of Verona*. Just as Speed refuses to serve without pay, Feste does not entertain without cash payment (5.1). In this respect, Feste does not respond to the lingering traditional expectations of the nobility that servants serve unconditionally. Perhaps the play cannot afford direct contact between the source of Feste's domestic governance in Olivia and the patron tied to his absences from her household in Orsino. In this respect, the brief nexus of economic exchange and clown-service between Feste and the Duke achieves the play's balancing point of late feudal and proto-capitalist domestic economics.

THE CLOWN LIVES BY THE CHURCH

The dialogue in Act 3 scene 1 between Feste and Viola has been frequently quoted as a comment on the service and payment in *Twelfth Night*. Feste puts his fooling to good use to be able to extract coins from Viola even as they trade insults. Much noted is Feste's ability to get money for his songs and verbal wit. In his seminal work in *Wise Fools*, Robert Hillis Goldsmith suggests that Feste receives more money for fooling than for singing (54). Like Shakespeare, thinks Goldsmith, Feste must live solely by his art. For C. L. Barber, this clash of wits illustrates that Viola's speech projects mockingly, much like Feste's. Barber fuses language and service to score a win for Viola. He posits that Feste's negative reaction stems from his verbal defeat (254). However, more important to this scene than tips and insults are service implications. In a play primarily concerned with issues of service, the exchange between Feste and Viola provides a closer look at proto-capitalist service for profit versus feudal service for duty.

Most obviously, Feste's clowning makes him a dangerous character with whom Malvolio should not trifle lightly. Similarly, Viola lightheartedly spars with the clown through quick flurries of candid witticisms that Feste volleys with clownish ease. Viola as Cesario represents a feudal messenger bonded to a noble lord. Unlike Feste, a cash-man, Viola subsists not on tips but on the benevolence of her master's house. By refusing Olivia's money (5.1.279), Viola distances herself socially from servants who, like Feste, make a living by taking cash profits from those they serve. Throughout the play, the rivalry between Feste and Viola represents opposing ways to serve nobility. Viola (as Cesario) represents the feudal messenger of late medieval England whose primary task is to deliver messages for his noble lord. In a study of medieval households, historian Kate Mertes finds that

> Unlike the royal household, nobles had no official messenger service. From the performance of mundane secretarial tasks of buying, preparing, providing for the lord's political requirements— probably often without full knowledge of the significance of such provisions—individual servants could be removed temporarily from the normal sphere of household activities to carry and receive letters, to convey and return instructions, and to assess the attitudes of opposite parties. (122)

Viola's masked identity and feelings for Orsino give her "full knowledge" of Orsino's desire for Olivia. Orsino immediately appoints Cesario his messenger, positioning Cesario comfortably with the feudal order of the house. It is perhaps for this reason in part that Feste seeks to separate himself from Viola's (as Cesario's) traditional service to a master. Viola uses her feudal authority, her connection to nobility to inquire abruptly into the clown's business. Yet she prefaces her attack by first praising Feste's craft. Feste perhaps senses Viola's challenge of wits and spares nothing verbal, answering Viola's query with double entendre:

Viola.	Save thee, friend, and thine music. Doest thou live by the tabor?
Clown.	No, sir, I live by the church. (3.1.1-3)

Feste is well aware of Viola's intensions and is immediately on his clown-guard. His triple pun falls on the word *by* and its prepositional meanings. First, Feste deliberately clouds the issue by treating Viola's curiosity to a healthy dose of clowning. In other words, Feste provides Viola with an avenue to bid a hasty retreat from the intricacies of his wit. Feste's answer does suggest that he indeed lives physically *by* a church. Feste's answer further complicates his job description since Viola is under the impression that Feste is Olivia's fool and resides in her house. Viola's questions whether or not Feste lives by free-lancing, an act that, like Maria, she suspects. However, unlike Maria who is willing to resist Malvolio's authority, Viola remains tied to Orsino's feudal household.

Second, the comic device at play in the pun, to live "*by* the church," follows the same pattern of contradiction between Feste and Olivia in Act 1. Feste is a comic and lives by fooling, as does a clown, not by virtue as do holy men. The supposition of the joke is that the church and the aristocracy are entities competing for the title of most-socially-oppressive. Viola really seeks to know whether Feste works for Olivia or the Duke, both aristocrats. Delany suggests that "no matter how greedy, inefficient, and exploitative the feudal church and the aristocracy may have been, their fervent idealism sustained man's sense of his own place in the social hierarchy" (430). Feste's play on words shows that he is no more a holy man of the church than Olivia is a practicing fool. Feste's role as clown is to present the play's paradox and inconsistencies, especially concerning matters of economics. For Feste, comic inversion is the primary tool of good fooling to thwart any verbal adversary, even Olivia.

> *Clown.* Wit, and't be thy will, put me into good fooling! Those wits that think they have thee do very oft prove fools; and I, that am sure I lack thee, may pass for a wise man. For what says Quinapalus? Better a witty fool than a foolish wit.

Feste suggests that the nature of his fooling is to prove an ass of those who deem themselves more wise than fools, and at the same time, prove himself sage to those who think him fool. "Wit," one spirit of his fool nature, must endow Feste with the comic power of inversion not just to outwit Olivia and Viola, but also to defend his proto-capitalist practices of living by his tabor. As in Act 1 scene 5, when Feste makes his bid to prove Olivia a fool, he resorts to inverting language to divert attention away from the status of his service. And on both occasions, Feste's worth is measured by his ability to pun and cleverly invert language to produce unexpected meanings. Although there is no direct evidence that for Feste, Viola's shoptalk reflects her inner fear of possible unmasking, Feste's rhetoric does suggest that his mastery of inversion makes him a wise-danger to Viola. Much speculation surrounds Feste's Latin quip from that scene with Olivia: *Cucullus non facit monachum.* The reality that "the hood does not make the monk" (1.5.52-3) applies most obviously to Feste's later comic portrayal of Master Topas. It is also the comic force that drives the play. *Twelfth Night* revolves around disguises and mistaken identities. Yet, Feste, the verbal champion of the play, will not allow Viola to build confidence in her reality nor in her disguise at the expense of his fooling. Note how Viola attempts the same comic style of inversion:

> *Viola.* So thou mayst say the king lies by a beggar, if a beggar dwell near him; or the church stands by thy tabor, if thy tabor stand by the church. (3.1.8-10)

Humor occurs as Viola simultaneously gets the drift of Feste's pun and quickly duplicates its structure. Humor secures a comically safe place not only in the joke but also in Illyria's servant society. Thus, Viola's word play on "beggar" completes the incongruous pun on Feste's proto-capitalism. In other words, Viola completes the pun by becoming Feste herself. It is not surprising that Viola offers Feste a payment from safely within the contest of the pun.

Nevertheless, once Viola becomes the fool and is pleased with her part in the verbal exchange, she attempts to return to her previous mode of speaking. But her effective fooling only piques Feste's anger. The shift in Viola's language from verbal sparing to direct inquiry occurs once she concedes to Feste through complement: "I warrant thou art a merry fellow and car'st for nothing" (3.1.26-27). Courtly music and fooling—and playacting, as Viola discovers for herself—are forms of work carried out by people who need to earn a living (Yachnin 777). As seen with Malvolio, Orsino, and now Viola, once Feste engages in a battle of wits, the contest does not end until the clown has the final word. Feste then amplifies wit to insult: "Not so sir, I do care for something; but in my conscience, sir, I do not care for you" (3.1.27-28). Partly, the jest lies in Feste's meanings of the "something' and "nothing" for which he cares. First, the "nothing" for which Feste cares represents the play's nobles and noble-minded characters who question his work ethic. Feste defends his proto-capitalist business sense from characters that attempt to affix feudal restrictions to his custom. Coddon states: "Like Orsino before her, Viola attempts to constitute Feste as merely the embodiment of the mirthful court jester, the abstract spirit of song and festivity" (319). For Viola, dialogue with Feste does not jeopardize her servant status. She approaches Feste not only as fellow servant, but also as "friend." As one who serves, Viola uses the exchange of wits to hone the verbal skills upon which she relies through the play.

However, for Feste, any dialogue that questions his labor practices may possibly jeopardize his servant status. The exchange serves to side Viola with the nobility, the feudal order that restricts his enterprise and tethers him to one feudal household and master. The "something" for which Feste cares forms the dual bases for his economic perspective. Evidently, Feste cares for cash. Money for services rendered is part of Feste's economic philosophy. Viola is as aware as other characters and audiences of Feste's emphasis on monetary payment. Once Viola is unable to return Feste's verbal volleys, she re-adopts the direct speech of a page and drops the wit of a fool: "I saw thee late at the Count Orsino's" (3.1.37). Yet, this return to proper station as court servant does not break Feste's fooling. Nonetheless, Viola resorts to giving Feste coins.

When he accepts the money, Feste couples his vituperative insults with saucy allusions to the crass nature of commercial exchange between Troilus and Lord Pandarus (Coddon 320). On the surface, to bring a Cressida to a Troilus in terms of money points to Feste's additional wit to garner an additional payment from Viola. He alludes to the classics and creates a play on words to double his money. On a deeper level, the reference parallels the acts of the play's nobles, acts that Feste openly critiques in his songs and puns. Coddon notes that "Pandarus, of course, evokes the activity for which Orsino has engaged 'Cesario'; like Feste, Viola is playing the role of servant, and her actual social superiority is undercut by the clown's suggestion of a kind of material equivalence between them" (320). To this effect, Feste's final disrespect of Viola is redolent with humorous vulgarity: Orsino, like Troilus feels impotent to woo alone. Thus, Orsino, like Troilus employs as intermediary, a servant to woo for him, to obtain his love. However, Pandarus does not woo; but instead, becomes a "sailing Pandar" to procure an objectified Cressida, "a Pearl" (*Troilus and Cressida* 1.1. 103, 106). Viola as Cesario becomes Orsino's Pandarus, and Feste implies that her service to Orsino is as monetarily seedy as is Pandarus' service to Troilus. Feste responds to being labeled "beggar'" by retorting that in business of service it is better to be a beggar than a pimp. Even though Viola does not appear to feel the full brunt of Feste's insult, she respects his verbal ability as well as his knowledge of the classics:

> This fellow is wise enough to play the fool,
> And to do that well craves a kind of wit.
> He must observe their mood on whom he jests,
> The quality of persons, and the time;
> And like the haggard, check at every feather
> That comes before his eye. This is a practice
> As full of labor as a wise man's art;
> For folly that he wisely shows is fit,
> But wise men, folly-fall'n, quite taint their wit.
> (3.1.60-68).

Barber reads Viola soliloquy as the play's overall approval of Feste's fooling, sagacity disguised in mirth (252-3). Coddon hears "homage to the theater" in Viola's lines (320). Perhaps the final couplet sheds light on Viola's meaning. Viola observes that Feste, the clown, manipulates words just as a wise man works at his craft. Feste's wit that is full of folly is an attribute that infuses his jests with wisdom. Viola's reference to wise men that are "folly-fall'n" points to characters like Malvolio and Orsino who portray characters with tainted wit.

"Nothing that is so is so."

The brief scene of Feste and Sebastian is significant to the economic action of the play (4.1). The dialogue in the scene continues from the previous meeting between Feste and Viola (3.1). Feste's return to his pun "nothing" (in 3.1) facilitates a closer look at Feste's economic perspectives on money. In both scenes, Feste's word-play earns pay in gold coins and thereby provides Feste with economic incentive to continue the banter. He reasons that Sebastian's failure to acknowledge him continues the prior volley of insults with Viola . A point made clear by Feste's presumption that Sebastian keeps up the earlier rhetoric of "nothing" (3.1.30), he addresses Sebastian: "Well held out, i'faith" (4.1.5), and argues:

> No, I do not know you; nor I am not sent to you by my lady, to bid you come speak with her; nor your name is not Master Cesario; nor this is not my nose neither. Nothing that is so is so. (4.1.5-8)

Feste tells that his dislike for Viola/Cesario as the embodiment of nothingness stems from his "conscience" (3.1.29). Feste's conscience, like Launcelot's conscience in *The Merchant of Venice*, is the seat of his loyalty to domestic hierarchal decorum. In his conscience, not to care for Sebastian (as Viola) as "nothing" dictates that his dislike targets Viola's (as Cesario's) position of service. For Feste, Viola/Cesario seems more connected to noble sentiments of decorum than to orientations of servants. She exists on the high-side of service. In mistaking Sebastian for Viola, Feste unknowingly transfers his dislike to the twin brother. Prior to paying Feste, Sebastian attempts to dismiss the clown-servant in an aristocratic manner consistent with Viola's earlier high-mindedness. Feste's "nothing" illustrates his disregard for the service placements of Viola and now Sebastian. Just as Malvolio is no more than a steward, a member of the servant-class, Viola (as Cesario) and now Sebastian appear as no more than pages.

Feste's "nothing" represents a world where what one sees is often not what it appears to be, but words create a reality where laws of order that govern the reflection of a material world no longer operate (Freund 478). His tasks of being "sent" and having to "bid" (4.1.6) are not acts pertaining to his freelance endeavors but are traditional commands, "words" from his domestic employer. If servants disregard the commands of masters as Feste's "No" and "not" (4.1.5-8) signal, and if titles of identity like "Master" (4.1.7) become merely "wanton" words, then his "nose," the very embodiment of the late feudal domestic servant becomes "nothing."

To view "nothing" in terms of late feudal order is to see "something" in terms of money. The "something" for which Feste does care for throughout the play is money. His services of wit fluctuate with the availability of cash payment from his noble employers. Whether in Olivia's house or Orsino's house, Feste prefers to be in the presence of cash payment. In *Twelfth Night*, money reflects not only the disparity between the classes, but also it provides a sense of safeguarding reality and one's place in it. Feste's scene with Sebastian (4.1) shows that even in identity confusion, money retains its fluidity and its ability to influence social outcomes. In a moment of panic, Sebastian seeks to protect his nobility by throwing money at Feste. Just as the nobility pays to summon service, it may pay it off to go away. Yet, in the same moment, Sebastian's act of payment reassures Feste of the ability to sell verbal wit in a non-traditional fashion. Sebastian's act to preserve his nobility, in actuality, works to collapse it.

It must be pointed out that money is not the only cause of the move away from late feudal order in seventeenth century England (Hilton 198). Money allowed servants (like Feste) to devote more of their time to their holdings and less to traditional demands of service by the nobility (198). The accumulation of peasant-surplus promoted the buying and selling of land. As more land became available for sale on the market, the resulting dissolution of traditional holdings further assisted the social differentiation of the peasantry as some farmers became relatively wealthy yeomen (199). Feste comments about Sebastian's unsolicited payment of cash in terms of land acquisition for the peasantry: "By my troth, thou hast an open hand. These wise men that give fools money get themselves a good report--after fourteen years' purchase" (4.1.20-22). Feste's comments suggest the possibility of land ownership through a system of income-earned investments for the non-noble. Bevington connects Feste's lines to land, land originally valued at the price of twelve years rental; Feste adds two years to this amount (417). Perhaps Feste's addition of two years points the inflationary conditions in the Elizabethan economy and that hard work rather than superficial class climbing achieves wealth. He is by no means of the same class-climbing notions as Malvolio, yet he does recognize the ability of money to move a small part of the material of noble wealth within the grasp of the poor. Feste's income illustrates that the money nobles pay servants only further insures the dissolution of the values of master-servant relations. This dissolution points to the innate characteristic of late feudal dependence on "solidarity" and "articulation" (Hilton 197). In *Twelfth Night*, it is the solidarity of the upper class and the articulation of socioeconomic stratification along class lines that Sebastian's gold coins uphold and Feste's freelance sales of wit decries.

MASTER TOPAS

In Act 5 scene 1, Feste participates in Malvolio's imprisonment because the steward's earlier insults (1.5) illustrate Malvolio's attempts to have Feste dismissed from Olivia's household. The steward disapproves of Feste's absence and insults both his ability to do his job and his position of domestic clown-servant in Olivia's household. This act undermines both Feste's commercial and traditional employment. Laroque notes that Malvolio "uses his authority as the defender of his mistress, Olivia, and the shield of his virtue to wreak his vengeance upon people whose social position he envies yet whose behaviour he despises" (255). Malvolio envies Feste's wit and despises his ability to market his wit to the nobility. His offense against Feste is the use of his domestic position as steward openly and crassly to subjugate Feste and belittle his labor as witless. Malvolio's insult of Feste as "a barren rascal" (1.5.81) suggests a characteristic that would make Feste unfit for domestic service. The term "barren" insults Feste's on two levels, both of which discredit his job performance and incite the clown-servant to vengeance. From one perspective, "barren" refers to Feste as stupid (Barnet 884), as shown in his inability to outwit a common fool beneath his station (1.5). For Malvolio, Feste lacks wit, an assessment that he harbors until his imprisonment (4.2). Yachnin reads the "meanness of spoilsports" in Malvolio's use of "barren" (777). If seen as a domestic "spoilsport," Malvolio appears both jealous of Feste's wit and his means of self-employment that remove him from the steward's domestic authority. Another meaning of "barren" as fruitless or the failure to produce points to Feste as an economic drag on Olivia household economy. If Feste is without wit, he does not produce a service and in turn consumes Olivia's assets without work. However, an imprisoned Malvolio confesses, "I am as well in my wits as thou art" (4.2.82). His claim that his wits are equal to Feste's recants his earlier pompous deprecation of Feste's wit in Act 1 scene 5. From his confession, he aims to reconcile clown-servant and steward on the grounds of shared domestic service.[7] Either he admits that he too is a barren rascal, a claim that is likely to delay his release. Or more aptly, he admits that Feste does possess wit on a level comparable to his own in order to enlist Feste's help to freedom. Before Malvolio confesses Feste's wit, he admits his inflated ambition to marry Olivia and is subsequently imprisoned.

In addition to the claim that Feste lacks wit, Malvolio compounds the insult by voicing his opinion in the presence of Olivia. His deliberate slander of Feste's credibility leads to the dishonoring of his own dignity by the clown-servant. As a domestic servant, Feste's job hinges upon the approval of his wit by his employer. When Malvolio tells of the "ordinary fool" (1.5.82) against whom Feste competed, in essence, he outs Feste's freelancing practices. In an act that jeopardizes Feste's employment, Malvolio plays the tattler as well as the underling who desires the authority of the mistress. Coddon note that "Malvolio, rather than Olivia, takes offense at the fool's impudence" (317), an act that points to his self-conceptualization as "Count Malvolio" (2.5.34) rather than Steward Malvolio. For Malvolio, Feste's lack of wit is reason enough that Olivia should sever his services from her household. But, because the dismissal of a witless clown-servant falls to the master or mistress, not the steward, Malvolio apes the nobility and inflates his criticism as if in possession of the power to control household economics. He covers an indirect insult of his mistress in a master's critique of her clown-servant.

Feste's sole command of the stage as Sir Topas then as himself (in 4.2) points to the important connection between Malvolio's insults of Feste's wit and economics early in the play and Malvolio's detention that follows. Toby and Maria lock Malvolio away, but do not torment him. They seem to sate their vengeance with the beguiling letter and following custody. Feste alone is left to torture Malvolio. He aims his spirited masquerade at Malvolio's charge that he is witless and dishonest. Doubtless, the scene gave to the clown-servant actor (to Armin and later clown actors) the spotlight to enliven his torment for prior insults with indulgence in buffoonery. John H. Astington is in part concerned that Feste, having the entire platform stage to himself, 'would naturally have broadened his antics" (55). David Carnegie suggests that "another potential of keeping Malvolio out of sight is that Feste is given the entire stage for what may well have been by Shakespeare as an opportunity for bravura performance by the company clown" (412).[8] Feste's buffoonery, complete with his voice shifts and mock dialogue from Topas to himself, builds to a specific point in the scene that highlights Malvolio's earlier insult of Feste's livelihood. Particularly, the dialogue that builds to Malvolio's confession (4.2.86-96) deserves a closer look.

Malvolio confesses that his wit is equal to Feste's and he signals his surrender. When Feste departs as Topas and returns as himself, the dialogue begins with his question that broaches the topic of Malvolio's insult, wit. Feste asks: "Alas, sir, how fell you besides your five wits?" (4.2.86). Bevington identifies the five wits as "common wit, imagination, fantasy, judgment, and memory" (419), all senses that Feste uses to corrupt words into wit in both his traditional and proto-capitalist income earning, all aspects of foolery encompassed by Malvolio's insult. Malvolio's answer, "Fool, there was never a man so notoriously abused: I am as well in my wits, fool, as thou art" (4.2.87-88), places the steward on an even domestic plane of service with the clown-servant. But Malvolio's mistreatment of other domestics directly ties to his sense of superiority. Playing the devil's advocate, Feste plays to Malvolio's earlier insult, a product of his high-mindedness: "But as well? then you are mad indeed, if you be no better in your wits than a fool" (4.2.89-90). Feste not only suggests that reconciliation between clown-servant and steward is an impossibility, but also that he is ever dedicated to the demise of the steward based on their ill association in domestic service. However, from Malvolio's place of arrest, he must be at even wits with the clown-servant to move a step closer to emancipation.

Malvolio's acceptance of the comparison to Feste represents the turning point of captivity: "They have here propertied me; keep me in darkness, send ministers to me, asses, and do all they can to face me out of my wits" (4.2.91-93). It is at this point in the play that Feste gets Malvolio to recant his insult, a point at the height of Feste's buffoonery. He signals this moment of triumph by ensuring Malvolio's sincerity: "Advise you what you say; the minister is here" (4.3.94). Feste, as Sir Topas, adds the atmosphere of confession to Malvolio's declaration. Upon accepting Malvolio's defeat, Feste, in the voice of Topas, absolves Malvolio of his earlier transgression against Feste's clown-service: "Malvolio, Malvolio, thy wits the heavens restore!" (4.2.95-6). The voice shifts and mock dialogue allow Malvolio to experience Feste's full range of wit. At the play's end, the knowledge of Feste's dual role further incenses Malvolio and heightens his hasty departure.

CONCLUSION

Feste of *Twelfth Night* illustrates Shakespeare's most developed clown-servant whose entrepreneurial wit ties directly into the socioeconomic fabric of the play. Feste is the principal link between the other characters. Through his clown-services, he interacts with upstairs and downstairs characters alike yet retains his service identity and connectedness to the working class. As suggested, Feste's proto-capitalist enterprise moves away from late feudalism to show a dramatic reflection of the decline of traditional domestic economics in the play and in Elizabethan England.[9] This viewpoint examines a character who labors in a period of transition. Feste profits from both the progressive marketing of his wit and songs and traditional ties to the domestic staff of a noble household. His profits represent money gained through freelancing, money that provides the early modern poor with the capital incentive to gain material wealth, a condition that accelerates and that alters traditional household order.

In addition, Feste's wit and cash earnings constitute a proto-capitalist approach to profitable exchange of money for the contrivance of words. By linking Feste's foolery to wit and money, that is, his ability to outwit his superiors with puns, innuendo, and double entendre for cash, his foolery changes as does the value of his cash payment from the nobles that he entertains. In other words, Feste's entertainment serves the coin not the count. By the late sixteenth century, London audiences would not have missed the prospects for profit that cash offered Feste. Yet, cash not only affords Feste the money to enjoy goods and services, also it compromises his ties to faithful domestic service. At the same time, they would also understand Feste's reluctance to sever completely his ties of domestic service to Olivia's house. His freelance singing and jesting and the money he earns are economic occurrences that point to changes to customary domestic order.

Furthermore, Feste's labors within domestic late feudal order break fixed restraints on his cash income earning. He uses wit to profit from proto-capitalist monetary exchange. It is important to the play's economics that Feste accepts his class and station as a clown-servant to profit from the monetary implications of his job. He does not manage the other servants like Malvolio, tend the lawn like Fabian, or organize household stuffs like Maria. Rather, Feste is a clown-servant who commands his wit as an object of trade. He does not expect any amount of cash payment to change his occupation from clown-servant. Yet, he does earn cash profit from the talent of entertainment and the ability to outwit the nobles, money that his freelance practices add to his domestic ties of service. In this time of transition experienced by Feste and also by Shakespeare's players, his development of entrepreneurial practices must occur within an accepted late feudal atmosphere.

NOTES

—

Quotations and line numbers from Shakespeare's texts are from *The Complete Works of Shakespeare*. ed. David Bevington. (Glenview IL.: Scott, Foresman and Company, 1980).

INTRODUCTION

1. Examinations of the role of clown-servants vary. Robert Armin evaluates the roles of stage clowns and outlines various types performers and performances. David wiles traces the development of clown actors and the texts they inhabit. Wiles presents history, development, and stage histories for Tarlton, Kemp, Armin, et al. Karen Greif chronicles the stage history of *Twelfth Night's* Feste from the early modern to post modern stages.

2. I also rely on Judith Weil's interpretation of Shakespeare's wide range of the terms "serve" and "service": "Although a sizeable majority of these terms refer either to the performance of particular tasks or to functions and agencies. . . majority of his 'servant' references apply to work; only a handful appears in respectful

forms of address" (2). Weil notes that the verb "serve" usually refers to acts as an agent or to work. By far, the largest number of references to "service" also concern work, followed by polite behavior and military occupations.

3. Natasha Korda expands the definition of "household" to include not only domestic subjects (husbands, wives, children, servants, etc.), but also as domestic objects (household goods, chattel, or furniture) (1).

4. Bente A. Videbaek categorizes and evaluates Shakespeare's clown characters as rustic clowns in *Titus Andronicus*, *The Taming of the Shrew*, *Antony and Cleopatra;* servant clowns in *Romeo and Juliet*, *Othello*, *Macbeth*, *Timon of Athens*, *The Tempest*; and miscellaneous clowns in *Richard III*, *Hamlet*, *Pericles*, *Cymbeline*, *The Winter's Tale*. According to Mary Springfels in her article, "Music in Shakespeare's Plays," relatively minor characters are those who sing the songs of Shakespeare's plays: "Servants …, clowns, fools, rogues, and minor personalities" (4).

5. Immanuel Wallerstein and Andre Gunder Frank, among others, agree with Marx's statement in *Das Kapital* that dates proto-capitalism to the early modern period: "the modern history of capital dates from the creation in the 16th century of a world-embracing commerce and a world-embracing market" (*Moscow*: Progress Publishers, 1954). This book acknowledges Wallerstein's evaluation of medieval and early modern economies in terms of proto-capitalist forces: "Many of these [previous] historical systems had what we might call

proto-capitalist elements. That is, there often was extensive commodity production. There existed producers and traders who sought profit. There was investment of capital" (35).

Michel Beaud depicts the economic climate that primed Elizabethan England for entrepreneurial endeavor: "Thus in the sixteenth century the conditions for the future development of capitalism were put into place," . . . "banking and merchant bourgeoisies having at their disposal both immense fortunes and banking and financial networks; national states having available the means of conquest and domination; and a conception of the world which valued wealth and enrichment. It is in this sense only that one can date the capitalist era as beginning in the sixteenth century" (23).

6. My study takes as a point of departure Paul Delany and his view of "cultural superstructure" within the transition from feudal to capitalist. This approach allows Delany to evaluate the emergence of the bourgeoisie and the wane of feudalism in both *King Lear* and in Elizabethan England. I apply Delany study to this transition to emphasize the shift in approach from legal and political discourse to analysis of service relationships and domestic economics.

7. For earlier studies on the 16th century origin of "feudal order (or feodalité), see J. G. A. Pocock's work on the history of England from the Middle Ages through the 17th century. D. R. Kelly's historical research examines feudal order from a legal perspective.

8. Kate Mertes notes that by the 16th century, "extensive enclosures had begun to eat away at wasteland which an expanding peasant population could have colonized" (119). As early as 1548, Edward VI saw the emerging economic dilemma in the decay of houses and husbandry as a direct threat to the family (Korda 160). Where once "diverse families in work and labor" dwelled as, "faithful subjects" who might serve both God and the King, now "into one or two men's hands" fall these lands and have thereby brought the realm "to marvelous desolation, houses decayed, and parishes diminished" (246).

9. Consequently, to approach feudalism as an economic society leads to questions of historical economic development: If the urban middle class of medieval Europe is said to have begun its notorious career as early as the 10th century, why was it not until the 17th and 18th centuries that this class became the dominant force in society (Hilton 195)? Why did it take 700 years to reach this position if during the whole period it was 'rising" (195)? This study accepts that the most important pre-condition for the development of capitalist industry is the "concentration of moneyed wealth" (198). The shift from "labor rent" to "money rent" illustrates that peasants worked for themselves rather than for nobles and were able to accumulate wealth through "retail trading" and capitalist farming (135, 198).

10. Heather Dubrow's chapter, "'No Place To Fly To': Loss Of Dwellings" gives a detailed analysis of vagrancy in relation to homelessness. Dubrow offers social economic as well as literary examples of weakening feudal order that led to

an exponential population increase in London. Helpful are Dubrow's oscillations between literary texts and Elizabethan life to illustrate the complexities of homelessness on social interactions among people of differing classes.

11. The Act for the Punishment of Vagabonds states: "All & every person and persons beynge whole and mightye in Body and able to labour, having not Land or Master, nor using any lawful Merchandise, Craft or Mystery whereby he or she might get his or her living, and can give no reckoning how he or she doth lawfully get his or her living; and all Fencers, BearWards, Common Players in Interludes and Minstrels, not belonging to any Baron of this Realm or towards any other honourable Personage of greater Degree... shall be taken adjudged and deemed Rogues, Vagabonds and Sturdy Beggars" (Gurr 19).

12. Early in the twentieth century, Frederick Warde evaluates Feste of *Twelfth Night* as an itinerate beggar, rather than as a proto-capitalist entrepreneur, an evaluation made popular in more recent Shakespeare studies. By emphasizing beggary rather than profit-driven marketing, Warde, A.C. Bradley, Robert Hills Goldsmith, and others restrict Shakespeare's servant-clowns from the economic actions of their plays. However, proto-capitalist shifts in the economy caused Elizabethans to redefine beggary.

13. In terms of mercantilism, Hilton suggests that "it is only when capital 'takes hold of production' that merchant's and usurer's capital becomes subordinate to industrial capital, and only then that it becomes possible to speak

of a capitalist 'mode of production'" (198).

14. This study views the term "mercantilism" as it applies to the movement of money on national and global levels. Richard T. Gray, in "Buying into Signs" argues that the "mercantilist theory of monetary circulation," consistent with the transformation of money from "substantial" to "functional," downplays the significance of money as a commodity, and began to see it as a stimulator of trade, commerce, and exchange" (98-9).

15. Lacey Baldwin Smith offers an overview of Londoners' reactions to crime, vagrancy, and beggary to paint vivid pictures of urban life. Smith describes a rough intersection of late feudal expectations and the reality of a changing economy: "Beggars were a common sight [in London]; Officials whose duty was to check crime often aided it . . . 'Proper' citizens reacted in two quite different ways. They passed more laws and harsher ones: some two hundred crimes warranted a death penalty. The other reaction was surprisingly humane: poor laws were passed requiring each parish to provide work for the able-bodied" (21).

16. John Astington joins the views of J. Leeds Barroll on the relationships between actors and patrons coupled with William Ingram's view on conditions in the mid sixteenth century. Astington posits that "The function of a nominal patronage which served as official protection for the commercial career of actors has often been commented on in histories of Elizabethan theater, and the tropes which bore royal names, as all major companies did after 1603, were no different in any essential

respect from those patronized by the nobility" (6). Astington makes the point that the business of playacting, from the players' perspectives, continued to be a mixture of itinerate playhouse performances and infrequent royal performances.

17. I view that in the spirit of dramatic production, Elizabethan players took advantage of performing in the most elaborate venues, that royal theaters complemented the aesthetics of theatrical performance. Astington comments: "The result was that the court was seeing the best—presumably—of the dynamic professional theater of London, as if, in the 1970s, the Royal Shakespeare and National Companies were to have played several of their best production of the year for a few nights of command performances at Buckingham Palace" (109).

18. M. D. Jardine expresses the limitations of studying early modern English patronage as a synecdoche of national unity and British absolutism (287). I operate under Jardine's caution against accepting Elizabethan drama as mere monarchal propaganda in order to evaluate the business of theater in relation to Elizabethan market economies.

19. Andrew Gurr argues that, with the advent of public playhouses, "Whereas when traveling the players could sustain themselves with the same play repeated in constantly changing venues, once the venue was fixed, the repertory had to keep changing. As the chief determinant of this novelty there had to be an intimate interaction between the settled expectations of playgoers and the fare they fed on. The result was a constant,

pressurized evolution in the players' repertoire of plays, a kind of aesthetic Darwinism" (115).

20. The act of playing produces the "commodity" of the play with several marketable qualities: it seeks to entertain, to induce pleasure, to offer something suitable, advantageous and timely on a particular and convenient occasion; and it benefits both parties, bringing entertainment to its audiences and financial gain to the players (*Company* 43).

21. This discussion of lawful "public" theater and patronage does not negate the problem of unregulated patrons and unlicensed players in the 1590s. I view unregulated patrons and unlicensed players as a commercial response to market demands. Regulation of proto-capitalist theater fosters the existence of an unregulated theatrical underground, a means of profit for actors and patrons without the taxation of licensing.

22. Roslyn Lander Knutson notes that players who were freemen of their respective guilds include John Alleyn (innholder), James Burbage (joiner), Robert Armin (goldsmith), Ben Jonson (bricklayer), and Richard Tarlton (vintner) (22). The company affiliations of these men include Admiral's/Strange's Men, 1589, Alleyn; Chamberlain's Men, 1594, Burbage and Armin; Pembroke's Men, 1597, Jonson; Queen's Men, 1583, Tarlton (22).

23. For example, owner and guilded grocer John Brayne, not completely distraught with the financial failure of the Red Lion playhouse, accepted the proposal of his brother-in-law, James Burbage to build and profit-share in the Theater (Knutson 22). In addition, Philip Henslowe, dyer,

used his business skill to construct and operate the Rose; and Oliver Woodliffe, haberdasher, assembled a partnership that later financed construction of the Boar's Head in 1598 (22).

24. Knutson directly relates the artistic triumphs of Elizabethan playing companies to the commercial practices of "cluster marketing" and instances of companies playing together (38). In *A Midsummer Night's Dream*, Shakespeare depicts guildsmen players who produce *Pyramus and Thisby* without regard to their respective crafts.

25. Knutson suggests economic factors rather than social feuding played a greater part in the development of playing companies. Based on the notions that *Histrio-mastix* was not played at a commercial playhouse, the little eyases passage in *Hamlet* is unrelated to the War of the Theaters of 1600-1601, and *Poetaster* and *Satiromastix* endorse the business of playing (22-3).

26. I assert that the joint efforts of playing companies signal a greater shift towards proto-capitalism and breaks from Knutson's view that deems joint efforts as retro-feudal.

27. Henslowe's records show that the Admiral's Men played the provinces with the following companies: " Ipswich, 7 August 1592, with Darby's Men; York, April 1593, with Morley's Players; Newcastle, May 1593, with Morley's players; Shrewsbury, sometimes after 24 July 1593, with Strange's Men; and Bath, 1593-4, with Lord Norris's players" (HD 276) (qtd. in Knutson 23-4).

28. This book works from the premise that the Elizabethan clown was directly influenced by the Vice of the English stage. Wiles points out

that "the Tudor Vice traditionally had the task of mediating between play and audience, breaking down the boundary between them. The Vice's descendant, the clown, retained this function. It was his task to lead the audience out of the play and into a different type of entertainment in which vigorous participation was expected" (55).

29. Italian influence on Tudor and Stuart drama may be limited to specific playwrights and characters like the clown-servant Nimble in *Thomas of Woodstock*. Quick wit and horseplay like tumbling were just as much a part of the English fair and surrounding country-life as they were dramatic arts of the Italian Renaissance.

30. Olive Mary Busby acknowledges the resemblances between the Italian zanni and English stage clowns, yet notes that similarities moreso may result from parallel development (22).

31. David Wiles notes the absence of pictured court jesters wearing motley and cockscomb outfits in the sixteenth century (183). He cites Thomas More's fool, Will Somers of Henry VIII, and Armin as instances of standard livery as the clown's uniform in relation to the accolade of the fool coat worn on occasion. However, if we accept Robert Armin's Foole upon Foole, or, Six Sortes of Sottes (1600) that describes natural fool Jack Oates' as "motley his wearing, yellow or else greene, a collores coate on him was seldome seene . . . ," then we must accept Wiles' uses of the term motley as parti-colored (Hotson 8).

32. "As it was sundty [sic] times publiquely acted in the honourable citie of London, by the right Honourable the Lord Strange his Seruants."

London: Printed [by J. Haviland] for Iohn Wright, and are to be sold at his shop at the signe of the Bible in Guilt-spur street without New-gate, 1631.

33. In his opening soliloquy, Launcelot reasons: "I should be ruled by the fiend, who, saving your reverence, is the devil himself" (2.2.23-4).

CHAPTER I

1. On the meaning of a star, Phillip Vannini uses the term "commodified personae" to refer to stars and celebrities of current popular culture. This study treats a commodified personae as one that is subject to ready exchange or exploitation within a market such as stars as individuals and as *commodities* of the film industry (Merriam-Webster).

2. According to Marx, the commodity has a dual character. Commodity is a use-value (*Gebrauchswert*), a "thingly" existence that allows its exchange. Commodity is also a value (*Wert*), the amount of work needed to produce the object, the "thingly." For Igor Kopytoff, a commodity is a thing that has use value and can be exchanged, transacted for a counterpart, a thing that can be bought for money, and/or a thing with salability (68-9). I add to Kopytoff's Marxist notion of commodity, Christopher B. Balme's theatrical criticism. Balme examines Marxist commodity theory in relation to political economies and applies it to theater economics. His view of the human actor as a commodity, as a thing of trade together with objects, theatrical properties, allows this study to apply notions

of commodities and marketing to human actors and the characters that they portray.

3. This more general use of the term "commodity" has reached current criticism by such critics as Max Thomas and Mary Bly.

4. The observation of that lineage of the stage clowns resides in the tradition of the court fool does not negate the influences of country rusticity. David Wiles notes that according to the writings of Robert Armin, Richard Tarlton was a seminal influence in the development of Shakespeare's clowns who "studied real rustic simpletons to create his own clown character". Wiles points out that "modern clowns prefer to copy Tarlton's counterfeit rather than real jest. By "counterfeit jests," Wiles' refers to the theater and dramatic performance as opposed to "real jests" by country simpletons.

5. By the terms familial association, I refer to the court practice of maintaining the status and daily necessities of the clown-servant without the direct payment of a wage or commodities to be exchanged for profit.

6. Perhaps a current example of this cycle of commodity development is the production and marketing of the popular soda Coca Cola, from "Coke," to "New Coke," back to "Classic Coke." Nonetheless, like the development of "Will Summer," the characterized clown-servant, Coca Cola, the product, retains integral characteristics that allow it to be recognized as the soda, Coke.

7. *Misogonus* was written by the year 1577, but a likely production date is 1564. Categorized as a University play, *Misogonus* was a Cambridge

play and was prepared for performance at
Cambridge by Cambridge students (Barber, L 26).

8.   Richard Bond notes that *Misogonus* indeed
     affords us a most life like representation of
     English rural life and gives us, too, the earliest
     known dramatic reflection of the institution
     of the domestic English fool (xxvi).

9.   In reference to Will Summer in *Summer's Last
     Will and Testament*, C.L. Barber discusses "the
     role fancifully assigned to the Ghost of Will
     Summer, Henry VIII's famous fool, whose name
     was a by-word for jesters" (61). When viewed
     through economic lenses, the by-words Will
     Summer take on the commodified connotation
     of a brand name product representative of a
     service (theatre) that is exchanged for a fee.

10. According to Southworth, Somer's contemporaries
     relished him as more than a "token court natural"
     maintained through alms, capable only of
     miniscule tasks and rewards of kindness (70-1).

11. Bevington notes that "Beneath God , the
     hierarchy is as follows: angelic creatures (pure
     intelligence), man (intelligence and "sense,"
     or instinct, or feeling), animals (sense), plants
     (growth but no sense), inorganic matter (mere
     existence), and finally chaos. Within the given
     rank, there are sub- hierarchies: just as God
     is the highest spiritual being, so the sun is the
     chief planet, the king is the chief human being,
     man is the superior of woman, the lion is the
     king of beasts, gold is the best metal" (29).

12. Noteworthy, the symbol of bacon as a commodity
     that acts as a monetary source is later repeated by
     Launcelot Gobbo in Shakespeare's *Merchant*: "This

making Christians will raise the price of hogs: if we grow all to be pork-eaters, we shall not shortly have a rasher on the coals for money" (4.5.21-24).

13. In his chapter, "Warrior Fools," Southworth traces the "truth-telling function" of the fool from Greek and Hellenistic origins through the Middle Ages, with emphases on the influences of religions and the court.

14. Roeckelein reviews the origins of the pun, with emphasis on types of puns and examples of their usages (64-6).

15. David Wiles's chapter "The Vice: from *Mankind to Merchant of Venice*" poignantly asserts that the stage clown's ancestry is firmly planted in the Tudor Vice. He further asserts that an examination of the Vice tradition of the early modern English morality plays is central to understanding the clown's role on the Elizabethan stage (1).

16. In the "The First Fytte" of *A Gest Of Robyn Hode*, Robyn is a outcast yeoman (or knight) who maintains feudal order and decorum. The tale tells that he is "a gode yeman" (in line 12) even though "bisshoppes and these archebishoppes, [he and his men] "bete and bynde" (57-8). These acts illustrate the feudal hierarchy that he maintains with his men in light of the anti-feudal economic practices of wealth redistribution. In terms of service, Richard Almond and A. J. Pollard suggest that "The Middle English word, probably derived from *yongman* or *yongerman*, began to be used in the fourteenth century as a translation of 'valet'. Valet was the rank of service, and 'yeoman' continued to be employed in this sense throughout the fifteenth

century. It was an indicator of a stage in a career, the stage through which a young man in service passed on the way to becoming a squire" (52). But during the early modern period, when contempories complained that servants like Cacurgus did not know their place anymore, the term yeoman came to cover diverse socioeconomic groups (52).

17. The clown-servant enjoys elevated servant status that keeps him in the company of nobles while at the same he is a domestic servant and must interact as a servant with other servants. Cacurgus accomplishes a great feat for a servant by convincing the master of his natural insanity.

18. Armin notes that "There was in the time of Will Sommers, another artificiall Foole or Iester in the Court, whose subtiltie heapt vp wealth by gifts giuen him, for which Will Sommers could neuer abide him. This Iester was a big man of a great voyce, long black locks, & a very big round beard: on a time (of purpose) Will Sommers watcht to disgrace him, when he was iugling & iesting before the King. Will Sommers brings vp a messe of milk and a manchet, Harry saies hee lend me a spoone: Foole saies the Iester, vse thy hands. The King, the Iester and all gathers about him to see him eat it. Will begins thus to rime ouer his milke: *This bit Harry I giue to thee, & this next bit must serue for me, both which Ile eate apace: This bit Madame vnto you, and this bit I my selfe eat now, and all the rest vpon thy face.* Meaning the foole, in whose beard & head the bread and milk was thick sowne, & his eyes almost put out. Will Sommers he gets him gone for feare. This lusty iester forgetting himself, in fury drawes

his dagger, & begings to protest: nay sayes the King, are ye so hate, claps him fast, & though hee drawes his dagger here, yet let him put it vp in another place. The poore abused Iester, was Iested out of countenance, and lay in durance a great while, till Will Sommers was faine (after he had broken his head to giue him a plaister) to get him out againe: but neuer after came my Iuggler in the Court more, so neere the King, being such a dangerous man to draw in the presence of the King" (46-7).

19. R.J. (Richard J) Schoeck's work makes clear similarities between English Renaissance clowns and mid-twentieth century comedians: "Where the medieval fools on the whole remain anonymous, the Renaissance men in motley acquired something of the notoriety of a Hollywood comedian" (506).

In "Last Laugh, The," *Entertainment Weekly Magazine* describes George Carlin "the rabble-rousing, button-pounding comic has been working the circuit since the '60s, when his antiestablishment tirades made him one of the country's most talked-about talents. His legendary Seven Words You Can Never Say on Television bit is still a censor's worst nightmare--and even more relevant in a post-nipplegate universe--and crowds still flock to hear Carlin rant, rail, and mock every little thing that irks him. WHY WE LEFT HIM OFF in the hall of fame, no doubt, but his stuff hasn't been fresh since the Carter administration" (43).

Gallagher does not rely exclusively on props for

his comedy. Large portions of his shows feature Gallagher simply speaking to the audience on a variety of topics, displaying a wry observational wit and sharply pointed social commentary ("Leo Gallagher").

20. For performance dating, see E.K. (Edmund Kerchever) Chambers (327). *The Famous Victories of Henry V* with the Queen's Men was performed between at the Curtain, the Bell, and the Bull. Dericke is also referred to as "the Clowne," so this was evidently Richard Tarleton's part when the play was acted by the Queen's company in the 'eighties (Ward 274).

21. In King John, the Bastard reasons: "And why rail I on this Commodity? But for because he hath not woo'd me yet: Not that I have the power to clutch my hand, When his fair angels would salute my palm; But for my hand, as unattempted yet, Like a poor beggar, raileth on the rich. Well, whiles I am a beggar, I will rail And say there is no sin but to be rich; And being rich, my virtue then shall be To say there is no vice but beggary. Since kings break faith upon commodity, Gain, be my lord, for I will worship thee" (2.1.587-98).

22. Alexandra Halasz's work on the celebrity of Tarlton offers a multi-dimensional study of Tarlton's sixteenth century "Star" quality. Interestingly, Halasz situates her study of Tarlton's celebrity among modern theories and concepts of Motion Picture stardom within the Marxist notion of labor. Halasz asserts that as a star, Tarlton personifies the agency of labor power as opposed to the personification of capital in owners or monopolists that Marx discusses in *Capital*. In

addition, Halasz differentiates between Tarlton's theatrical and literary careers and cites the former as representative of star quality since it is Tarlton's theatrical fame that commodifies his name.

23. Goldsmith notes these similarities between Vice and stage fool in regard to ancient Greek drama, Shakespeare, and early twentieth century television. I assert that these eras of drama all share some degree of commodification (19).

24. According to Robert Weimann, "The Elizabethan platform stage--far from constituting a unified representational space—can itself be said to have provided two different, although not rigidly opposed, modes of authorizing dramatic discourse. One, the *locus*, was associated with the localizing capacities of the fictional role and tended to privilege the authority of what and who was *represented* in the dramatic world; the other, the *platea*, being associated instead with the actor and the neutral materiality of the platform stage, tended to privilege the authority of what and who was representing that world" (409).

25. Paul Slack points out that " by the end of the sixteenth century, London urban surveys begin to distinguish laboring householders who did not earn enough to pay for the upkeep of their families from able bodied men who failed to maintain gainful employment" (27).

26. By the late sixteenth century, notes Slack "they ['poor able labouring folk'] were much closer to the mainstream of society. Cobler represents an image of the poor of the late feudal period in England as no longer a marginal subset of the general poor (28).

Chapter II

1. According to David Bevington, the First Folio of 1623 is the earliest known edition of *The Comedy of Errors* and *The Two Gentlemen of Verona*. *The Comedy of Errors* is first mentioned on Innocents Day, December 28, 1594, when "Comedy of Errors (like to *Plautus* his *Menechmus*)" was performed by professional actors as a part of the Christmas Revel at Gray's Inn. Frances Meres' list dates *Two Gentlemen* in 1598 (Bevington 1611, 1613).

2. Charles Wells points out the following: "In the Roman plays together, Shakespeare employs some thirty-five servants, putting into their mouths more than 800 lines of text. These figures do not take into account the even broader category of 'follower' which, if included, would of course increase the figure very substantially" (142).

3. As discussed in Chapter 1, the English court, with Henry VIII as its monarchial head, is a macrocosmic household in relation to male householders and their more humble early modern homes as microcosmic households.

4. According to Korda, "These projects spurred expanded domestic production and consumption of a 'bewildering variety' of commodities beyond the staple necessities of life, including glass, iron, copper, and brass wares, stockings (of worsted, jersey, and silk), buttons, pins starch, soap, fine knives handles, liquorice, tobacco, tobacco pipes, pottery, ribbons, gold and silver thread, lace, linen, toys, new lighter 'draperies' (bays, tufted taffeties, cloth of tissue, wrought velvets, braunched satins,

silks, etc.), and 'innumerable fashion goods for women,' including ruffs, masks, busks, muffs, fans, periwigs, bodkins, and gloves" (Korda 17).

5. I stress Speed's proto-capitalist economy as the clownish interplay of words and logic to expand his workload.

6. According to Battelle: Consumer zones are areas of emerging value where changes converge to create particularly rich opportunities for consumer value. They will occur when new technologies and products meet marketplace trends and changing consumer behavior to create exceptional value for consumers (pars. 5). I suggest that the early modern theater was a consumer zone of new and innovative performance, marketed as indoor entertainment for a fee.

7. In *The Comedy of Errors*, the theme of hair's relation to wit begins the running of a comic gag that reappears in *Two Gentlemen of Verona*. Launce says: "Him we go to find: there's not a hair on's head but 'tis a Valentine" (3.1.190-191); 'Item: She hath more hair than wit, and more faults than hairs, and more wealth than faults' (3.1.345-346). In *Twelfth Night*, Sir Toby remarks that the witless Sir Andrew has "an excellent head of hair" (1.3.94).

8. For examples, E. Dromio (*Errors*) pairs with the kitchen wench, Launce (*Two Gentlemen*) with the milkmaid, and Launcelot Gobbo (*Merchant*) with the pregnant Moor. It is the most economically progressive of Shakespeare's clown-servants, Feste (*Twelfth Night*), whose plot is without the carry-over of domestic arrangements for the clown-servant.

9. In Shakespeare's comedies, proto-capitalist

clown-servants often develop their advisory qualities throughinteractions with female masters (mistresses). For example, these are some service bonds between female masters and clown-servant: Launcelot Gobbo/Jessica (*Merchant of Venice*), Lavatch/ Countess of Rousillon, and Feste/Olivia (*Twelfth Night*).

10. The natural "green world" found in *A Midsummer Night's Dream* and *As You Like It* stands in dramatic opposition to court life in these plays. Rather, this study approaches the forest of the fifth act as a reflection of social economic tensions evident in early modern London and not what Ronald R. Macdonald views as "anachronism" in an "unlikely band of outlaws" (20):
There's not a man I meet but doth salute me
As if I were their well-acquainted friend;
And everyone doth call me by my name.
Some tender me money, some invite me;
Some other give me thanks for kindness
Some offer me commodities to buy.
Even now the tailor called me in his shop
And showed me silks that he had bought for me.
(IV.iii.1-8)

11. By viewing *The Comedy of Errors* as a farce, I argue that the humor arises from attempts to re-establish identities that have been previously blurred by social economic change

12. To generate a sense of social economic harmony, E. Antipholus strives for the identity of both master of   and of the household. When S. Antipholus is mistaken constantly for E. Antipholus in the Ephesian Mart, his recollection paints an accurate picture

of E. Dromio's local economic stature:
There's not a man I meet but doth salute me
As if I were their well-acquainted friend;
And everyone doth call me by my name.
Some tender me money, some invite me;
Some other give me thanks for kindness
Some offer me commodities to buy.
Even now the tailor called me in his shop
And showed me silks that he had bought for me.
(IV.iii.1-8)

Unknown to S. Antipholus, these monies and
commodities of conspicuous consumption bolster
the reputation of E. Antipholus, consumption that
must highlight his late feudal domestic status in
the town to reinforce his household economics.
Although he strives without success to master the
Mart, his future marriage to the kitchen wench will
begin his own domestic hierarchy.

13. E. Dromio's beatings: (I.ii.92-3) [Beats him],
    (I.ii.46) [The clock hath strucken/My mistress
    made it one upon my cheek] (IV.iii.17-18)
    [Beats him], and (IV.iii.43-4) [Beats him].
    E. Dromio's threats of beating: (I.i.65), (II.i.77),
    (II.i.79), and (III.ii.21-2).
    S. Dromio's beating: (II.ii.23-4) [Beats him].
    S. Dromio's treats of beating: (II.ii.219).

14. Gurr views "Singing Simkin" as either "Kemp's
    newe jygge betwixt, a souldiour and a Miser and
    Sym the clown' or a very close resemblance (114).

15. Shakespeare uses "dog" or "dogs" over two
    hundred times in his works. He also was the first
    writer to use the compound noun "watchdog"
    in *The Tempest* (I.ii.390) (About Shakespeare).

16. References to dogs as bread servants continue later in *Timon of Athens* in the form of Lord Lucullus's conditional gift of greyhounds to Timon. The gift and reception of the dogs continue to illustrate expectations of service relationships.

CHAPTER 3

1. It is only in the face of this already occurring feudal change that cash exchange and other forms of proto-capitalist change took hold. For as Rodney Hilton points out, "Unfortunately, for the advocates of the money-as-solvent theory, cash scutage is found as early as the beginning of the 12th century, and money fiefs not much later . . . Nor did big cash incomes transform the behaviour of the feudal ruling class . . . If anything, it was the declining cash incomes of the feudal aristocracy, which was the first symptom of the end of the feudal mode of production; for these incomes to the end represented peasant surplus, coercively extracted, and their diminution was the monetary sign of the failing grip of the aristocratic domination of the old type. The solvent qualities of money only came into operation once the holistic processes of the dissolution of the feudal modes of production were well under way" (217).

2. Walter Cohen states: "To the English, and particularly to Londoners, Venice represented a more advanced stage of commercial development than they themselves were experiencing" (*"Merchant"* 50). G. K. Hunter states of Jacobean theater that "Italy became important to English dramatists only when 'Italy' was revealed

as an aspect of England" (95). C.L. Barber
notes that "despite the terrible suffering some
sections of society were experiencing, the 1590s
were a period when London was becoming
conscious of itself as wealthy and cultivated,
so that it could consider great commercial
Venice as prototype" (*Merchant* 207).

3. An inevitable connection according to Karl
   Marx who states: "life is not determined
   by consciousness, but consciousness
   by life" (Marx and Engels 155).

4. Here, I quibble over Mentz's twice applied term
   "debate" to Launcelot's opening soliloquy (180,
   181). The term "debate suggests the possibility
   of triumph and defeat for both side. I suggest
   that Launcelot has already decided to run and
   what we the audience hear and see is a character
   berating half of his consciousness for even
   suggesting that he remain with the Jew. For more
   on Launcelot's soliloquy as inner debate, see
   John Scott Colley, "Launcelot, Jacob, and Esau:
   Old and New Law in *The Merchant of Venice.*"
   Colley works from a biblical parallel of Jacob and
   Launcelot's family struggles concerning money.

5. A gambling card-game, very fashionable
   from about 1530 to about 1640, in which
   four cards were dealt to each player, each
   card having thrice its ordinary value.

6. See Susan McLean for analysis of Bassanio
   as a Prodigal Son and the social, economic,
   and religious ramifications of "thrift"
   or "profit" on other characters (5).

7. Of risk, Mentz states that "His [Launcelot's]
   confusion about whether he will stay with

Shylock or seek more speculative employment with Bassanio parallels other risky economic decisions in the play: like Bassano he will trust himself to one desperate throw, and like Antonio he will place himself in potentially dangerous bondage, in this case to a poor master" (180-181).

8. Psalm 12 states: 1. Help, LORD; for the godly man ceaseth; for the faithful fail from among the children of men. 2. They speak vanity every one with his neighbour: with flattering lips and with a double heart do they speak. 3. The LORD shall cut off all flattering lips, and the tongue that speaketh proud things: 4. Who have said, With our tongue will we prevail; our lips are our own: who is lord over us? 5. For the oppression of the poor, for the sighing of the needy, now will I arise, saith the LORD; I will set him in safety from him that puffeth at him. 6. The words of the LORD are pure words: as silver tried in a furnace of earth, purified seven times. 7. Thou shalt keep them, O LORD, thou shalt preserve them from this generation for ever. 8. The wicked walk on every side, when the vilest men are exalted (*King James Bible*).

9. Catherine Belsey argues: "The Prince of Aragon thinks of his own desert, and the silver casket acts as a mirror of his narcissism, revealing the portrait of a blinking idiot" (143). Mackenzie says that "The silver casket is selected by the Prince of Aragon, another foreigner and one who also emphasizes that his mission is one entirely committed to the will of fortune" (198). He reasons that a man who sets out bravely to "cozen [beguile] fortune" (II.ix.36) deserves reward. Aragon's fault is that he is arrogant, an overconfidence that takes priority over his business sense. He displays an

economic notion that meritocracy should discern the haves from the have-nots and deems himself most deserving of Portia based his own merit.

10. I share Japtok and Schleienr's uneasiness in projecting modern meanings of words like "race" into the early modern period (169). Emily C. Bartels notes that "Critics have been hesitant to ascribe racism to early modern culture, in large part because the idea of race and homosexuality seemed poorly formed at best" (9). Once these anxieties are acknowledged, Bartles states: "Racism, homophobia, xenophobia, and the like, though they did not have a local habitation or name, had their beginnings here, with cross-cultural and domestic discourse whose uncertainties amplified difference, allowing the self to impose its terms of supremacy on the world, over the alien abroad and the alien at home" (9).

11. The Italian physician Hercole Sassonia (or Saxonia) in his *Luis venereae perfectissimus tractatus* (1597) writes: "But one needs to inquire into what I have heard was experienced by some people in Venice: they claim to have been cured instantly of gonorrhea by having intercourse with a black woman [*mulier Aethiopis*]. The *experimentum* is true and it seems can be confirmed by [Julius Caesar] Scaliger's *exercitatio* 180, c. 18, according to whom Africans are cured from lues venereal by sleeping with a Numidian or Ethiopian woman" (Sassonia c. 37, fol. 40).

CHAPTER 4

1. The hood does not make the monk.

2. David Schalkwyk notes in recent analysis of love and service that "*Twelfth Night* is as much a study of service and master-servant relations as it is a comedy of romantic love . . . Every instance of desire in the play is intertwined with service" (86-7).

3. In *All's Well That End's Well*, the Countess of Rossillion inherits the Count's aged clown-servant Lavatch who offers a Feste-like verbal wit. Feste's claim for the omnipotence of "foolery" echoes in Lavatch's "Oh Lord, Sir! Spare not me" (2.2.49), an attempt to coin a single answer of foolery for situations of socioeconomic disparities between masters and servants.

4. There are at least seven dramatic instances in which scripting directs that characters [Give money] as payment to Feste for his entertainment: from Sir Toby for singing/jesting (2.2.31-2), from Sir Andrew for singing/jesting (2.2.33), from Duke Orsino for singing (2.4.69), twice from Viola (Cesario) for witty word-play (3.1.43, 53), from Sebastian as an acknowledgement of his perceived station of clown-service (4.1.18), and twice from Duke Orsino from witty word-play (5.1.25, 32).

5. Ben Kingsley comments on playing the role of Feste: "I think there is something Shamanistic about Feste . . . he seems to have been given by the author more than his fair share of knowledge about what's going on. His powers of observation are very acute. He can probably walk into any room and within seconds know how to play the room because of the various flaws, arrogances, and bits of narcissism that are in that room" (Schwartz pars. 4, 2).

6. Curio tells Orsino that "Feste the jester . . . a fool that the lady Olivia's father took much delight in (2.4.12). Following Feste's witty response he claims to "know them well" (5.1.9).

7. In Act 4 scene (*Malvolio within*), the steward attempts to enlist Feste's assistance in return for the promise that he will use his stewardship to Feste's benefit rather than to his demise as in the past. Malvolio pleads: Good fool, as ever thou wilt deserve well at my hand, help me to a candle, and pen, ink and paper: as I am a gentleman, I will live to be thankful to thee for't. (4.2.80-3)

1. Yet, it must be noted that Malvolio need only be out of Feste's line of sight not necessarily out of the audience's sight. The scene has been staged differently by different production companies. For example, in 1995, the Bell Shakespeare Company sets Malvolio visible through the mesh of a rubbish dumpster and threatened by an unseen Feste atop the container (Carnegie fig. 7. 404).

2. It is only in the face of this already occurring feudal change that cash exchange and other forms of proto-capitalist change took hold. For as Rodney Hilton points out, "Unfortunately, for the advocates of the money-as-solvent theory, cash scutage is found as early as the beginning of the 12th century, and money fiefs not much later . . . Nor did big cash incomes transform the behaviour of the feudal ruling class . . . If anything, it was the declining cash incomes of the feudal aristocracy, which was the first symptom of the end of the feudal mode of production; for these incomes to the end represented peasant surplus,

coercively extracted, and their diminution was the monetary sign of the failing grip of the aristocratic domination of the old type. The solvent qualities of money only came into operation once the holistic processes of the dissolution of the feudal modes of production were well under way" (217).

WORKS CITED

Adelman, Janet. "Her Father's Blood: Race, Conversion, and Nation in *The Merchant of Venice*." *Representations* 81. (Winter 2003): 4-30.

Adler, Moshe. "Stardom and Talent." *The American Economic Review* 75.1 (Mar., 1985): 208-212.

Agnew, Jean-Christophe. *Worlds Apart: The Market And The Theater In Anglo-American Thought, 1550-1750*. Cambridge: Cambridge UP, 1986.

Ajzenstat, Samuel. "Contract in *The Merchant of Venice*." *Philosophy and Literature*. 21.2 (1997): 262-278.

Anderson, Linda. *A Place in the Story: Servants and Service in Shakespeare's Plays*.Newark: Delaware UP, 2005.

Angelo, Sidney. "The Court Revels of Henry VII." *Bulletin of the John Rylands Library* 43 (1960-61): 12-45.

Armin, Robert. *A Nest of Ninnies*. T. E. for Iohn Deane. 1608.

_ _ _.*Fools and Jesters With A Reprint Of Robert Armin's Nest Of Ninnies, 1608, With An Introduction and Notes*. London: Printed for the Shakespeare society, 1842.

Arnold, Janet. *Queen Elizabeth's Wardrobe Unlock'd: The Inventories Of The Wardrobe Of Robes Prepared In July 1600, Edited From Stowe MS 557 In The British Library,*

MS LR 2/121 In The Public Record Office, London, And MS V.B.72 In The Folger Shakespeare Library, Washington DC. Leeds: Maney, 1988.

Astington, John, H. *English Court Theater 1558-1642.* Cambridge, New York: Cambridge UP, 1999.

Baines, Edward. *Baines's Account of the Woolen Manufacture of England.* New York: Augustus M. Kelly, 1970.

Balme, Christopher B. "Selling the Bird: Richard Walton Tully's The Bird of Paradise

and the Dynamics of Theatrical Commodification." *Theatre Journal* 57.1 (2005): 1-20.

Barber, C. L. (Cesar Lombardi). "The Merchant and the Jew of Venice: Wealth's Communion and an Intruder." In *Modern Shakespearean Criticism: Essays on Style, Dramaturgy, and the Major Plays.* Ed. Alvin B. Kernan. New York: Harcourt, Brace & World, 1970.

_ _ _ . *Shakespeare's Festive Comedy: A Study Of Dramatic Form and Its Relation To Social Custom.* Princeton, N.J.: Princeton UP, 1959.

Barber, C. L., and Richard P Wheeler. *The Whole Journey: Shakespeare's Power Of Development.* Berkeley: California UP, 1986.

Barber, Lester E. *Misogonus: Edited with Introduction.* New York: Garland, 1979.

Barnet, Sylvan. *The Complete Works of Shakespeare.* Harcourt Brace Jovanovich, 1972.

Barry, Jonathan. "Bourgeois Collectivism? Urban Association and the Middling Sort." In *The Middling Sort of People: Culture, Society, and Politics in England, 1550-1800.* Eds. Jonathan Barry and Christopher Brooks. New York: St. Martin's, 1994.

Bartels, Emily C. *Spectacles of Strangeness: Imperialism,*

Alienation and Marlowe Philadelphia: Pennsylvania UP, 1993.

Baskervill, C. R. *The Elizabethan Jig and Related Song and Drama*. Chicago: Chicago UP, 1929.

Battelle. "Battelle Predicts Future Consumer Value Zones." *The Chief Engineer*. 3 May, 2007. <http://www.chiefengineer.org/content/content_display.cfm/seqnumber_content/2474.htm>.

Beaud, Michel. *A History of Capitalism 1500-1980*. Trans. Tom Dickman and Anny Lefebvre. New York: Monthly Review, 1983.

Belsey, Catharine. "Love in Venice." *New Casebook: The Merchant of Venice*. Ed. Martin Coyle. New York: St Martin's, 1998.

Bentley, Gerald Eades. *The Profession Of Player In Shakespeare's Time 1590-1642*. Princeton, N.J.: Princeton UP, 1984.

Berry, Ralph. *Shakespeare and the Awareness of Audience*. London: Macmillan, 1985.

_ _ _ .*Shakespeare and Social Class*. Atlantic Heights, NJ: Humanities Press International, 1988.

Bevington, David. *The Complete Works of Shakespeare*. 3rd. ed. Glenview IL.: Scott, Foresman and Company, 1980.

Billington, Sandra. *A Social History of the Fool*. New York: St. Martin's, 1984.

Boehrer, Bruce. "Shylock and the Rise of the Household Pet: Thinking Social Exclusion in *The Merchant of Venice*." *Shakespeare Quarterly* 50 (1999): 152-170.

Bradbrook, M. C. *The Rise Of The Common Player; A Study Of Actor And Society In Shakespeare's England*. Cambridge: Harvard UP, 1962.

Braddock, Robert C. "The Rewards of Office-Holding in Tudor England." *The Journal of British Studies* 14.2 (May, 1975): 29-47.

Brown, Ivor John Carnegie. *How Shakespeare Spent the Day.* London: Bodley Head, 1963.

Brown, John Russell, ed. *The Merchant of Venice.* London: Methuen, 1955.

Burnett, Mark Thornton. *Masters And Servants In English Renaissance Drama And Culture: Authority And Obedience.* Basingstoke, 1997.

Busby, Olive Mary. *Studies In The Development Of The Fool In The Elizabethan Drama.* London: Oxford UP, 1923.

Carnegie, David. "'Maluolio within': Performance Perspectives on the Dark House." *Shakespeare Quarterly* 52.3 (Autumn, 2001): 393-414.

Coddon, Karin S. "'Slander in an Allow'd Fool': *Twelfth Night's* Crisis of the Aristocracy." *Studies in English Literature, 1500-1900.* 33.2, Elizabethan and Jacobean Drama (Spring, 1993): 309-325.

Cohen, Walter. "*The Merchant of Venice* and the Possibilities of Historical Criticism." *New Casebook: The Merchant of Venice.* Ed. Martin Coyle. New York: St Martin's, 1998.

_ _ _ . *Drama Of A Nation: Public Theater In Renaissance England And Spain.* Ithaca: Cornell UP, 1985.

Comensoli, Viviana. "*Household Business*": *Domestic Plays of Early Modern England.*Toronto: Toronto UP, 1997.

Delany, Paul. "King Lear and the Decline of Feudalism." *PMLA* 92 (1977): 429-440.

Drakakis, John. *The Merchant of Venice.* Ed. Nigel Wood. Buckingham: Open UP, 1996.

Draper, Ronald P. *Shakespeare, The Comedies.* New York: St. Martin's, 2000.

Dubrow, Heather. *Shakespeare And Domestic Loss: Forms Of Deprivation, Mourning, And Recuperation.* Cambridge, U.K.: Cambridge University Press, 1999

Earle, Peter. "The Middling Sort in London." *The Middling Sort of People: Culture, Society, and Politics in England, 1550-1800.* Eds. Jonathan Barry and Christopher Brooks. New York: St. Martin's, 1994.

Engle, Lars. "Money and Moral Luck in the Merchant of Venice." *Shakespearean Pragmatism: Market of His Time.* Chicago: Chicago UP, 1993.

_ _ _ ."'Thrift is Blessing': Exchange and Explanation In The Merchant of Venice." *Shakespeare Quarterly* 37.1 (Spring, 1986): 20-37.

Everett, Barbara. "'Or what You Will.' in *Twelfth Night.*" In *Twelfth Night.* Ed. R. S. White. New York: St. Martin's, 1996.

Famous Victories of Henry V [The] quoted text: Bullough, Geoffrey. ed. *Narrative and Dramatic Sources of Shakespeare.* "*The Famous Victories of Henry the Fifth.*" Vol. IV. London: Routledge and Kegan Paul, 1962.

Ferguson, Arthur B. *Chivalric Tradition In Renaissance England.* Washington D.C.: Folger Shakespeare Library, 1986.

Fortin, René E. "Launcelot and the Uses of Allegory in *The Merchant of Venice.*" *Studies in English Literature, 1500-1900* 14. 2, Elizabethan and Jacobean Drama. (Spring, 1974): 259-270.

Freud, Sigmund. "Wit and Its Relation to the Unconscious." In *The Basic Writings of Sigmund Freud.* New York: Modern Library, 1938.

Freund, Elizabeth. "Twelfth Night and the Tyranny of Interpretation." *ELH* 53.3 (Autumn, 1986): 471-489.

Fripp, Edgar Innes, d. 1931. *Shakespeare, Man And Artist, By Edgar I. Fripp* . . . Ann Arbor, Michigan: University of Michigan Library, 2005.

Goldsmith, Robert Hillis. *Wise Fools in Shakespeare*. East Lansing: Michigan State UP, 1955.

Greenblatt, Stephen J. *Will in the World. How Shakespeare Became Shakespeare*. New York: W.W. Norton, 2004.

_ _ _ ."Invisible Bullets: Renaissance Authority and Its Subversion, *Henry IV* and *Henry V.*" In *Political Shakespeare: New Essays in Cultural Materialism*. Eds. Jonathan Dollimore and Alan Sinfield. Ithaca: Cornell UP, 1985.

Greif, Karen. "A Star Is Born: Feste on the Modern Stage." *Shakespeare Quarterly*. 39.1. (Spring 1988): 61-78.

Grock (Adrian Wettach). *Grock: Life's A Lark*. trans. Madge Pemberton. London: William Heinemann, 1931.

Gurr, Andrew. *The Shakespearean Stage 1574-1642*. Cambridge: Cambridge UP, 1970.

_ _ _. *Playgoing in Shakespeare's London*. Cambridge: Cambridge UP, 1987.

Haberdashers' Court Minute Book. Guildhall Library MS 15842/1. First published it in David Kathman, "Grocers, Goldsmiths, and Drapers: Freemen and Apprentices in the Elizabethan Theater" *Shakespeare Quarterly* lv (2004): 1–49.

Halasz, Alexandra. "'So Beloved That Men Use His Pictures for Their Signs': Richard Tarlton and the Uses of Sixteenth-Century Celebrity." *Shakespeare Studies* 23. (1995): 19-38.

Harrison, William. *Descriptions of Britaine and England*. Bk.

II. Ed Frederick J. Frunviall. New Shakespeare Society Series IV, 1887.

Hilliard, Stephen S. *The Singularity Of Thomas Nashe.* Lincoln: Nebraska UP, 1986.

Hilton, Rodney H. *Class Conflict and the Crisis of Feudalism: Essays in Medieval Social History.* London: Verso 1990.

Hinely, Jan Lawson. "Bond Priorities in *The Merchant of Venice*." *Studies in English Literature, 1500-1900* 20.2. Elizabethan and Jacobean Drama (Spring, 1980): 217-239.

Hollender, John. "*Twelfth Night* and the Morality of Indulgence." In *Modern Shakespeare Criticism: Essays on Style, Dramaturgy, and the Major Plays.* Ed. Alvin B. Kernan. New York: Harcourt, Brace & World, 1970.

Holton. R. J. *The Transition from Feudalism to Capitalism.* London: Macmillan, 1985.

Hornback, Robert. "Staging Puritanism in the Early 1590s: The Carnvialesque, Rebellious Clown as Anti-Puritan Stereotype." *Renaissance and Reformation* 24.3 (2000) : 31-67.

Hunter, G. K. "English Folly and Italian Vice-The Moral Landscape of John Marston." In *Jacobean Theatre.* Ed. John Russell Brown and Bernard Harris. London: Stratford-upon-Avon Studies, No. 1., 1960.

Japtok, Martin., and Winfried Schleiner. "Genetics and 'Race' in *The Merchant of Venice*." *Literature and Medicine* 18.2 (1999): 155-72.

Jardine, M. D. "New Historicism for Old: New Conservatism for Old?: The Politics of Patronage in the Renaissance." *The Yearbook of English Studies* 21 (1991): 286-304.

King James Version. Holy Bible : 1611 edition: Peabody, MA: Hendrickson, 2003.

Knutson, Roslyn Lander. *Playing Companies and Commerce in Shakespeare's Time*. Cambridge: Cambridge UP, 2001.

Korda, Natasha. *Shakespeare's Domestic Economies: Gender and Property in Early Modern England*. Philadelphia, Pennsylvania UP, 2002.

Lamb, Mary Ellen. "Tracing a Heterosexual Erotics of Service in *Twelfth Night* and Autobiographical Writings of Thomas Whythorne and Anne Clifford." *Criticism* 40.1 (Winter 1998): 1-25.

Laroque, Francois. *Shakespeare's Festive World: Elizabethan Seasonal Entertainment and the Professional Stage*. Cambridge: Cambridge UP, 1991.

Laslett, P. *The World We Have Lost--Further Explored*. London: Methuen, 1983.

Leech, Clifford. ed. "*The Two Gentlemen of Verona*." London, Methuen, 1969.

Leggatt, Alexander. "The Audience as Patron: The Knight of the Burning Pestle." In *Shakespeare and Theatrical Patronage In Early Modern England*. Eds. Paul White Whitfield and Suzanne R. Westfall. Cambridge: Cambridge UP, 2002.

Leinwand, Theodore B. *Theater, Finance and Society In Early Modern England*. Cambridge: Cambridge University Press, 1999.

Like Will To Like quoted text: Hazlitt, Carew W. *A Select Collection of Old English Plays: Originally Published by Robert Dodsley in the Year 1744*. "*Like Will To Like*." Vol. 2. New York: Benjamin Blom, 1964.

Lippincott, H. F. "*King Lear* and the Fools of Armin." *Shakespeare Quarterly* 26 (1975): 243-253.

Logan, Thad Jenkins. "Twelfth Night: The Limits of Festivity."

Studies in English Literature, 1500-1900. 22.2 *Elizabethan and Jacobean Drama* (Spring, 1982): 223-238.

Lukács, Georg. "Shakespeare and Modern Drama." In *The Lukács Reader*. Ed. Arpad Kadarkay. Oxford: Blackwell, 1995.

_ _ _ .*History and Class Consciousness; Studies in Marxist Dialectics*. Trans. Rodney Livingstone: Merlin, 1967.

Macdonald, Ronald. *William Shakespeare: The Comedies.* New York: Twayne, 1992.

MacFarlane, Alan. "The Origins of English Individualism: Some Surprises." *Theory and Society* 6. 2. (Sep. 1978): 255-277.

MacHovec, Frank J. *Humor: Theory, History, Applications.* Springfield, Ill.: C.C. Thomas, 1988.

Mackenzie, Clayton. G. "Ionic Resonance in *The Merchant of Venice*." *Neohelicon* 27.2. (2000): 189-209.

Marx, Karl. "Critique of Hegel's Doctrine of the State" (1843), in *Early Writings*, trans. by Rodney Livingstone and Gregor Benton. London: Penguin, 1992.

_ _ _ . "On John Mill." In *Selected Writings*. Ed. David McLellan, Oxford: Oxford UP, 1977.

_ _ _ . *Pre-Capitalist Economic Formations*. New York: International, 1976.

_ _ _ ."Economic and Philosophic Manuscript of 1844." In *Marx-Engels Reader*. New York: Norton, 1972.

_ _ _ .*Capital*. Vol. 1 Moscow: Progress, 1965.

_ _ _ ."The Communist Manifesto." *The Essential Works of Marxism*. Ed. Arthur P. Mendel. New York: Bantam 1961.

Marx, Karl., and Frederick Engels. *The German Ideology Part One, with Selections from Parts Two and Three, together* with Marx's *"Introduction to a Critique of Political Economy."* New York: International, 2001.

Maza, Sarah C. *Servants and Masters in Eighteenth-Century France: The Uses of Loyalty.* Princeton: Princeton UP, 1983.

McBride, Kari Boyd. *Domestic Arrangements in Early Modern.* Pittsburgh: Duquesne UP, 2002.

McCracken. Grant. *Culture and Consumption II: Markets, Meaning, and Brand Management.* Bloomington: Indiana UP, 2005.

McIntosh, Marjorie K. "Poverty, Charity, and Coercion in Elizabethan England" *Journal of Interdisciplinary History* 35.3 (2005): 457-479.

McLean, Susan. "Prodigal Sons and Daughters: Transgression and Forgiveness in *The Merchant of Venice*," in *Papers on Language & Literature* 32.1 (1996): 45-62.

McRae, Andrew. *Renaissance Drama.* London: Oxford UP, 2003.

Mendel, Arthur P. *Essential Works of Marxism.* New York: Bantam, 1961.

Mentz, Steven R. "The Fiend Gives Friendly Counsel: Launcelot Gobbo and Polyglot Economics in *The Merchant of Venice*." *Money And The Age Of Shakespeare: Essays In New Economic Criticism.* Ed. Linda Woodbridge. New York: Palgrave Macmillan, 2003.

Mertes, Kate. *English Noble Household, 1250 To 1600: Good Governance and Politic Rule.* Oxford: B. Blackwell, 1987.

Mish, Frederick C. ed. *Merriam-Webster Dictionary Online.* 5/15/07.<www.m-w.com>.

Misogonus, quoted text: Ed. Barber, Lester. New York: Garland, 1979.

Moisan, Thomas. "'Knock me soundly": Comic Misprision and Class Consciousness in Shakespeare." *Shakespeare Quarterly* 42.3 (Autumn 1991): 276-290.

Muldrew, Craig. *Economy Of Obligation : The Culture Of Credit And Social Relations In Early Modern England.* Houndmills: Macmillan, 1998.

_ _ _. "'Hard Food for Midas': Cash and Its Social Value in Early Modern England." *Past and Present* 170. (Feb. 2001): 78-120.

Nicoll, Allardyce. *Masks Mimes and Miracles: Studies in the Popular Theatre.* New York: Harcourt, Brace and Company, 1931.

Niklaus, Thelma. *Harlequin.* New York: G. Braziller, 1956.

Pandit, Lalita. "Emotion, Perception and Anagnorisis in *The Comedy of Errors*: A Cognitive Perspective." *College Literature* 33.1 (Winter 2006): 94-126.

Parish Register of Chelmsford St Mary, St Peter, and St Cedd, Essex Record Office. MS D/P94/1/2. First published it in David Kathman, "Grocers, Goldsmiths, and Drapers: Freemen and Apprentices in the Elizabethan Theater" *Shakespeare Quarterly* lv (2004): 1–49.

Porter, Gerald. "'Work the Old lady Out of the Ditch': Singing At Work By English Lacemakers." *Journal of Folklore Research* 31.1-3. (1994): 35-55.

Pugliatti, Paola. *Beggary and Theater in Early Modern England.* Aldershot, Hants, England: Ashgate, 2003.

Raman, Shakar. "Marking Time: Memory and Market in *The Comedy of Errors*." *Shakespeare Quarterly* 56.2 (2005): 176-205.

Redfern, W.D (Walter D.). *Puns.* Oxford: Basil Blackwell, 1984.

Rivlin, Elizabeth. "Mimetic Service in *The Two Gentlemen of Verona.*" *ELH* 72.1 (2005): 105-128.

Sacks, David Harris. "The Metropolis and Revolution: Commercial, Urban, and Political Culture in Early Modern London." In *Culture of Capital*. Ed. Henry S. Turner. New York: Routledge, 2002.

Sassonia, Ercole. *Luis venereae perfectissimus tractatus.* Patavii, 1597.

Schalkwyk, David. "Love and Service in *Twelfth Night* and the Sonnets." *Shakespeare Quarterly* 56. (2005): 76-100.

Schleiner, Louise. "Voice, Ideology, and Gendered Subjects: The Case of *As You Like It* and *Two Gentlemen.*" *Shakespeare Quarterly* 50.3 (Autumn 1999): 285-309.

Schwartz, Stan. "Ben and the Bard's Clown: Stan Schwartz Interviews Ben Kingsley." *Urban Desires* 2.6. (Nov./Dec. 1996): 01/14/07. <www.desires.com/2.5/Performance/Kingsley/kingsley.html>.

Shaughnessy, Robert. ed. *The Cambridge Companion to Shakespeare and Popular Culture*. Cambridge: Cambridge UP, 2007.

Shishko, Robert, and Bernard Rostker. "The Economics of Multiple Job Holding." *American Economic Review.* 66.3 (June 1976): 298-308.

Shumway, David R. "The Star System in Literary Studies." *PMLA* 112.1. Special Topic: The Teaching of Literature. (Jan., 1997): 85-100.

Simpson, J.A., and E.S.C. Weiner, prep. *The Oxford English Dictionary.* 2nd. ed. Vol. III, V, XI. Oxford: Clarendon, 1989.

Slack, Paul. *Poverty and Policy in Tudor and Stuart England.* London: Longman, 1988.

Slights, Camille. "In Defense of Jessica: The Runaway

Daughter in *The Merchant of Venice.*" *Shakespeare Quarterly* 31.3 (Autumn, 1980): 357-368.

Southworth, John. *Fools and Jesters at the English Court.* Thrupp: Sutton, 1998.

Springfels, Mary. "Music in Shakespeare's Plays." *Britannica Student Encyclopedia.* 2007. Encyclopædia Britannica Online. 1 Mar. 2007 <http://www.britannica.com/ebi/article-9396030>.

Sweezy, Paul. "A Critique." In *The Transition from Feudalism to Capitalism.* Ed. Rodney Hilton. London: New Left Books, 1976.

Thaler, Alwin "The Traveling Players in Shakespeare's England." *Modern Philology* 17.9 (Jan. 1920): 489-514.

Thompson, Peter. "Clowns, Fools, and Knaves: Stages in the Evolution of Acting." *The Cambridge History of British Theatre.* Eds. Jane Milling and Peter Thompson. Vol. 1. Cambridge, Cambridge UP, 2004.

Timpane, John. "'I am but a foole, looke you': Launce and the Social Functions of Humor." In *The Two Gentlemen of Verona: Critical Essays.* Ed June Schlueter. New York: Garland, 1996.

Turner, Frederick. *Shakespeare's Twenty-First Century Economics: The Morality of Love and Money.* Oxford: Oxford UP, 1999.

"Up in the morning." Bedfordshire, c. 1904. *Old Songs Sung in Bedfordshire* 1904:3.

Vannini, Phillip. "The Meanings of a Star: Interpreting Music Fans' Reviews." *Symbolic Interaction* 27.1 (Feb. 2004): 47-69.

Veblen, Thorstein. *The Theory of the Leisure Class: An Economic Study of Institutions.* New York: The Macmillan, 1899: 35-67.

Videbaek, Bente A. *The Stage Clown in Shakespeare's Theater* Westport CT: Greenwood, 1996.

Vintners' Freeman Book 1. Guildhall Library MS 15211/1. fo 171ʳ. First published it in David Kathman, "Grocers, Goldsmiths, and Drapers: Freemen and Apprentices in the Elizabethan Theater" *Shakespeare Quarterly* lv (2004): 1–49

Wall, Wendy. *Staging Domesticity: Household Work and English Identity in Early Modern.* Cambridge: Cambridge UP, 2002.

Wallerstein, Immanuel. *The West, Capitalism, and the Modern World- System.* 1989 b. Prepared as a chapter in Joseph Needham, Science and Civilization in China, Vol. VII: The Social Background, Part 2. Sect. 48. Social and Economic Considerations. Published as "L'Occident, le capitalisme, et le systeme-monde moderne" in Sociologies et Societ,s (Montreal) Vol. XXI, No. 1, June 1990.

Weil, Judith. *Service and Dependency in Shakespeare's Plays.* New York: Cambridge UP, 2005.

Weimann, Robert. "Laughing with the Audience: *Two Gentlemen of Verona* and the Popular Tradition of Comedy." *Shakespeare Survey* 22. (1969): 35-42.

Weller, Barry. "Identity and Representation in Shakespeare." *ELH* 49.2. (Summer 1982): 339-362.

Wells, Charles. *The Wide Arch: Roman Values in Shakespeare.* New York: St. Martin's, 1992.

White, Whitfield Paul and, Suzanne R. Westfall eds. *Shakespeare And Theatrical Patronage In Early Modern England.* Cambridge: Cambridge UP, 2002.

Wiggins, Steven N., and David G. Raboy. "Price Premia to

Name Brands: An Empirical Analysis." *The Journal of Industrial Economics* 44.4 (Dec., 1996): 377-388.

Wiles, David. *Shakespeare's Clown: Actor and Text In The Elizabethan Playhouse.* Cambridge: Cambridge UP, 1987.

Willeford, William. *Fool and His Scepter; A Study in Clowns And Jesters And Their Audience.* Evanston, Ill.: Northwestern UP, 1969.

Womersley, David. "The Politics of Shakespeare's *King John*." *The Review of English Studies.* New Series.40.160. (Nov., 1989): 497-515.

Woodbridge, Linda. *Vagrancy, Homelessness, and English Renaissance Literature.* Urbana IL.: Illinois UP, 2001.

Yachnin, Paul. "Reversal of Fortune: Shakespeare, Middleton, and the Puritans." *ELH* 70.3 (2003): 757-786.

Yancey, Diane. *Life in The Elizabethan Theater.* San Diego: Lucent Books, 1997.

INDEX

—

Lightning Source UK Ltd.
Milton Keynes UK
UKOW04f0611121217
314301UK00001B/13/P

9 781440 153518